BLESSED ARE
THE SPIRALING

BLESSED ARE THE SPIRALING

**How the Chaotic Search for Significance Can
Lead to Joy Through Life's Shifting Seasons**

LEVI LUSKO

W PUBLISHING GROUP

AN IMPRINT OF THOMAS NELSON

Blessed Are the Spiraling

© 2025 Levi Lusko

Published in Nashville, Tennessee, by W Publishing, an imprint of Thomas Nelson. W Publishing and Thomas Nelson are registered trademarks of HarperCollins Christian Publishing, Inc.

Published in association with the literary agency of Wolgemuth & Associates, Inc.

Thomas Nelson titles may be purchased in bulk for educational, business, fundraising, or sales promotional use. For information, please email SpecialMarkets@ThomasNelson.com. Unless otherwise indicated, Scripture quotations are taken from the New King James Version®. Copyright © 1982 by Thomas Nelson. Used by permission. All rights reserved.

Scripture quotations marked ESV are from the ESV® Bible (The Holy Bible, English Standard Version®). Copyright © 2001 by Crossway, a publishing ministry of Good News Publishers. Used by permission. All rights reserved.

Scripture quotations marked MSG are taken from *The Message*. Copyright © 1993, 2002, 2018 by Eugene H. Peterson. Used by permission of NavPress. All rights reserved. Represented by Tyndale House Publishers, a Division of Tyndale House Ministries.

Scripture quotations marked NLT are taken from the Holy Bible, New Living Translation. Copyright © 1996, 2004, 2015 by Tyndale House Foundation. Used by permission of Tyndale House Ministries, Carol Stream, Illinois 60188. All rights reserved.

Any internet addresses, phone numbers, or company or product information printed in this book are offered as a resource and are not intended in any way to be or to imply an endorsement by Thomas Nelson, nor does Thomas Nelson vouch for the existence, content, or services of these sites, phone numbers, companies, or products beyond the life of this book.

ISBN 978-1-4003-4560-1 (audiobook)
ISBN 978-1-4003-4559-5 (ePub)
ISBN 978-1-4003-4558-8 (softcover)

Library of Congress Control Number: 2024949147

Printed in the United States of America
25 26 27 28 29 LBC 5 4 3 2 1

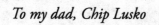
To my dad, Chip Lusko

CONTENTS

Contents

FOREWORD

I WAS IN a spiral of my own a few years back, and in the midst of it, I flew to Montana to spend some time with my good friend Levi Lusko.

After I arrived, he asked if I wanted to hike up a mountain. If you know Levi, then you know this is a very typical Levi kind of question to ask. I accepted the challenge, and off we went.

The route was short and steep—only 1.75 miles long but a considerable 2,100 feet of elevation gained. As we went straight up this mountain, lungs and muscles burning, we talked. And as we talked, I was changed.

Levi opened up to me about his own few years of spiraling.

The fears and the questions.

Uncertainty about how to get his footing in life's shifting seasons. Struggling to resist lies the Enemy was trying to get him to believe about his worth and his future. Ultimately his rediscovering the majesty and worth he found in Jesus as he walked with Him to the other side of it all.

It will go down as one of the most memorable and formative conversations of my life. Yes, the beauty of the landscape was breathtaking, and the wild huckleberries were delicious. But more than that, it was our conversation on the mountain that stirred my heart. It turned out to be what we American evangelicals call a "God Moment." It was exactly what I needed to hear for the season I was in.

When he told me this was going to be the theme of his next book, I all but cheered, because I know I am not the only one who needs what Levi shared with me that day. Whether you're going through a midlife crisis, struggling as a single parent, facing an empty nest, or feeling disoriented for any reason, this book holds road-tested truths to guide you through whatever mountain you are up against.

I pray that as you read this book, you will have your own God Moment like I did on that Montana mountain, because I know you will come through better for it.

There is blessing waiting for you in your spiraling.

—Phil Wickham, award-winning singer-songwriter

INTRODUCTION

I AM LOST on the mountain.

It's cold and I'm slipping. I can't see.

I have been here before, but it's dark now. Nothing looks like it did on other days. There is a treasure I am looking for. I'm scared by everything.

Lying on the bathroom floor, sweating and crying, I can't breathe. I pace the halls at two a.m. wishing I could just go to sleep.

Who will take care of my family if something happens to me?

Is this as far as I can go? Are my best and brightest days behind me? Am I yesterday's news?

Who am I if I can't perform?

There seems to be no treasure in the past; it's all in the present and future. Or maybe it *is* all in the past and there's no more treasure to be found.

Why is it so hard to enjoy where I am without fearing that it will be lost or taken away?

How much blessing will it take for me to be happy?

I am now forty years old. This is, presumably, the halfway point. Of the hill. The mountain. And I am over it. In every sense of the word.

Have I peaked? Am I able to progress? Where is there to go from here?

Do I have worth beyond my role and my accomplishments? Is there purpose beyond productivity?

As they say, the only constant in life is change.

Will I still find meaning when my path takes a turn and I no longer have or can do the things that have made me "successful"?

Is there significance to discover when life gets in the way of what I enjoy?

Will life be full when the nest is empty?

For so long the kids we have been raising have taken so much oxygen and energy in our home, but the day is quickly coming when they will be out living life on their own.

What will I do when physically, mentally, emotionally, or verbally I inevitably decline? When the little man in my brain who hands me files goes on longer and longer vacations, then decides to relocate to the south of France permanently?

These were the types of questions that stormed my mind during a full-on midlife crisis and sent me spiraling. Far more than a cliché, this was legitimately the most disorienting time of my adult life, a tumultuous stretch of months when I kept grasping for anchors as my inner battles waged on.

Maybe for you it wasn't a midlife or quarterlife crisis that sent you spiraling. Perhaps it was a divorce. A death or diagnosis. A nightmare work situation. A transition into a different stage that turned your life into a foreign country.

It doesn't have to be a bad thing; it could be a good thing you were looking forward to—a graduation, a promotion, or retirement. Spiraling comes in all shapes and sizes and can show up when least expected. Blessings and burdens are both heavy and can be easily confused.

Whatever brought you here, you are asking really painful but important questions—about your worth, your purpose, your future, your story.

GETTING LOST

I had plenty to eat as a child, but you wouldn't think I did by my appetite for *more* in life, which motivated me throughout my later teenage years and on into my twenties and thirties. There was fire in my belly to spare. I had places to go and things to do. Drive, intensity, and focus.

At thirty-eight the bill showed up for the pace I kept in those two decades. Leading and writing and dreaming and speaking and traveling. I went to Africa in that period twice, just for the weekend. I don't recommend it.

It's all one big, beautiful, and nauseating blur. One made even more intense because of the death of Lenya, our daughter who went home to be with Jesus unexpectedly in 2012. We buried her on the day after Christmas. And then I tried to bury myself in ministry. None of it was bad. The books and the sermons and the church plants and the speaking tours. It was just an unsustainable pace. Man cannot live by sugar-free Red Bulls alone.

My mantra became "I can't get out of this trial, but I can get something out of it." Turn the pain into power, convert the loss into fuel. All good things. (And I truly believe it was God's will, as far as I can tell.) That is the essence of the Beatitudes—blessed are the brokenhearted, those who mourn, those who are persecuted, those who spiral. But it can become unhealthy and untenable if not tempered, conditioned, and refined. The Sabbath is a weekly and yearly principle for a reason.

Preaching around the globe to "make the devil pay" did not bring Lenya back, but it ticked miles in dog years on my internal odometer without my realizing it. Ironically, in time, her death would be revealed to be the least of my worries. A gaping wound of that magnitude got my undivided attention. It was the myriad other ones that I had been dragging around untreated for decades that would cause the most problems.

Death from a thousand paper cuts.

No one gets off this planet unscathed.

It was a perfect storm, and going into the pandemic, I was a ticking time bomb. I had flown a million and a half miles in ten years, and then travel screeched to a halt. When the music stopped, I was left without the distraction and novelty of the scenery constantly changing. My ever-faithful TUMI carry-on suitcase sitting at the foot of our bed wasn't the only thing that needed to be unpacked.

The body keeps score.

And, as Warren Buffett once said, when the tide goes out, you find out who has been swimming without a bathing suit.

GETTING FOUND

My midlife crisis rocked my world. And then it surprised me with *delight*. Ultimately it was a death that led to life. An end followed by a new beginning.

Getting lost on the mountain allowed me to be found.

It positioned me to recalibrate, see what truly matters, and become aware of my mortality. I no longer seek to be the young warrior but instead embrace my place as a father who is on the path to becoming an elder and eventually a sage of the tribe. I now see the stages of development as nothing to fight against but everything to embrace.

I still have battles to fight, but I am gladly accepting my current season of life and looking ahead to the next one with more excitement than dread. I have a game plan, and you can have one too. It's what we don't understand that scares us, and things are much less terrifying with the lights on.

Don't misread what I am saying—life is still plenty chaotic. But a surpassing joy has opened up in the midst of it that has warmed and comforted me like a hot-water bottle in a cold cabin bed.

I hope to be a Sherpa, a guide for you on the mountain. (Or if you are reading this on behalf of a spouse who is facing a disorienting season, a guide to help you help them.) You have to face this season of spiraling *for* yourself but not *by* yourself. I can't walk it for you, but I intend to walk with you. Not because I am any better than you but because it appears I got disoriented first and have been able to get my bearings. I was lost, but I've been found. I have moved from a human view of the mountain to a divine one, and it has changed everything.

So, walk with me from an earthly understanding of the arc of life to a divine one.

We are headed from Valentine's Day to Good Friday.

From love to LOVE.

From human to divine.

It was C. S. Lewis who observed that once God's *agape* (unconditional) love lights our fire, we won't look for the human loves of *eros* (sexual), *storge* (family), or *phileo* (friendship) to fulfill us. They will stop being a substitute for the transcendent and take on real meaning and beauty. They will go from disappointing you to fulfilling you, because you won't expect them to do what they can't. No person can fill a hole in your soul. But once God does that for you, you will be able to enjoy the relationships in your life for what they are—a gift to enhance your life, not the sole source for your life's meaning.

This is what I believe you will find on this journey. Not just human love, but a divine love so enchanting, intoxicating, and all-consuming that it will change how you approach human love. Loving God so fiercely doesn't make other loves lesser; it makes them possible.

You don't have to live full of dread and desperation. The gloomy mountain you now look at in fear and terror, once it is aflame with the glory of God, will transform before your eyes.

Joy is waiting.

LEVI LUSKO
Valentine's Day
Whitefish, Montana

GET YOUR BEARINGS, FACE YOUR SHADOW, AND STRATEGIZE FOR THIS SEASON

PART ONE

CHAPTER 1

GOING UP

I FELL DOWN a flight of stairs at our church in Pueblo, Colorado, when I was a one-year-old. I was in one of those walkers with a tray that allows babies to move around a room at will, all while drooling and eating Cheerios to their hearts' content.

Somehow, I managed to evade the bounds of captivity while the nursery worker was distracted. Newly emancipated, I roamed the building wearing my footie pajamas, eventually steering my mobile saucer straight for a set of stairs that led to the basement. Unluckily for me there was no door at this open stairway. Clearly, I had no idea what I was doing, but I like to imagine that I saw myself as an eeny-weeny Evel Knievel as I headed straight for the top step and floored it.

The stairs were made of concrete, trimmed by metal, and the landing was cement. Not ideal.

I tumbled down each step, going head over wheels again and again, before violently crashing at the bottom. While all this was happening, my dad was preaching in an adjacent auditorium space. The crash of the walker and my subsequent screams echoed throughout the entire school building, and everyone came running at once. Fortunately, one of the first to reach me was a nurse who began assessing me in my adrenaline-spiked, hyperventilating state.

My mom says she had to wait for a minute and pray to summon the courage to walk over to me because she could tell it was serious. She didn't know whether she would be able to handle it if, for instance, her son's head was caved in.

The entire church congregation prayed as my parents took me to the hospital. Remarkably, I was completely fine. I am convinced we will see guardian angel involvement when replaying in heaven the stored file from this day.

Experiencing my midlife crisis at age thirty-eight felt exactly like that violent, unstoppable somersault down a concrete, metal-lined stairway. One moment I was going along fine; the next, the bottom dropped out and I was in a free fall.

Debilitating panic attacks. Heart pounding, palms sweaty, mind racing. Complete chaos emotionally, fear of the future, suicidal ideation, constant dread.

Most terrifying of all was my lack of desire for the one thing I have always been most confident about: my calling to preach God's Word. There was even one episode backstage when I was crying uncontrollably, grasping for the motivation to go out and preach. For the first time in decades, I didn't know if I wanted to continue pastoring or leading a team and ministry. I consistently had dark, scary thoughts that sent me downward.

Where did this come from? Tumble.

Why is this happening? Tumble.

How will I survive this? Tumble.

Where do I go from here? Tumble.

Will I ever feel like myself? Tumble.

Who am I? Tumble.

It's terrifying to spiral. Adrenaline does not de-escalate an adrenalized response; you can't fight and win in a fight-or-flight reaction. Trying to reason your way out of a panic attack is useless too; you might as well pour gasoline on a fire. Instead, you must slow down and stare down what is actually going on.

So I did.

I saw my doctor and counselor, started meeting with a psychologist, and spoke to friends and other pastors. I confided in my wife, was vulnerable with my kids about what I was facing, and depended on God for every next breath. I made serious changes to my pace of life, prioritized activities that replenished me, and took up a new hobby. I examined everything I was putting into my body and, for a time, took a prescription drug that helped. I adopted breathing activities that regulated me and faced some emotional wounds I thought I had resolved. I left no stone unturned and began a long process of deeply personal inner work and healing.

Through it all I came to realize, with stunning clarity, that I was at a turning point, and I needed to get my bearings as I headed into the next season. The transition, as hard and dark and painful as it was, represented a curtain falling on a chapter of my life. But what that meant was that another curtain could rise on something new.

And new seasons require new strategies.

I was at the stage of life when, biologically speaking, catabolism was exceeding anabolism. On a cellular level my rate of decomposition was beginning to exceed the rate at which new cells were being formed. My connective tissue was degenerating as soft tissue grew weaker. The inevitable process of physically aging was barreling forward, and there was nothing I could do about it.

NEW SEASONS REQUIRE NEW STRATEGIES.

Over the hill. Past my prime. *This is it; don't get scared now.*

But I *was* scared. And that is important. The free fall got my attention in a splashing-water-on-my-face way, waking me up to what God was trying to teach me, giving me the healthy respect I needed to take it seriously. I wasn't *just* scared because my outward man was perishing or because I likely had less time in front of me than behind me. I was terrified to have my sense of identity—and all that was so tightly wound around it—tampered with. My mind, which had always been my greatest strength, was now spinning out of control. Would I ever get it back? And who would I be if people weren't calling me brilliant or looking to me for input, advice, or product reviews? My breakdown was screaming of the inevitability of decline and change, a preview of coming attractions.

Do you still matter if what makes you *you* withers?

Try as we might, none of us are powerless to stop the crushing onslaught of time and forces outside of our control that will conspire to take everything that forms how we see ourselves that is not connected to our relationship with God.

Woe was me.

I was in a spiral free fall, and I was undone.

THE NATURE OF TRANSITIONS

Poet William Butler Yeats viewed life as "a spiral, a twisting down closer to the center around and around in smaller and smaller circles." His description is profound and seems to line up with my experience. But if it's possible to be in a downward spiral, why can't we spiral in the right direction and go up?

As I picture us all rising up this spiral staircase, I see the higher views bringing us new perspective and insight. Increasingly, we care less about things we once obsessed over; we now see they don't matter like we once thought they did. As we get closer to the end of the journey, we (hopefully) better understand what is truly meaningful. There is significance in the spiral. It is not meaningless. The goal is to get closer to the center as you go around and around in smaller and smaller circles.

One of the most important things I learned through my crisis was that, in the grand scheme of my development as a human, it doesn't have to be a circular movement going down but can be one going up. Your spiraling can send you in the *right* direction.

One of my counselors explained that human growth isn't a straight line slowly angling up; it is more jagged than that. We rise, and then our path flattens and is seemingly stagnant for a season; then another growth spurt surges, followed by a flat line; then another up. The line looks more like stairs. But what that means is each time you are about to grow, you hit a proverbial wall, which is always hard, messy, and uncomfortable.

How do you feel when you slam into the upward plane of a new phase?

If you're like my son, Lennox, you are elated. When he lost his first tooth while eating a burrito, he took the tooth out of his mouth and held it high. With blood dribbling down his chin, he beamed and shouted, "Puberty! Puberty! Puberty!" He took it as a badge of honor.

Most of us, however, are more like my daughters, who freaked out when they lost their first teeth. It is indeed quite shocking to have something fall from your body that you were very much attached to. You have the foreign sensation of feeling the gaping hole it left behind and eventually the rough edge of the new tooth pushing through. Without your consent the childhood you were enjoying—*thank you very much*—is being torn from your fingers.

One of my daughters actually declared war on puberty after she learned about it. She resolved to do everything in her power to outwit it, avoid it, and defeat it. She meant business. Dug battle lines. Decided she would not be taken without a fight.

Change is scary.

It's scary to know acne and turbulent emotions are around the bend. It's also scary to have your children graduate from high school and prepare to move out. To lose a job you love. To watch a marriage end. To discover thinning hair, ear hair, a slowing metabolism, or a thickening midsection and realize you are getting older.

These all are potentially disorienting moments, stirring fear about sources of identity, purpose, and gratification slipping away. You feel like you're running straight into a wall. *Smack.*

But the truth is, you don't have to dread transitions. You can view them as catalyzing forces preparing you for the coming attractions of joy and development. The key is in how you choose to interpret them.

An end and a beginning.

Studies show that on average we face a developmental shift every eighteen months. Hitting these walls, or crisis moments, is not a necessary evil; it is *simply necessary*.

Panicking can be a sign that you are simply misunderstanding the nature of growth. You were expecting it to be a diagonal line, like floating up a mountain in a ski lift—not climbing up a staircase. Smashing your nose into a solid object understandably leaves you drawing the wrong conclusion about what happened.

But nothing, in fact, has gone wrong; something has gone right.

"You just reached the end of your latest developmental shift," my counselor told me repeatedly, "and it is time to take a step up to another level." It wasn't a wall that had bloodied my nose; it was a stair.

It is in the coasting moments that we are tempted to take our most recent growth mode for granted and assume it will carry us forever. All the confusion and pain and bumping into stairs is meant to supply us with the energy for the next jump. We just have to look up.

Author Bruce Feiler calls these transition moments "lifequakes" and believes that successfully navigating them is the key to how you handle life. Unsurprisingly, it is in these brutal moments that you will be tempted to make your greatest mistakes. Hit the wall, and you might be tempted to quit the job, leave the relationship, or abandon the new language you were learning or the trip you were saving for.

Haste makes waste. Don't call the plastic surgeon, the divorce lawyer, the old college boyfriend, or the Corvette dealer just yet. Instead, take a breath, get your bearings, regroup, and evolve for the next season. The factory that once produced a now-obsolete technology doesn't need to be burned to the ground; it needs to be retooled for what's next.

Properly understood, these moments don't have to prompt terror or hysteria. They are the cue to grow. To morph. To mature.

THE WALL YOU'VE HIT IS A CHANCE TO GROW.

Have you hit a wall? Do you fear that something is terribly wrong? Don't jump to conclusions. Put the label maker down. Maybe you've simply gone as far as possible with the tools you currently possess. You've reached the necessary end of one step, and the wall you've hit is a chance to grow—to rise to the next level on a spiral staircase of blessing. Round and round you are meant to go, tighter and tighter in smaller circles, toward what really matters.

The worthless burning away, the Worthy remaining.

And at the end of your journey, you will find not something but Someone.

FROM OVERNIGHT SUCCESS TO DEATH ROW

John the Baptist's entire life story is one of clarity and confusion, revelation and relegation, ecstasy and exile as he struggled and grew step after step.

It had been four hundred long years of silence since the prophet Malachi had hit send on his theologically rich email. The angel Gabriel showed up and promised Zacharias, a weathered old priest, that he was going to be a father. Zacharias had the nerve to ask the angel for a sign so he could know it was legit.

Let me run that back for you because it shocked the angel also.

You are burning incense in a temple and *poof!* Out of thin air a bright, powerful angel shows up and gives you an announcement. And you ask this heavenly creature, who has just miraculously appeared—presumably with some glory, pomp, and perhaps some circumstance—for some heavenly assurance. Like, what? You want a double rainbow during the drive home?

The angel was so stunned by this demand for confirmation that he sassed Zacharias pretty hard: "I am Gabriel!" he shot back. "I dwell in the presence of God! Is that not enough of a sign for you? But since you want some guarantee, here's what you'll get. You will be mute until the baby is born."

And just like that, Zacharias was speechless.

Later, Mary and Joseph received similar visits from Gabe, sans the sass, then John the Baptist and Jesus each were born. The new covenant was afoot.

J the B was a bridge between the Old Testament and the New Testament. A point of transition. Living, breathing, spiritual puberty. It began during a dark period for John—he was in a holding pattern, having dwelled in the desert for several decades, eating bugs and wearing camel skin.

Then God nudged him, and he began to preach. Successfully. Suddenly his name was on everyone's lips.

"Can you believe what he wears?"

"Yeah, he is, like, so savage. Doesn't even care!"

"Did you hear he fearlessly throws shade on the Pharisees?"

"He called them snakes! That guy is my spirit animal. We *have* to go hear him this weekend."

He was a one-man Coachella, out in the desert eating weird food, dressed in strange clothes, and attracting massive crowds of people. And right when he was at the top of his game, he hit a wall.

Jesus asked John to baptize him. The clouds parted; the Holy Spirit descended from heaven like a dove; the Father spoke. Definite stairstep.

But afterward, Jesus started preaching, and everyone followed *Him*—including people who had been following the camel-skin-wearing, locust-crunching Jedi master. John's remaining padawans were defensive of him; he'd once been the newest, freshest thing on the block. "Jesus is baptizing more than you, John," they might have grumbled. "We need to do something to get our momentum back!"

"He must increase, but I must decrease," John said, confident about transitioning into a new season (John 3:30). They were words he probably had to preach to himself over and over as his podcast numbers nose-dived when Jesus popped off and went viral.

It would be disorienting to feel like you were no longer thriving at the one thing you had given your entire life to. But John consoled himself: Jesus was going to inaugurate the kingdom soon and it all would be okay.

Then John preached a sermon that offended the wrong person, and he ended up in jail. There's a wall for you! *Smack.*

Panic set in and he began to question everything. Not only was he at a low point in his life, he was afraid he'd made a huge mistake. He was middle-aged and having a full-blown existential crisis.

From death row, John sent word to Jesus that he was afraid he'd been wrong; maybe Jesus wasn't who John had thought he was. Matthew 11:2–3 says, "When John had heard in prison about the works of Christ, he sent two of his disciples and said to Him, 'Are You the Coming One, or do we look for another?'"

The emotion in the question is unmistakable. He had thrown everything into his calling; now it seemed his gamble might have been foolish. *Who am I if I'm not the one who prepared the way for the Messiah? If you're not it, what does that make me? A fraud. A failure. An impostor.*

Jesus sent back a message that would have been hard to receive but also could serve as a nudge up another step of faith: "The blind see and the lame walk; the lepers are cleansed and the deaf hear; the dead are raised up and the poor have the gospel preached to them. *And blessed is he who is not offended because of Me*" (vv. 5–6, italics added).

This was an invitation for John to see the blessing in his spiraling. To rise up in trust. Tighter and tighter, round and round, closer to the center.

It also helped him summon the courage to prepare to face what every human needs to: death. Ours might not be coming as quickly as John's death was, but we must reckon with the tangled and traumatic reality of our mortality. To grasp that every day matters, and it's up to us to make each one count. Only then will we be able to make it up the next stair with a fresh perspective to face whatever God puts in front of us.

No one wants to die, but I bet you would rather die well than poorly. Living a glorious life and dying a glorious death is what Jesus invites us to do as we deny ourselves, pick up our crosses, and follow Him. And remember, in Christ, death is just the *beginning.* As Jesus exhibited by rising on the third day, death is not the end of the road but a bend in the road. All that and more was in His communication to His cousin who was in crisis.

We don't know exactly what John's reaction was to this cryptic message from Jesus, but we do know what Jesus' true thoughts about John the Baptist were. After the messengers had left, Jesus turned to the crowd and gushed about how proud He was of John. He confirmed John was indeed the promised forerunner to the Messiah, then doubled down with this mic drop: "Among those born of women there has not risen one greater than John the Baptist; but he who is least in the kingdom of heaven is greater than he" (Matthew 11:11).

IS IT POSSIBLE THAT WHEN YOU AND I ARE SPIRALING, JESUS CALLS US BLESSED?

Did you catch that?

When John's wheels had to have been spinning, when he was heading into a free fall and feeling like a failure, Jesus didn't chastise him. Jesus described his cousin as the greatest man ever born of women.

Let that sink in. John was spiraling, but Jesus called him blessed.

Is it possible that when you and I are spiraling, Jesus calls us blessed?

YOU CAN DO THIS

Sometimes part of our angst is that we are struggling at all; we feel thrown by it. But if the greatest person ever born of a woman was continually subjected to ongoing dramas, disappointments, and forced development—even as he passionately followed God—why would it be different for us?

Things for J the B were awesome for a while, but it was

impossible for him to hang on to his spot at the top forever. It is the same for you and me. There will come a time when we can't hang on to our youthful physique or robust health, maintain our relevance in the industry we work in, keep up with every new social media platform, or cling to some other earthly crown. Do me a favor and picture whatever prominence you are most tempted to be defined by. See it in your mind. Okay, now listen . . . Do you hear footsteps? The "executioner" is coming. Not for your head, but for your spot at the top of whatever ladder you are on.

It's not a matter of if but when.

The goal then is not to try to win at a losing game but to play a game where victory is possible: pleasing God and running your race faithfully, loving selflessly, and then finishing obediently. Strive to win an *imperishable* crown that you can keep forever. Don't zero in on a temporary one you will lose when the pieces go back into the box at the end of this life.

John struggled yet still checked all those boxes—faithfulness, selflessness, obedience. He didn't die the most popular preacher, but he pleased the only audience that counted: his Savior. Flawless victory. Jesus deemed John a smashing success, the very model of significance.

According to Jesus, even if we are the least in the kingdom, we are even *greater* than John! This is because we are in Christ in a different way than John was as an old-covenant believer. John had the Holy Spirit *working* in his life; we have the Holy Spirit *living* in us! Jesus took us off the grueling treadmill of law and drew us into a relationship where pleasing God is our passion. It's not rooted in slavish fear but in ever-increasing power, love, and a sound mind.

And so this is what it comes down to: *It's possible to come through crisis and be better for it.*

You can do this.

No, it won't be easy.

But every time you smack into a disorienting wall of transition, you can make it your goal to see your life through Jesus' eyes. From the wise vantage point high up on the spiral staircase, closer to the end of your life, you can keep rising in levels of obedience. You can keep trusting Him as you move forward and up, one shaking step at a time.

This is desiring for God to increase and for us to decrease. What we do on the stairstep above might not be bigger, more epic, and grander—it might be unseen, smaller, and quiet. Jesus fed a hungry crowd of four thousand people after He fed the famous five thousand. The ENTJ in me chafes at that. *Come on, Jesus, let's go for six thousand!* But bigger isn't always better.

The stages of spiritual development don't promise more quantity but instead proximity to Him. They trade impressing the world for welcoming more of heaven's beauty. They take you around and around, further up and further in, closer to the center, in smaller and smaller circles. What is waiting for you on the next step is guaranteed to be glorious.

The fact is, you can make it through the stairs unscathed just like I did as a child. Not by pretending the steps aren't scary and disorienting and painful, but by embracing the lack of equilibrium and doing exactly what John did—reaching out to Jesus in your confusion.

As you learn to breathe and reevaluate, you will realize it wasn't a dead end you smacked into; it was an opportunity to ascend to another level on the way to glory. And as you do, God will send angels to help you so you don't strike your foot on a single step.

So, if you feel you're in free fall, you are not alone. I've been there. And I know for sure I have many more spiraling encounters with stairs of development and puberty-like moments to come. But I am less afraid than I once was because of who I know is at the top of the stairs.

A PICTURE BY THE BED

I once rode on a chairlift with a woman who noticed I was with my son, Lennox. As we chatted, she shared her strategy for getting her kids to love skiing. Though they didn't start until they were two, she put them in ski outfits and skis when they were one and took a picture of them in the snow. Then she framed two prints of the photos and put one on each of their nightstands. And whenever they pointed to the pictures, she told them they were amazing skiers. There was never a time in their lives when they didn't see themselves as belonging on the snow.

"Did it work?" I asked.

"Yep," she said, grinning proudly. "All five of my children are now adults, and they all are fantastic skiers who love the sport."

Some of the story didn't sit well with me; there was a slight manipulation and heavy-handedness to it. But there was also gospel truth.

God doesn't call you to get your act together and hope you can rack up enough points to cash in for a halo one day. Instead, He puts a picture by your bed of who you are in Christ and how He sees you. God's righteousness isn't based on you but placed on you. And the day-to-day goal isn't to get something

GOD'S RIGHTEOUSNESS ISN'T BASED ON YOU BUT PLACED ON YOU.

by doing the right things, but remembering who you already are and then being what He has legally once and for all decreed is true about you.

So, if it's been awhile since you have glanced at the pic by your bedside, allow me to reintroduce you to yourself.

In Christ you are the righteousness of God.

You are more than a conqueror.

Your testimony and the blood of Jesus overcome the Enemy.

You are a child of the King.

You are the temple of the Holy Spirit—the same Spirit that raised Jesus from the dead lives in you.

You are chosen, forgiven, called, and equipped.

You are seated in heavenly places and your prayers pull down strongholds.

You are indestructible in the will of God and headed for heaven when you have finished your mission.

So, as for those spiraling stairs you are bound to face? Let me assure you, you have what it takes.

CHAPTER 2

FROM DEATH TO RESURRECTION

HOW MANY REJECTION letters would it take for you to give up on your dream? One? Four? Nine? Would you keep going after opening the mailbox and receiving eleven letters crushing your hopes and dreams?

As a small boy growing up in a Mexican-American family that picked produce nine months of the year up and down the California coast to survive, José Hernández had a dream of becoming an astronaut. Against all odds, he achieved that impossible dream in 2009 when he flew to the International Space Station on the space shuttle *Discovery*. But the process of getting there was anything but easy, and he had every opportunity to give up on his dream along the way.

Before José was finally accepted into the intensive Astronaut Candidate training program, NASA rejected him *eleven* times. Yet he reapplied again and again. Every year. For twelve long years he received letters informing him that he had failed to qualify. He didn't waste his waiting. Through the years, while he waited, he added skills that would help him become a more desirable candidate, including a scuba certification, a pilot's license, and a proficiency in speaking Russian. It wasn't until the twelfth time he applied that he was selected.

During his period of rejection, while working as an engineer, José pioneered a mammography machine for early detection of breast cancer that has saved hundreds of thousands, if not millions, of lives. This accomplishment would not have been possible had José not been rejected as many times as he had. Think about this: His stack of rejection letters, which were, on their own, a humiliating, disappointing, embarrassing death, were in fact a resurrection. Not just for José but also for the many lives all around the world that the machine would save.

In that story is a glimmer of the diamond at the center of the gospel.

I want you to really absorb this next sentence: "Christianity, like its founder, does not go from strength to strength but from death to resurrection."

Pastor Tim Keller wrote these words in an article about the increased secularization of our country, citing how American churches are closing and more and more people are identifying as "nones" (having no religious affiliation). And those who do identify as Christian have declining attendance patterns.

The picture is bleak, and yet Keller was pointing out the nature of heart-soaring, pulse-pounding, casket-splitting, phoenix-rising, hope-stirring, death-shattering, eternity-altering resurrection. *Resurrection* is the key word to understanding Christianity. Take it away and everything else comes crashing down.

But no one can take it away. We have come to a kingdom that cannot be shaken. Our God raises the dead, and Jesus has conquered the grave!

So for the church in the West—and the East, North, and South—the tide of popularity can rise and fall, people can come less regularly, watch online, or seemingly not be watching at all. Gen Z can turn to TikTok and microdose shrooms; churches can turn into weed dispensaries, and Joe Rogan can become the high priest of a new form of alien-infused spirituality. We need not despair, for all is not lost.

Jesus said, "On this rock I will build my church, and the gates of hell shall not prevail against it" (Matthew 16:18 ESV).

When it might seem like it is dying, Christianity is in fact preparing for a glorious spiral step of resurrection. It can be struck down, but in so doing, it will spin closer and closer, round and round, and become far more powerful than the Enemy could imagine. In fact, the church castigated, relegated, and persecuted is often the church glorious, purified, and indefatigable. The great struggle has always been how to thrive in abundance, blessing, and prosperity without being ruined by it. As novelist G. Michael Hopf wrote, "Hard times create strong people, strong men create good times, good times create weak people, and weak men create hard times." And sadly, the cycle continues.

But have no fear. Down through the ages this truth rings out—Jesus will build His church!

These words have comforted my heart again and again in the two decades I have been in pastoral ministry. It helps me remember that the church is Jesus' problem and His responsibility. Being faithful is ours.

When the FBI called to tell us there were credible death threats on my life—Jesus' problem.

When we ran out of money in a building campaign during the 2008 recession—Jesus' problem.

When we lost staff members in crucial roles—Jesus' problem.

> THE GREAT STRUGGLE HAS ALWAYS BEEN HOW TO THRIVE IN ABUNDANCE, BLESSING, AND PROSPERITY WITHOUT BEING RUINED BY IT.

"CHEER UP, WESLEY; I'LL MOST LIKELY KILL YOU IN THE MORNING"

"Down, down, down into the bricks" is our family's code to laugh at the irony of a bleak situation. Alivia said that to me as we drove home one day about fifteen years ago. We were talking about someone on the church team who had recently quit. This was during a season when we had a smaller team and when several families, all for various reasons, had decided to worship elsewhere in a compressed time frame. Unfortunately, every departure had been emphatic. She asked, "What about so-and-so?" She unknowingly picked someone else who had also felt called to serve God elsewhere. At the tender age of six she quipped, "Wow, if this keeps up . . ." and her voice trailed off. I sensed the reverse crescendo, and my heart dropped into my stomach along with her tone. "What?" I asked.

Dramatically quiet for a moment, she mimed an airplane falling from the sky, saying, "It'll be down, down, down . . . into the bricks!"

The look on her face in the rearview mirror was equal parts solemn acceptance and stoic resignation, which made me explode into laughter. We laughed and laughed and laughed, and it functioned as a release valve, breaking the tension as the tears rolled down my cheeks. From then on it has become a dark joke in our family anytime someone quits or people we thought would never leave move on. It's our little way of coping by fake catastrophizing with a resigned shrug of the shoulders. "If this keeps up . . ." one of us will say, and then the other will quip, ". . . it'll be down, down, down into the bricks." It's one of my favorite weird, insider Luskoisms. It has helped us to normalize a disappointment and then "keep buggering on," as Winston Churchill liked to put it, in times that would otherwise discourage us.

It reminds me of the ten steps of sadness Tiger Woods allowed himself when he made a mistake on the golf course. He permitted a pity party of no more than ten steps before forcing himself to move on in his emotions, putting the failure completely behind him so he could hit the next ball. This whole "forgetting the things behind you so you can run your race with endurance" is a key ingredient in not letting your past paralyze you.

You don't need to panic when you feel you are in a free fall, because the fate of the universe is *not* in your hands! You must do what only you can do, then trust Him for what only He can do. So when a blow comes, go ahead and feel bad for the time required to take ten steps, then shake it off. But know that it's not into the bricks you are falling—it's into His grace and His love, which has no end to its height or depth or width. It never runs out.

Obedience is our responsibility. The outcome is His.

There is such a comfort in sovereignty—the Most High God rules the universe! We can have a relaxed confidence in that. And so when we remember that Jesus will build His church, we are telling our hearts that it is not for us to stress or strive or wear an ulcer into our stomach lining with anxiousness. The sovereignty of God is a safety net to fall into when the circumstances of life feel overwhelming. He is in control, and that feels really wonderful when our hearts are weary because things are out of our control.

> THE SOVEREIGNTY OF GOD IS A SAFETY NET TO FALL INTO WHEN THE CIRCUMSTANCES OF LIFE FEEL OVERWHELMING.

"You will face trouble," Jesus warned His followers. "But don't lose your cool! I have overcome the world" (John 16:33, paraphrased). Do you see how bad to the bone His tense is? His sovereignty is so final that He is describing future victory in the past as though it were already accomplished! That is metal. Why could He do that when He hadn't even gone to the cross yet? Isn't that counting His chickens before they hatch? No. Because there's nothing that God can't do. That means you and I can sleep tonight, because He never does.

Even if church doors close in one place, the church will continue to grow.

Even if your family faces hardship, your spirits can thrive.

Even if a job is lost, a new opportunity will open up.

If you or someone you love ends up in the ICU, God will be there in the hospital.

Not even death can stop God, so why would we stop trusting in the midst of our trial?

THE ROOT SYSTEM

In Utah there is an aspen grove that has been described as the largest organism ever discovered on earth. It spreads over one hundred acres and consists of forty thousand individual trees. You can cut down trees in one place but they will continue to grow in another because the aspen tree originates from a single seed and spreads by sending up new shoots from the expanding root system.

The church is like that. An aspen grove made of one organism showing up uniquely in different times, seasons, and places, yet still one. One faith, one Lord, one baptism, one Spirit. While the church may not be having its finest moment in some places in America, there are still extraordinary works of God happening. From sea to shining sea there are glimmers of revival in many places, including our Fresh Life Church. In addition, the global church has been experiencing explosions of growth in the Southern Hemisphere—South America, South Africa, and South Asia.

What I'm saying is that even if the church where you live seems to die, the root system would make sure that a new explosive resurrection would pop up somewhere.

This is paradigm altering because God's promise of protection and blessing is as true for your house as it is for His. Internalizing this truth, and truly believing it, will give you a completely different way of looking at every crisis. So whether it is a job situation or medical issues, deep grief after the loss of a child or other family member, dating after a divorce, anxiety about the future, or witnessing your spouse go through a valley of depression—what should by all rights freak you out can be an occasion for calm confidence.

Remember, you are climbing stairs.

In your life, as you face what seems to be a free-fall swan dive toward the bricks, believe that the death will lead to a resurrection. How many relationships have ended only to lead to unimaginable happiness in a new beginning? How many new companies have been started by someone laid off—a person whose job was a safety net and who would never have had the courage to start their own company without losing that net? How many incredible songs have been written by people who endured extraordinary tragedy that turned into inspiration for beauty?

SUFFERING SERVES A PURPOSE.

When you smack into a wall, it might feel like an end, but it is a new beginning. When you are nowhere near your dream—like José—you don't have to waste your waiting time. Suffering serves a purpose.

WAIT FOR IT

Resurrection is what God does. It's also who He is. John 12:24 reminds us of this principle by explaining that unless a seed goes into the ground and dies it will remain alone. But if it dies, it will produce a harvest.

God has a completely different way of looking at death. We are often tempted to stand at the graveside ceremony, shed our tears, and then walk away. Consider God with His arm out to block our departure, like a true Marvel fan does when someone new to the franchise gets up to leave at the end of the movie. As the credits begin to roll, He says, "Wait for it . . ."

Staring at the ground, we are confused. All we can see is dirt on a casket.

God whispers, "One one thousand, two one thousand . . ."

Looking at the best-loved stories in the Bible, we are given the inescapable reality that to suffer is a gift, a gateway to glory. Would Esther have married the king and saved her people had her mom and dad not died, leaving her to her cousin Mordecai?

Would Daniel have become a trusted advisor to the king without first having been kidnapped from his home? Would we have the knowledge that songs can shake the ground and set the captive free had Paul and Silas not been imprisoned in Acts 16?

Joseph would never have been the top project manager under Pharaoh, riding around in the royal backup chariot, aka Air Horse Two, had it not been for the unspeakable difficulties he had faced— betrayal by family members, imprisonment under false charges, and being forgotten by people he had helped. His pain wasn't a barrier to his dreams coming true; it was the gateway.

Our faith story is not one that goes from strength to strength but from death to resurrection. This means that the death you are experiencing in your life, in your body, in your career, or in your walk with Jesus is not a curse; it is a catalyst. As Paul said of the hardships he faced in Ephesus, "We were burdened beyond measure, above strength, so that we despaired even of life. Yes, we had the sentence of death in ourselves, that we should not trust in ourselves but in God who raises the dead, who delivered us from so great a death, and does deliver us; in whom we trust that He will still deliver us" (2 Corinthians 1:8–10).

The King is dead. Long live the King! And His Spirit is in you, so you don't have to fear any kind of dying. You are immortal.

If you are flat on your back and gasping today, do not fear.

It's time to rise again.

THERE CAN BE BREAKTHROUGH IN WHAT IS TRYING TO BREAK YOU.

My friend Cody Carnes wrote a powerful worship song that has been sung around the world called "Firm Foundation (He Won't)." The song poses the question "So why would He fail now?" then answers with an emphatic "He won't." This is why it is not a mistake to build your life on Him. He'll never let you down.

When I asked Cody about the circumstances of writing the song, he said he wrote it after one of the first and worst panic attacks he had ever had. *Smack*. (It is worth noting that it came at a midlife point for him. Cliché or not, I don't know very many people who have made it through the halfway point of life without some spiraling.) Cody's response to his out-of-breath struggle was to open his mouth and praise. And a song was born.

Here's the insight that can turn what feels like a wall into a spiral staircase: When you sing in the pit of despair, there can be breakthrough in what is trying to break you.

THE EYE OF THE BEHOLDER

When my daughter Clover was eleven, she was looking for a jewelry box to make her own, and to her delight she came across one at a thrift store for three dollars. She showed it to me with joy and admiration as though she had unearthed a treasure. I took one look at it and immediately knew she had overpaid. Battered and filthy, it looked as though it had survived a long life at the hands of an unloving owner.

"Oh, Clover, it is . . . very nice," I managed. "How much did you pay?"

"Three dollars," she gushed, beaming with pride as though it was the bargain of the century.

"I think you might have overpaid. This thing has been well-loved . . . a little *too* well-loved."

With a look of betrayal, she clutched it close to her. "Just wait until I get done with it. I can clean it up."

And she did. Snapping latex gloves into place like a surgeon preparing for an intense procedure, she laid out Q-tips, cleaning cloths, disinfectant, and polish on our table at home and got to work.

Half an hour later I heard a squeal of joy from the other room. While cleaning out dust between the velvet cushions—the spots designed for storing rings—she had found a tightly rolled-up one-hundred-dollar bill.

She strode over to me with a mischievous smirk and held up the Benjamin. "I overpaid, huh?"

How could I argue with that? She made ninety-seven dollars and ended up with a freshly restored jewelry box. Sparkling with character and personality, it is in her room to this day. Not only did she get to see something dilapidated—which I had written off— come to new life, but in the process she found something hidden that was contained within.

She saw what I couldn't, and so she found what I didn't.

This, dear reader, is why you must not reject the dirty and beat-up thing that is your life as one season gives way to another. It may feel like a mess, but there is treasure hidden within. You must believe this even in the most painful, disappointing, or dreadful of circumstances and go all in with Jesus, the One who went from death to resurrection so we could, too, yet again.

So take another step toward Him. I know it may feel discouraging if that step seems small, but do not underestimate its impact.

Maybe it will be buying a fresh journal to write in, running a 5k, or getting a library card and checking out books to read in the park instead of doom-scrolling or binge-watching. Maybe it's joining a volunteer team at your church or signing up to spend time at a senior citizens home—resolving to put yourself in places where you'll spend less time feeling sorry that you're no longer twenty-two or that your children have adult lives and aren't home with you anymore. Maybe you need to buy a blender instead of hitting a drive-through, so you can make a smoothie that's good for you. One small step for man can be one giant leap for being kind to yourself.

I don't know what makes your life feel like a throwaway box right now, but I know that the Holy Spirit has something precious tucked away in the dusty velvet, something for you to discover as you once again go all in and continue to climb.

In the next chapter we are going on an aerial adventure, a thirty-thousand-foot view of your life to see it from beginning to end so we can get some perspective and have a vision for old age. Not just to tolerate it but to actually find beauty and purpose in it. For now, though, I hope you'll close this chapter and talk to God about what you are feeling. He's right here with you.

CHAPTER 3

DON'T BLOW IT

WHAT IS THE goal of life?

This isn't a gotcha question. There is a "right" answer, according to the Westminster Shorter Catechism, which states, "Man's chief end is to glorify God, and to enjoy him forever." Translated, it means to do what will bring God praise, fame, and credit. This goal is to be the motivation and the source from which everything else flows.

In some ways God's will for you is the same as it is for me—to be saved, sanctified, and thankful, worshiping Him in spirit and in truth. But beyond bringing God glory, there are more specific callings. Things like woodworking and welding. Getting married and giving sermons. Raising children, doing laundry, lassoing cattle, and playing the bassoon.

We each have location-specific situations and a unique mix of personality traits and gifts, aptitudes and appetites. There are things that, for you, would be obedience that for me would be turning my back on what God has called me to do. For instance, if you are called to sing soprano or advance science, then giving sermons would be a sin. But for me to stop preaching to give myself over to opera or chemistry would be Jonah-like disobedience. I have long suspected if I tried to leave Montana to take a job in Brooklyn or Beijing, a giant moose would come out of the woods, swallow me alive, then spit me back out in the West where God has called me to serve Him. As James 4:17 reminds us, if we know the right thing to do and don't do it, we have missed God's mark.

With that groundwork laid, let me ask the question again: What is the goal of life? I mean, assuming you are saved, sanctified, thankful, and doing science, not singing—or singing, not doing science—whatever God's specific will is for you. Within that framework or sweet spot, what is the exact goal you should aim for? The benchmark or metric of success *within* that calling?

Perhaps you are thinking *improvement*, *faithfulness*, and *progress*.

Check. Check. Check.

When Jesus gave His last instructions to the disciples before His arrest, He said it was His Father's will that we bear fruit, *more* fruit, and *much* fruit (John 15). So you can certainly make the case that the goal should be that you do science, *more* science, and *much* science—or whatever your calling is—to the glory of God. Both quantity and quality. Giving it your all.

What this means is for the next ten thousand hours, and then plus, plus, plus after that, you ought to run in such a way as to win the prize, as the apostle Paul said, giving it everything you've got. No sloppy living. You should be seeking to receive gold, not bronze or silver, as far as it lies within you, so you can receive an imperishable crown.

This is important.

Jesus made wine once, and it was the best wine anyone ever tasted. Surprisingly, shockingly, outrageously good. It wasn't boxed wine sold on the cheap in a supermarket. He crafted the finest vino—not Two Buck Chuck.

For thirty years Jesus was a carpenter, building things like furniture, chicken coops, and sheep pens. There is no doubt the results of His handiwork were excellent, judging by the intricacies and the extravagancies of our universe, which He made by the power of His word. I would venture a guess that Jesus' chairs weren't rickety, and his tables didn't require a ton of sugar packets to kill the wobble. (Don't you hate that?)

Since you are made in His image, you are to do things to honor Him, not just with lip service but with the sincerest form of flattery: imitation. So, as you lead in business, finance, or medicine, you follow His sandaled footsteps and strive for your God-given best. If you are a guitar player, you do not settle for subpar but strive for Clapton, Hendrix, or Mayer proportions, because when He meets you face-to-face, He will ask you what you did with what you were given. If you had just three talents, He would never hold you to what the five-talent person could have done—but He will expect you to have grown your gift of three. God wants a return on investment. "Whatever your hand finds to do, do it with your might," reads Ecclesiastes 9:10. Growth and excellence should be your goal.

WHEN WE CAN'T GO "UP AND TO THE RIGHT"

But what about when you are at a low point emotionally or physically? Or when you're decades older? You can't go up and to the right forever, can you?

No, there will come a point when you are as good as you will ever get. You will hit the top. And you won't be able to stay there, standing strong in the prime of your life, forever. Sometimes it is our life crises that pull us away from excellence; other times it is simply due to the nature of our humanity. You will inevitably hit a point when you can't get good-er.

The science on this is clear. If you think the bull's-eye on the target of life accomplishments is continuous improvement, then this will depress you. (I guess this was a little "gotcha" after all . . . but keep reading, and it won't be for long.)

According to data where Dean Keith Simonton has studied progress in careers, you have twenty years where you will get better and better at a job, and then progress will stall out. If you start your career at age twenty-five, your progress will begin to diminish by age forty-five. And if you start a job at thirty, you can expect to do your best work at fifty and then go into decline soon thereafter.

Benjamin Jones, a professor of strategy and entrepreneurship at Northwestern University's Kellogg School of Management, studied the accomplishments of major inventors and Nobel Prize winners over more than a century and found that the typical age for producing a magnum opus is the late thirties. Thereafter, "the likelihood of a major discovery . . . declines dramatically through one's forties, fifties, and sixties."

Simonton found that poets peak in their early forties, and novelists generally take a little longer (i.e., in their forties and fifties). Many tech entrepreneurs are in creative decline by age thirty. *Harvard Business Review* reported that tech-company founders valued at one billion dollars tended to cluster in the twenty to thirty-four age range—with the average being thirty-four—and the majority of successful start-up founders are under the age of forty.

We don't have to be inventors or Nobel Prize winners for the principles to apply to us. There *will* come a day when the surgeon will need to put down the scalpel because their hands shake. The mind of a lawyer, once quick, will slow. Someday I will find it impractical to hop on planes to speak at events or preach forty new sermons a year.

Sylvester Stallone once said, "I want to do a screening where I present *Rocky 1* next to *Rocky 6* and show how fast life goes by." No matter what title you might win in a prize fight, a board room, a beauty pageant, or a soccer pitch, you can't hang on to your spot for long.

What goes up must come down.

When this sets into your mind and body, it can feel like a crisis.

According to researchers, three out of four people ages twenty-five to thirty-three experience a *quarterlife* crisis. One in four Americans between forty and sixty years of age have a midlife crisis. One in three people over sixty experience what's called a *laterlife* crisis. In reality, the numbers for each category may be higher, since you don't always realize what's going on when you are in a storm. What's the takeaway? Transitions are hard.

Destabilization can happen to any of us in any stage of adulthood. One study even reported that most midlife crises were triggered not by age but by types of major life events known to be associated with psychological distress, including divorce, separation, job loss, marriage and remarriage, serious health problems, and other major life crises. If you are not experiencing the spiraling effects of transition disorientation, someone around you probably is; maybe you are reading this so you can help them. The kindness of my wife, Jennie, in my times of heavy spiraling was a massive blessing to me. She prayed for me, stroked my back, and told me everything was going to be all right while I did breathing exercises and tried to ground myself while in the throes of a panic attack. Just being able to tell her how scared I was at two a.m. gave me incredible comfort.

RECALIBRATING AND EMBRACING SEASONS

If you are the one spiraling, I know it may seem like an unlucky position, but I believe it is a gift. It is the chance to recalibrate and get your bearings before your time on earth is over. You get to explore the big questions it's easy to forget to give time to in less-turbulent seasons.

What is the goal of life?

How do you handle not being able to do the thing you were uniquely gifted and called to do?

What do you do when your emotional or physical state keeps you from top-shelf excellence?

You come back to Ecclesiastes 3 and remember life is meant to have different seasons or "times." A time to be born, and a time to die; a time to plant, and a time to pluck what is planted; a time to gather stones and a time to scatter them; a time to speak and a time to be silent.

Incremental improvement can't be our only goal in life, for that is a losing battle. It is more about seeking to thrive in every season, whatever limitations we may have, and depending on God through all the transitions and crises. This of course includes aging and eventually dying.

The world does not train us to age with class, style, and generosity. We don't know how to die a glorious death because we are conditioned to avoid decay, entropy, and death at all costs (when we are brave enough to even acknowledge it). Our culture's strategy for elderly celebrities is outright cruelty. Banish them if they show signs of aging, and mock them if they take steps to hide it. A few lucky ones get to be Denzel Washington, Anthony Hopkins, or Helen Mirren, the elderly statesmen and women of an industry. The rest are in a "darned if you do, darned if you don't" situation.

THE GOD WHO DOES ALL THINGS WELL HAS A PLAN NOT JUST FOR OUR DAYS OF DOMINATION BUT ALSO FOR OUR DAYS OF DIMINISHED CAPACITY.

But I believe the church can lead the way in embracing the natural course of life instead of living in denial of it. It is indeed possible to glorify God through it. Because the God who does all things well has a plan not just for our days of domination but also for our days of diminished capacity. There can be power and glory in both the gathering of stones and in their scattering.

We live and serve His glory in myriad ways—in faithfulness, fruitfulness, and progress, but also in diminishment, in letting go of a previous season, and in seeing the beauty of life and significance in what is in front of us.

In learning how to prepare to die well.

In shifting from a success mindset to a significance one.

In trusting Him enough to greet each new season with a smile.

We have the chance to glorify Him as we experience different aspects of our humanity. Even if we are unsure how. What does it mean to face a dementia diagnosis with grace? To bravely suffer the loss of memories and motor function? To watch a loved one lose their dignity while keeping yours intact? These are the messy but beautiful, painful but powerful realities of being human, and we can lean on Him to guide us through them.

Secularism is bankrupt when it comes to hope-filled answers for aging; it is no wonder suicide and euthanasia are often on the table where God is rejected. Epicurean "eating, drinking, and being merry" is often the result of nihilism, the rejection of all religious and moral principles. Seek pleasure now, because ahead there is despair. If you believe there is only nothingness after death, then you will see no reason to live once you are old and infirm and no longer producing. The only treasure available to you is on earth, and there is no heavenly life to taste here and now.

But we believe in a God who raises the dead!

He is a God who meets us in our need and weakness and has goodness and love to give every day.

Decay, weakness, feebleness, hospice—these are some of the crevices and corners of your life that Jesus wants to inhabit just as much as He does your vitality and strength. He is there for you as you perish just as much as He is when you are in your prime.

From life's first cry to life's last breath—all of it has been ordained from before the foundation of the earth was laid. All of it. Not just the good stuff.

> FROM LIFE'S FIRST CRY TO LIFE'S LAST BREATH—ALL OF IT HAS BEEN ORDAINED FROM BEFORE THE FOUNDATION OF THE EARTH WAS LAID.

According to Psalm 139, God numbered your days in His book. Before any of them took place, He planned them.

In case it's been a while since someone told you (if ever), *you are not an accident*! Your Father in heaven has a plan for you. A plan for all four quarters of your game clock on earth.

And what is your role? Walk closely with Him, listen to what He says, and hold on to Him more than to anything else.

LETTING GO AND FINDING TREASURE

There was a man who once found a treasure in a field, so he sold all he had to buy the field to obtain the treasure. This, according to Jesus, is what the kingdom of God is like. You let go of what you have in order to receive Jesus.

People often think this passage applies to the moment of salvation, when you deny yourself and take up the cross, laying down your life to find eternal life. But it is not a one-time thing; it is a way of life. Throughout your days, you are always accumulating more stuff, both in your hands and your heart, so there is always more to lay down—and more of Jesus to take in.

It was in my midlife crisis that I had to discover the power of repeatedly laying down my life and selling what I had so I could hold the Treasure. This is what it means to grow. Transform. Adapt. I had to die daily, and when I did, there was always new Treasure to find in the wounds and worth of Jesus. His glory has no end.

In each season you will be tempted to get comfortable in what you fought to rise to and attain. You will always want it to remain. That is when you know it is time once again to "sell" that earthly gain for the greater Treasure. Meaning, don't become infatuated with the blessings *of* God and forget they came *from* God. They are a poor replacement for Him.

It is foolish to put anything God has given in the place that only He is worthy of.

It is wise instead to choose daily crucifixion. Dying again and again to the flesh that longs to be in control. Crucifying the desire to freeze time as it is and to stay in a season of usefulness or any particular blessing.

Let's not cling to the accolades of what was always meant to be a transient season, refusing to face reality and gracefully transition. There's nothing more awkward than seeing someone in denial about their age—still shopping at Forever 21 in their sixties or replaying the glory days instead of cashing them in for an even greater Treasure.

No matter what we do for God or what God does through us, at some point we will have to let go. Of all of it. But the good news is we get to decide when that happens. We can't have something ripped from our grasp if we hold it with a light grip. It only hurts to have things taken if we hold them with a clenched fist. If we can learn to use a light touch, we can be trusted with much more, and we won't have to fear the sting of the seasons changing.

We will never be able to see the beauty of our current season, and prepare for the next one, until we accept and mourn that change is happening and we say goodbye to past seasons. When we not only accept these things but glory in them, we humble ourselves to a position where we can be exalted. And life won't have to rip from us what has been joyfully surrendered.

Stop for a minute and think about your life. What is precious? What is worthless? And what season are you in today?

It is easy to mistake accomplishment, status, abilities, or accolades as treasure and attach them to our identity. They all are potential barriers to obtaining the true Treasure in that next season—the true Treasure of Jesus. Not what He does for you or does through you or entrusts to you; He alone is the prize.

LIFE WON'T HAVE TO RIP FROM US WHAT HAS BEEN JOYFULLY SURRENDERED.

Trade in your treasures for a greater Treasure while you still have them as currency—like the man who saw a treasure and bought a field to get it. He traded all he had to buy it.

Keep bringing God anything you are tempted to derive your identity from and that can be taken away. Cash it in for what can't. Only Christ is secure enough to anchor your identity both now and forever. In all the universe, He alone has pledged to you that He will never leave you or forsake you. All else will fly away from your hand.

A FUTURE SECURE IN HIM

When I first read C. S. Lewis's essay "The Inner Ring," it was a major light-bulb moment for me. It basically says that no matter what stage of life you are in, there is a social ring—an inner circle, pecking order, or hierarchy—you will be tempted to feel like you are just outside of and trying to get into. He points out the futility of this because each time you get into the next ring the target moves and you feel like there is another, more exclusive one you are still outside of. To put it bluntly, these inner rings are a dead end. For me, that essay explained so much of the striving in my life. My constant wondering and worrying about what I haven't been given, and my fear that I am not enough. While those things in me serve as a tremendous motivator to accomplish things, they do not lead to healthy places. They leave me needing to constantly *do* in order to *be*. In essence, they make me a human *doing*, not a human *being*.

Maybe you have these struggles too. When healthy, we can harness these forces in an explosive manner, driving and working and creating, not because we lack validation but because we have it and can't lose it. It's the ongoing quest for greatness.

Now, I am convinced that greatness and ambition have a glorious side, not just an icky self-serving one. I believe it's when you are happy with the ring you are in and not obsessed with reaching the next one that God may open up another ring for you—as many rings as He sees fit without it destroying you. The key for us is not to treasure those great works or try to use them to fill up some empty place in our lives.

This can be especially tricky when we've tasted some amount of success.

In an interview with *60 Minutes*, Hans Zimmer said he lives in constant terror that one day his phone will stop ringing. He is the master musician behind the epic soundtracks of *The Lion King*, *Gladiator*, *Pirates of the Caribbean*, *Top Gun: Maverick*, and many more. Yet he fears that opportunities to create more soundtracks will be taken from him. And it will. One hundred years from now, there will not be a movie in a theater (if we still go to movies in theaters) with a Hans Zimmer soundtrack (unless it's made by an artificial intelligence version of him, but that's pretty creepy).

When I heard his comment, I felt stabbed through my heart. It was like holding up a mirror, revealing how I can cling to whatever influence I perceive having as a speaker and author. Nothing I say or write will ever truly be helpful or creative if it comes from a place of trying to "keep my spot" or get into another ring. I cannot bless when I am trying to impress.

When I speak or write to keep the phone ringing, something in me sort of dies. That kind of motivation pollutes the well, and I begin to be defined by what is meant to be traded in for God's glory. My actions say that Christ alone is *not* enough to satisfy the deep cries of my heart.

Being successful has never been enough for anyone. It's like drinking salt water—the more you drink, the thirstier you become. But Jesus said that whoever drinks the water He gives will never thirst again! This is life everlasting. So we must stab the idols of accolades and status through the heart again and again, then offer open hands of surrender. If you don't kill your sin, it will kill you. Herod received the praise of the people instead of giving glory to God, and it ate him inside with worms. Don't let that be your story! Make Christ your all in all and let your fountains be in Him.

Here is my prayer (feel free to make it your own):

God, if You never do anything through me again, You are all I need.

If and when I can't preach or write or lead, You will be enough for me.

When I can't run or fly or feed myself, You are enough for me.

But when I am at that place of humility, and You allow me to fly, run, or speak without having those things above You, my identity won't be fazed.

Because it's in You my future is secure.

What does this ping inside of you? Perhaps you don't relate to my particular breed of crazy—my type-A drive may not be anything like your experience—but no doubt there are some things inside that you need to trade for fresh Treasure.

Is it the need to please?

The drive to acquire?

A craving for comfort?

A quest to control?

A penchant toward pleasure?

A compulsory drive to save so you will never go without?

See if you can pinpoint what you might be relying on for security in your future and talk to God about it.

STRENGTH AND GREATNESS THE JESUS WAY

We've talked enough about surrender and striving that, clearly, there is a tension we will live with. Here are a couple of teachings from Jesus we can keep in mind as we do.

At the Last Supper, Jesus chastised the disciples for their squabbling about who was the greatest in the kingdom. I don't think He was frustrated by the fact that they wanted to be great; that desire is hardwired into us. Their problem was that they were benchmarking what great *was*, based on a comparison of each other.

> BEING THE BEST IS NOT THE PROBLEM; ATTEMPTING TO BE BETTER THAN OTHER PEOPLE IS.

There is no doubt God wants you to be the fullest, greatest expression of the image He tucked inside you. But that will be stunted if you are looking to your left or your right.

Being the best is not the problem; attempting to be better than other people is.

On another occasion Jesus told the disciples that the greatest in the kingdom was the one who became like a little child. Young kids aren't impressed by outward appearances, and they don't worry about their social standing or many other things that light us up as adults. They live with imagination, curiosity, and authenticity.

It's true greatness, being comfortable in your skin—whether that skin is tight, wrinkle laden, or somewhere in between. It's part of why Paul was so steady and confident, saying, "I know how to be abased, and I know how to abound." He knew he could have a lot and be okay, and not have a lot and be okay. It didn't matter, because he knew his power originated outside of himself. "I can do all things through Christ who strengthens me," he resolved (Philippians 4:12–13).

Paul took everything of value to him—being a Pharisee, keeping the law, being a part of the tribe of Benjamin and of the Sanhedrin, writing most of the New Testament, being so full of faith handkerchiefs he touched healed people—and considered it as dung for a much greater, surpassing Treasure: knowing Jesus.

He did this again and again because he had the epiphany that trials can't separate us from the love of God. They drive us farther into His arms.

For Paul, knowing Jesus was the prize. The Treasure. The goal. As Paul perpetually held these other things in a category of less importance than knowing Jesus, it didn't sting as much when they were taken from him. This was how he lived up until the moment that, according to tradition, he was led to the outskirts of Rome and decapitated. Death didn't take him away from his Treasure; it brought him to Him.

You, too, are opened to an abundant life when you have laid yours down.

This is the goal in life.

Let's adventure together through the seasons of life to discover the joy of finding true and eternal, abiding and abundant life that comes from losing it and laying it down, again and again! We will discover beneath the dust of the field even more buried Treasure that we will get to keep forever. This is the paradoxical but powerful truth of God's upside-down kingdom, which we must fight to see in our world.

CHAPTER 4

PUT YOUR HANDS ON WHAT IS YOURS

I SOMETIMES TALK about the "surprising delight" of my midlife crisis—which may sound like a lie or like the words of an insane person. No, I didn't love the panic attacks. And no, I'm not spraying Febreze on a hardship by pretending it wasn't actually agonizing. It was. *Blech*, just talking about it takes me back to how out of control I felt while spiraling. And as a card-carrying control freak, that tampered with my sense of equilibrium in a huge way. At first blush there is nothing delightful about any crisis you go through in life's transitional moments. In the midst of it I really struggled.

I remember one particularly painful moment when I was driving with one of my daughters. I was feeling some really scary anxiety brewing like a storm in the distance, but I tried to act normal—including aiming to control my breath enough to calm myself down. At one point my daughter put her arm on my shoulder and said, "Dad, are you okay?" Looking into her eyes broke my heart because I saw loving concern and a little fear. I hated that I'd made her worry. Though I had to humble myself to acknowledge I was having a hard time, the vulnerability ended up bringing us closer together.

There is blessing in it.

If you're spiraling today, I am so sorry. I believe that if you keep going, even if it feels anything but joyful right now, you'll find delight of one sort or another before too long. I know you might have a hard time believing that right now. That's why it's going to be a *surprising* delight.

Jesus' words in John 12 help explain why: "Unless a grain of wheat falls into the ground and dies, it remains alone; but if it dies, it produces much grain" (v. 24). The delight comes when it produces fruit: It causes you to reevaluate what matters.

You go sell everything you have—metaphorically, or literally, but most importantly, doxologically—and buy the field because of the Treasure it contains.

You realize that what you wanted wasn't what you needed.

It's worth getting stopped in your tracks before you go too far down a road that leads somewhere you don't want to be.

Ask the man who came to Jesus wanting to follow Him but went away sorrowfully. He is normally called the rich young ruler, but—as my friend Jonathan Pokluda once pointed out—this man isn't rich, isn't young, and doesn't rule anything today. Those three defining features he had built his life and self-image on ultimately slipped away. His identity came from what seemed real but was sand. He let *what was temporary* keep him from *what is eternal.*

IT'S WORTH GETTING STOPPED IN YOUR TRACKS BEFORE YOU GO TOO FAR DOWN A ROAD THAT LEADS SOMEWHERE YOU DON'T WANT TO BE.

The formerly rich, once young, used-to-be ruler was given the chance to participate in a life built on rock, as a part of a kingdom of priests that can't be shaken and won't be stopped. But he turned it down. He might have gained the world but lost his very self.

This cautionary tale will keep you and me from following in his footsteps and losing what is most valuable—*if* we have ears to hear.

How will you spend your one precious life?

Have you forgotten it's a gift you get to steward?

THE FAITHFUL WORK OF PREPARING

You might need a wake-up call to jolt you away from obsessing over money, appearing youthful, or gaining influence. What should you do once you see how short-lived and fleeting sexiness, strength, speed, and style are?

"Let the lowly brother glory in his exaltation, but the rich in his humiliation, because as the flower of the field he will pass away. For no sooner has the sun risen with a burning heat than it withers the grass; its flower falls, and its beautiful appearance perishes. So the rich man also will fade away in his pursuits" (James 1:9–11). In the moments you gain clarity and perspective, you can shift your focus to more worthwhile pursuits.

Or maybe you need a wake-up call to look beyond your current season more. Solomon, the wisest person who ever lived, advised, "Go to the ant, you sluggard! Consider her ways and be wise, which, having no captain, overseer, or ruler, provides her supplies in the summer, and gathers her food in the harvest" (Proverbs 6:6–8).

While you may be in summer now, winter is coming, and you'll wish you had gathered and prepared. I'm talking about the winter of career, health, mobility, or vitality. You will not remain as physically beautiful, desirable, acknowledged, or sought after as you are right now. Clinging to these things, instead of anticipating their inevitable moment of being required of us, is to have your head hidden in the sand.

And so, even when your children are young, remind yourself there will be an empty nest in a later season.

Prepare yourself for the death of your parents, even when they are not sick or dying. It's the time to forgive, prioritize seeing them, preserve memories, and eulogize them, speaking well of them while they live.

Envision succession in your business or organization.

Form a plan for your legacy and estate right now, whatever your age. A 2024 survey showed that only 32 percent of US adults have a will. Even the simple precaution of choosing in advance who will look after your children is not always considered.

The trick with all of this? You have to hold every plan loosely.

Otherwise you will slip into arrogance or feel crushed by the weight of what-ifs and miss the gifts of *right now*.

THE WISDOM OF BEING PRESENT

Here's a worthy goal: Prepare for what is likely coming *and* be faithful with what is in front of you. Make smart plans for the future—but do it with open hands, without assuming you know what the future holds.

James wrote, "You do not know what will happen tomorrow. For what is your life? It is even a vapor that appears for a little time and then vanishes away. Instead you ought to say, 'If the Lord wills, we shall live and do this or that.' But now you boast in your arrogance. All such boasting is evil" (4:14–16).

You don't know when your earthly story will come to a close. All you have guaranteed is today. Right now. And that means you and I can stop worrying.

When I get caught up worrying about future issues, it is somewhat relieving to think that none of the things I'm worrying about may end up being a problem. The world could end, I could die, or Jesus could return. There is a plethora of ways that whatever I am worrying about might not actually be a factor; therefore, to rob today of peace by being troubled about something that might not even be an issue is a tragedy.

You might say, "Levi, that is not helpful. Now I am worrying about new things!"

No, you don't have to run that direction.

Remember, fear is faith in the Enemy. And our faith is not in the Enemy, it is in God who raises the dead! He is King of all, rules from outside of time, and simply wants you to trust Him in the here and now.

So breathe in, breathe out, breathe in. Do you feel that? It's His peace.

Try to ground yourself in the present moment. Focus on how the carpet feels under your feet. Or the sheets of the bed over and under you. Sense your lungs expanding and feel the sensation of your chest puffing out as you fill it with air. Hold on to that pleasant, tight feeling before you exhale.

As you take another breath in through your nose, imagine that air is a delightful blue or green and hold it for a beat. Then exhale slowly through tightly-pursed lips, and as you do, picture that the breath coming out of your mouth is red. You are breathing in God's grace and then releasing the stress and worry that come from not trusting Him. If you need to, go ahead and take ten minutes to do this. Feel the underlying dread or apathy melting away through the gift of breathing.*

You are alive! Right now. Your heart is beating, and that is a gift. Don't let that go. Be thankful. Can you turn a hair on your head either white or black (without chemicals)? No. You are not in control. The weight of the world is not on your shoulders. You are not promised more days, and that makes you lucky.

Philip James Bailey said, "We should count time by heartthrobs" (beats). I take that to mean you shouldn't measure life in years or decades but in moments. Every beat of your heart is a gift,

---

* Breathing was lifesaving during my worst moments of panic and is still a go-to when I need to reset, whether on an airplane where I feel the world is shrinking or whenever I feel overwhelmed. I consider this biological "hack" a gift God gave us when He breathed life into Adam in Genesis, as well as in the New Testament when the Spirit came on believers like a wind.

and if yours is throbbing right now it is because God has a plan. If you're not dead, He's not done. I once heard someone say, "When I am noticing the purple and yellow in a flower, I know I am in a good place mentally." This is sound advice. Slow down. When was the last time you took the time to appreciate the subtle nuances of the colors of a flower?

If you are a parent, about 936 weeks is all you get with your kids from their first breath to their high school graduation and emancipation. That's only 936 chances to make waffles together on a Saturday morning or chat on a lazy Sunday afternoon. And it's racing by.

Regarding time with your own parents, one writer did the math and worked out that on average, by the time you turn eighteen, you have spent approximately 90 percent of the total hours you will ever spend with your parents under their roof. It's astonishing to look back and think, *How did that happen so quickly?* You need to slow down enough to notice.

One day at a time. One heartbeat at a time.

If you often view your life in terms of years or decades, you will miss what is right in front of you. But if each day you think, *What will I do with the gift of this day?* you will approach the moments and opportunities that day brings with more intentionality.

Jesus said, "I must do the works of Him who sent Me while it is day" (John 9:4). This shouldn't make you frenzied and manic; it should help you be fully present and focused.

MAKING THE MOST OF YOUR DAYS

Consider the question, What would you do if you were going to die tomorrow?

"I would call my family to tell them I love them," you might answer.

"I would turn to that person I've been resenting and shower them with grace."

Or, "I would go share the faith of Jesus with a dozen people I haven't yet."

Martin Luther has often been attributed to saying, "Even if I knew that tomorrow the world would go to pieces, I would still plant my apple tree." There is beauty and nobility in doing a small thing, even if it seems like it won't make a difference. An act of beauty is defiance against despair in a world that can feel hopeless.

Live without regrets. Take the small moments you have to bless those God puts in front of you. Send a postcard. Ride a roller coaster. Call your mom. Plant an apple tree. Be nice to a stranger. Take the stairs.

You never know how one small interaction can change someone's life.

President Bill Clinton was raised in Arkansas with anything but a silver spoon in his mouth. His biological father died in a car accident while Bill was in the womb, so he was born into a single mother's home. At age four, his mom married a man who was an abusive alcoholic. By all rights, Clinton should *not* have ended up as president of the United States. But during a high school field trip to the White House, he shook the hand of President Kennedy just four months before Kennedy's assassination. According to one of Clinton's former classmates, while on the bus ride home, Clinton reflected on the handshake. He then turned to a group of school- mates and said, "Someday I'm gonna have that job. Someday I'm gonna be president." He was only sixteen at the time, but that touch shaped his future. What did it cost Kennedy? Very little. And it became a handshake of destiny.

God can use small acts of kindness when we are willing to show up in our daily lives in little ways. Many of Jesus' recorded miracles were interruptions. He would be headed somewhere, then someone would touch Him and He would allow it to redirect Him. His willingness to take a moment and give His attention was what changed the course of eternity for many people, reaching to the present moment.

This is also how Jesus was able to say to the Father at the end of His earthly ministry, "I have finished the work which You have given Me to do" (John 17:4). He had been present in His prayer life. Committed to the people closest to Him. Fully engaged with whatever was in front of Him at any given moment. And when he had the chance to take a nap, He took it.

That is what God intends for you too. Outcome is His responsibility. Obedience is yours.

Let me say it again. One. Heartbeat. At. A. Time.

Remembering that you are only promised today allows you to be more present, and it does not mean you neglect or fail to prepare for the future. Seek to fully honor God with what is right in front of you. This is how you change the world!

It is easy to get paralyzed with all that needs to be done around us and forget that when God does anything of consequence through someone, it always starts small. We are going to look at how Psalm 128 displays that—and I assure you, it is worth a careful look. Don't just skim this passage and jump down to the next

SEEK TO FULLY HONOR GOD WITH WHAT IS RIGHT IN FRONT OF YOU.

paragraph; actually read it and notice the progression from where it starts to where it ends.

> Blessed is every one who fears the LORD, who walks in His ways. When you eat the labor of your hands, you shall be happy, and it shall be well with you. Your wife shall be like a fruitful vine in the very heart of your house, your children like olive plants all around the table. Behold, thus shall the man be blessed who fears the LORD. The LORD bless you out of Zion, and may you see the good of Jerusalem all the days of your life. Yes, may you see your children's children. Peace be upon Israel!

This profoundly powerful passage is strikingly simple. It is thought to be the inspiration behind Jesus' famous parable given in Matthew 7 about the two men who built homes—one on rock, the other on sand. When the storm came, the house on the sand collapsed, but the one built on rock was still standing.

Jesus grew up singing the psalms found in our Bible, especially when He traveled to and from Jerusalem with Mary and Joseph or with His disciples. The Song of Ascents (Psalms 120–134) were part of the road trip playlist the nation of Israel sang whenever they journeyed to or from the Feasts of Passover, Pentecost, and Tabernacles.

But what these particular psalms do is shrink the change we want to see in the world to a manageable size. And then they end, soaring and sweeping, with *shalom upon Israel.*

Generational power. Children's children. Good in Jerusalem. But how does it start?

One person's soul fearing God. And from there, loving your spouse, if you have one. Then the concentric rings fan out to kids and grandkids, and the city being touched . . . to infinity and beyond! And if you are not married or don't have children, your impact can be felt just as powerfully. Think of your cousins, nieces and nephews, or neighbors. You can be a light to children in your church or your social circles. Paul wasn't Timothy's dad, but that didn't stop him from being a spiritual father figure.

What's the point?

The greatest thing you can do for the world is have strong, loving relationships.

The greatest thing you can do for your relationships is to have a strong, loving soul.

And the greatest thing you can do for your soul is to fear the Lord.

Boom.

So, LET IT SHINE!

With all the darkness, corruption, and crisis, it's easy to see how much needs to change in the world. But we don't enact change by being overwhelmed by what is in turmoil that is outside of our control. We honor God with what we can, not by yelling at the darkness but by lighting a candle and letting it shine.

There is a lot of talk in our day about a gun problem, but an even larger crisis exists: a son problem. Many children who grow up without dads are harmed and often do harm. And we will see even more of this if the family unit continues to unravel.

Instead of despair over what you *can't* do, ask this question: What *can* I do? Consider your marriage. Are you loving and serving your spouse and kids? Home is where you effect change that can bring God's peace to your city, your nation, and the world. What can be done to serve and help those who are growing up in single-parent homes? Godly men or women serving in Sunday school, youth group, and mentorship programs can make massive differences in the lives of those who don't have dads or moms in their lives.

Let's go back to Psalm 128 for a minute.

Why did the psalmist talk about a vineyard? Because grapes must be cultivated, protected, nourished, and connected.

Why an olive tree? It has generational staying power. Mark Twain called olive trees "those fast friends of a worthless soil" because of their ability to thrive in adversity and hang on in inhospitable places.

One of the oldest living trees on this planet is an olive tree. In Bethlehem of all places.

Estimates of its age vary, with some suggesting it could be as old as four or five thousand years.

There are olive trees in Jerusalem that are older than Christ. It is stunning to walk into the garden of Gethsemane knowing many of the trees were there when Jesus prayed in the garden. I love that this tree with longevity and legacy is the tree we are meant to associate with our children.

God wants you to have a bigger, longer, more impactful vision for your life and family. He desires rings of impact to ripple out from your family tree. But He is also faithful to keep His covenant for a thousand generations.

Look beyond where you stand! Believe for the little olive saplings that, by the way, take ten to fifteen years to produce meaningful fruit. And don't despair if it seems they aren't listening. Today, while it is still day, prioritize your soul,

your marriage,

your kids,

your closest relationships,

any children you get the chance to influence and open

doors for—

and bring people into your home to sit at your table and

witness the fruit and light of Jesus.

Your dinner table, be it a fancy setup from Restoration Hardware or a flimsy folding table from Walmart, is meant to be an extension of the kingdom and a powerhouse of advancing the love of God in and around the world. "The Son of Man came eating and drinking" (Matthew 11:19). And so can you.

Since you don't have a clue how much time is left on your clock, the response shouldn't be to make a bucket list and frantically eat, drink, and be merry, for tomorrow you die. But rather may it be, "Let's eat, drink, and have joy in the Lord because He is in control of tomorrow!"

Let's do this one day, one meal, at a time. Until we eat and drink in the kingdom, it's glasses up as we proclaim, "Here's to the King!" (I am convinced that communion should have this celebratory ring of cheers to it more than just the somber note of a funeral dirge.)

Focusing on these small and often overlooked areas of our lives is extremely important—because added together, they become massive over time. I am more convinced than ever that it is not the flashy big stuff but the faithful little things that God loves to bless.

We get trapped in big worries about our kids' futures and the problems in our world, but literally a box of Hamburger Helper and some Sprite are all it takes to start being the change you want to see in the world. Studies show that children who get to sit around the table with their families more often do better in school, develop a more robust vocabulary, do drugs less, are less likely to be sexually active, and are more likely to go to college. And it doesn't even have to be home-cooked food—it can be fast food, provided you take the time to sit around a table while you eat it. The number to shoot for is five meals a week. But with fast-paced lives, sports, and commutes, family meals are often eliminated. "In the typical American household, the average number of dinners eaten together is three per week, with the average length of dinner being 20 minutes. Many homes no longer even have a dining room."

IT IS NOT THE FLASHY BIG STUFF BUT THE FAITHFUL LITTLE THINGS THAT GOD LOVES TO BLESS.

This should give you hope and unlock your agency. It is easy to be paralyzed with fear, feeling like you can't do everything. But you *can* do something. And when you do, you move from a disempowered state to an empowered one. So make your bed in the morning and turn the TV off and gather your people around the table. Pile up the phones in a basket, break some bread, and look each other in the eyes. Eat until you are full and laugh until you cry. This is how you change the world.

We will continue answering the question of what we can do in the next chapter. It is time to face the shadowy things in ourselves that are holding us back from being who we have always wanted to be.

Buckle up.

CHAPTER 5

I REPLACED MY MOM WITH PORNOGRAPHY

YOU KNOW THE line in the sand that marks the before and after points around a critical event? One of those lines in my life story was at the end of fifth grade, when my family went through a tragedy involving abuse. My parents' marriage began to crumble, the strain of the lingering trauma eventually caused the hairline cracks to blow up, and ultimately it was too much for the relationship to bear. Trials don't destroy a foundation; they reveal what it is made of.

My memories before that horrific turning point have a rosy

glow, portraying Camelot. Afterward, my mom sank into a deep depression and coped by retreating emotionally. Then four things happened in my life like a series of chaotic dominoes.

I moved into middle school and began the sixth grade in a new public school knowing no one.

Puberty's murky darkness enveloped me, which affected my hormones and emotions but left my height untouched.

My vision failed, and I ended up getting glasses.

Smack. My nose hit the wall. While it might have been a stair, it seemed like a dead end.

At the same time, my next-door neighbor exposed me to pornography.

I know—how utterly shocking that, when I began shielding myself from being hurt by my mom's low ebb in life, I began looking to images of women to bring me comfort. You don't have to be a psychologist to connect those dots. Except I never really had until I was explaining it all *to* a psychologist.

It's funny how the dysfunction in your own life is much harder to see than that in people's lives. It's often invisible to us because we see it every day, and we just carry on with blind spots, completely oblivious to our obliviousness.

DYSFUNCTION JUNCTION

When my counselor and I first discussed the stranglehold porn had on me for years, he asked when it started. I told him that my next-door neighbor showed me a box of *Playboy* magazines his dad had collected, and as we sat there in his garage looking at one after another, a flood of warmth, pleasure, guilt, and shame washed over me. My heart pounded. I felt tingly and excited all over. I didn't know why I was feeling it or what to do with it.

But when my friend gave me a magazine to take home and I continually snuck looks at it, I knew what I was doing was wrong. So I didn't tell anyone about it. I just carried it around inside, keeping it tucked away and secret. Then I literally dug a hole, wrapped the magazine in a black trash bag, and buried it outside my bedroom window in our backyard. Each time I dug it up to take another look, I would tell myself it would be the last time.

After hitting a stretch of months of managing to avoid the temptation, I dug it up yet again and found that ground water had seeped into it, turning the images into a pulpy wet mess. I was horrified by the sight and sickened by the smell; still I couldn't resist trying to find a bit of pleasure from the stained, smeared, smiling women looking back at me through the ruined pages. Like a drug addict licking a baggie for residue or a desperate smoker picking butts out of an ashtray, I was at once caught in my frantic compulsion and disturbed by how pathetic I had become.

The worst part is that throughout this period I was singing and dancing as an actor in *Psalty the Singing Songbook*, a live worship event for children. I was so mad at myself for my hypocrisy. I spiraled into self-hatred and shame about how rotten I was and how disappointed God surely was with me.

"What else was going on when you were first exposed to these addictive images?" my counselor asked after hearing all of this.

"It was right about the time my mom stopped functioning relationally the same way she had in my childhood years . . . as though she had been struck by lightning emotionally," I answered. "But I don't think there's a connection."

Evidently I had predecided that there wasn't a connection,

because he looked at me the way counselors do. Not quite smug, but not entirely *not* smug.

Dang it, I thought.

In truth I was annoyed about simply being in his office. I vehemently resisted the cliché I was becoming. Seriously, how original. All your problems result from the sad things in your childhood and ultimately point back to your relationship with your mom? I deeply resented it all.

Except, when presented with the facts, I could not deny it was *true*. Painfully, obviously, abundantly true. Much of my life could be traced back to my mom's emotional collapse and coping mechanisms and my reaction of pushing her away to protect myself from her unavailability. I had gone searching for sources that would resolve my unmet needs—and this became a pattern that played out in multiple areas of my life. It impacted my interactions with my wife and my children and showed up where I least expected.

> I HAD GONE SEARCHING FOR SOURCES THAT WOULD RESOLVE MY UNMET NEEDS—AND THIS BECAME A PATTERN THAT PLAYED OUT IN MULTIPLE AREAS OF MY LIFE.

It started with porn. Then it carried over to the key relationships in my life and ministry. For decades.

IT'S CALLED A PATTERN

After my parents divorced, I "sided with" my dad. I lived with him, believed he'd been wronged, and wouldn't listen to anything my mom had to say about him. This was the easiest way for my young brain to make sense of things; obviously the reality was much more complicated than who was right and who was wrong. In this way, my dad was the next "mom replacement" I clung to after I found porn.

Eventually I moved on to the newer, shinier object of whatever youth pastor or mentor would affirm me, see potential in me, and invest in me. I searched for affirmation by being the most active participant or dedicated volunteer at church. I drank in the valida- tion of someone recognizing my efforts or inviting me into a new level of confidence. If I ever received access to an off-limits area, I'd go weak in the knees from the sense of importance that came with it.

Don't mishear me; I genuinely loved God and wanted to serve Him. But I was dragging along so many unnoticed, untreated wounds, and I had no clue they were driving me toward experiences that would allow me to feel separate and superior. My shadow side was operating behind the scenes, pulling me in particular direc- tions, and I never consciously noticed it.

I went on to burn through mentors at a rate of a new one every eighteen to thirty-six months for the next twenty years. I would perceive that they had let me down or I had grown beyond what they could give me, then I would distance myself from them and look for someone new to attach myself to. I also would wall up the moment I sensed any betrayal or loss of love. *You can't push me away if I push you away first!* was my unspoken relational theme.

It wasn't until I was sitting in the counselor's office that I looked back and saw the trail and where my searching had begun. All along, deep down, the disruption in the relationship with my mother had me on a quest to find unbroken love. And whenever someone I had latched onto would disappoint me, I put them at arm's length—much like I had with my mom during a significant developmental time in my life.

This even crept into my relationship with Jennie. I met her during a time when she'd committed to not dating anyone, so for six months we could only be friends, and we did so in earnest. I became obsessed with her and constantly flirted with her.

Even so, when we began dating months later (after her commitment to not date had ended), I started to cool my jets and pull away—because she was now close enough to make me uncomfortable. I retreated inside my shell, terrified I would get hurt, or she would let me down, or I would let myself down.

While I could feel it happening, I didn't know how to explain it or what to do about it. So I defaulted to my tried-and-true defense mechanism and—you guessed it—put her at arm's length.

Jennie wouldn't stand for the drama and was fine with sending me to the curb. "If you don't want to be with me, then don't be with me," she said with finality, breaking up with me with tears in her eyes.

It was a shock, for sure. But what became more disturbing was the realization that there were things happening below the surface that did not make sense and were not entirely connected to the situation with Jennie. The power of those things under the things scared me.

Sometimes when I've explained a circumstance that triggered a huge emotional response in me, my counselor has asked, "Levi, how old does this feel? Is it fresh or historic?"

It is such an annoyingly, vexingly helpful question.

The things that were influencing my relationship with Jennie at that time did not feel current; they felt ancient. I was pushing away a woman who was close to my heart because I feared being disappointed. In essence I was hurting her before she could hurt me.

When I became a parent and pastor, the same self-protective pattern resurfaced. When one of my children would hurt me, I'd feel myself becoming icy and want to put up walls. When staff members would leave our ministry, I would respond with a "You're dead to me" send-off. I didn't realize it at the time, but my core issue was not anger but rather fear of them leaving or rejecting me, like my mom had.

C. S. Lewis once postulated that a heart is not safe when it refuses to love out of a fear of being broken, because something much worse will happen: "It will become unbreakable, impenetrable, irredeemable."

It's real.

The last area where this pattern played out was in my relationship with myself. During the height of the "porn and family turmoil" period, I had a persistent phobia that I was going to take my own life. It was not suicidal intention ("I want to kill myself") but instead suicidal ideation ("I can see myself dying"). Depression was not the instigator for me. It was amped-up anxiety driving me to high-strung ruminating and panic.

Almost compulsively, I feared I would take my own life—even though I had no intention or desire to. I'd get stuck in a cycle of arguing with myself and insisting that it wasn't going to happen, that I didn't want that, that I wasn't going to do that—yet somehow, this would end up being my lot.

Problems in the so-called lizard brain can't be solved by the lizard brain. Once the fight, flight, or freeze process gets activated, it can't turn itself off. As I said before, you can't think or talk yourself out of a panic attack because problems can't be solved at the level they appear; you have to do an end run and go over their head. Deep breathing or singing work much better because they reset the autonomic nervous system; they are like having the code to shut off a blaring alarm instead of trying to reason with the system. So as I tried to argue with myself, I was only pouring gasoline on a fire.

I would go from, *Hosanna! Hosanna!*, cheering myself on when doing well, then quickly turn to *Crucify him! Crucify him!*, flipping on myself in disappointment. From deification to vilification. I expected perfection from myself, which was impossible, and when I failed to meet that standard, I turned on myself with a vicious self-loathing and buried myself in shame.

On and on this would go, bringing me as close to a panic attack as I could get—until my midlife crisis at age thirty-eight took it to the brink of a cliff, and I felt the chaotic force of it might hurl me over the edge.

Stepping back now and connecting the dots, it's easy to see the pattern: My parents let me down. Porn let me down. Mentors let me down. Jennie let me down. Naturally, I would let myself down.

Here's the thing, though: For years I viewed all of these struggles as completely disconnected. It wasn't until I went back through my life with a psychologist that I saw the ties between them and a theme emerging.

WHAT'S CONCEALED CAN'T BE HEALED

In reality only God, the perfect Parent, could meet my needs and heal my wounds. My problem was that I didn't let Him do that because I didn't know they existed, and the first step in healing is awareness. Even up to five years ago I would have told you, with a straight face, that my parents' divorce had no impact on me. Yes, it was hard, but I knew the Lord and His grace were sufficient for me.

Wounds that are concealed can't be healed.

They were shadowy and subtle. Imperceptible but powerful.

My counselor paraphrased the words of Carl Jung, explaining that unless we make the unconscious conscious, it will drive our lives without our knowing it. Knowing what is going on under the surface is half the battle. The other half is knowing what to do about it. In seeing these patterns and the big picture of their origination, I have been able to appreciate the magnitude of what I went through and how I was shaped by it.

WOUNDS THAT ARE CONCEALED CAN'T BE HEALED.

The next step is to invite the presence of the Holy Spirit in to help, heal, and transform. Then, with His help, I can be conscious of the old impulses, urges, and patterns. And instead of trying to fight fire by adding more fuel, I can neutralize the burn with normalization, sympathy, and even curiosity. I can now see myself as the little kid digging up a waterlogged magazine in a garbage bag without heaping shame on him. Instead, there's sorrow, compassion, and care.

"Take his hand," my counselor told me. "Tell him it's okay. He doesn't know what to do. He needs you. And you need him."

Tears.

Now, when someone lets me down (because of my unrealistic expectations) and I feel the old inclination to ice them or shut them out, I can grasp that they are touching an old wound. It's little Levi inside acting up. My feelings and reaction make sense.

Then I can remember they are humans and recognize that it's possible they are busy or unaware of my needs and not in a position to do what I wish they would do. In seeing how present moments touch an old wound and understanding where my reactions are coming from, my shadow side loses it menace and power. I can choose a different course instead of letting it pull me somewhere destructive.

This healing has not only helped me, it has helped me better love my family. Rather than pointing fingers, I have blessings to give and grace to extend.

My friend Louie Giglio told me that, for Christians, the sap can flow *up* family trees, not just down them—meaning a blessing can flow not only from parent to child but also from child to parent. It was extremely healing to have conversations with my mom and dad as a part of my journey. I spoke with them honestly and nonjudgmentally about the impact these early events had on me and shared with them some of the lessons I have learned.

This season of life allows me to be an agent of healing as I point other people to God, my perfect Parent. The big surprise has been how much this has changed how I view my actual parents, giving me more appreciation for their virtues and grace for their weaknesses. I am able to have compassion toward them and see them as children as well—realizing they, too, faced difficult things at key developmental moments that shaped them. So instead of blaming them for what the darkest chapters of their lives did to me, I can have sympathy and try to help them heal inside too. This inner work has helped me grow in compassion and understanding toward my wife and my children as well.

WHAT ABOUT YOU?

It's your turn. What are your old wounds? What seemingly unconnected struggles are you dealing with that might be connected?

How have the difficulties you have faced given you hot buttons that, when pushed, elicit a significant response that is disproportionate to the cause? When you get triggered, how old does it feel?

It would be helpful before we go on if you would take some time to jot down a timeline of the key difficulties in your life—when they happened to you and what else emerged around those times. Let's call it the "Top Five Greatest Traumatic, Life-Shifting Moments." After you list them, try to honestly answer these questions: What was the impact those moments had on you? How might they have led to behavioral patterns in your life?

Although the things you experienced in your early years are not your fault, they are your problem, and in time they can become a source of strength to steward. But it must be detected before it can be redirected. You and I are responsible for our conclusions and our responses to all we have endured. While it's essential that we understand how we ended up where we are, we have no excuse to stay there—God has more for us. We take the time to connect the dots on what brought us to where we are because it is key to getting to where God wants us to go. It will not be easy, but it will be good.

As you better understand what went into forming your shadow side, you can begin to anticipate your own reactions. You can learn to zig before the scared, younger version of you subconsciously zags.

This is, I think, part of what Paul meant when he said we are not to be ignorant of the devil's devices. Sometimes he will use the same tactics again and again—like the lust of the flesh, the lust of the eyes, and the pride of life. Fishermen don't change bait when the fish are biting. So, too, the Enemy will continue to bait us the same ways as long as we continue to walk into the same traps.

Let me encourage you. There is a way forward, and you can experience change. If you feel like there will never come a day when the wounds inside you will be whole, know this: Healing is absolutely possible.

Also, if all of this seems to be at odds with faith, let me remind you that Jesus told us to love God not just with our soul but with our heart, mind, and strength. That means our emotional and mental health are as important to God as our spiritual health. Perhaps you've been warned that therapy is an enemy of Christianity. Far from it. We get the word *therapy* from the Greek word *therapia*, which can be translated "healing." In Luke 9:11, Jesus announced the kingdom and healed those who needed *therapia*. In Revelation 22:2, we read that in heaven the river of life, which proceeds from God's throne, waters a tree, and its leaves are there for the *therapia* of the nations.

I firmly believe that biblically sound therapy is a tool God can use to build your faith. He wants you to sing and pray and go to church. Yes, yes, yes. But understanding toxic thought patterns and the lingering impact of traumatic events through the guidance of an experienced counselor is an act of worship too. I find that it's less about the wisdom you get from your counselor and more about the space to be honest with yourself and God. The best counseling focuses more on asking questions than on giving answers.

WHATEVER WILL YOU DO?

When you understand what is happening inside you, what can you expect? Is it going to be a Harry Potter situation, where the magic wand of not being ignorant cures all ills? No, I am afraid it is not like that. At times I still feel the old impulses to armor up and freeze out people, but it's now a muffled phone call inside me instead of a blaring fire alarm. And when it rings, I am more aware of what is going on. Plus, I have effective tools at my disposal. Instead of fighting and arguing, I can remain curious and empathic as I prayerfully talk myself through what is happening. (It's what I do on my best days—but trust me, there are days when Little Levi still gets rattled.)

Even as you're more aware of the old wounds and chatter in your mind, you will feel the occasional impulse to armor up, storm off, or bottle things up. To let your shame drag you down. To numb yourself with substances, social media, spending, or binge-watching. But gradually you will get better at developing new reactions and, in time, they, too, can become ingrained as overwritten habits. This kind of healing, as John Maxwell once observed, will not happen in a *day* but can happen if you work on it *daily*.

Let me end this chapter with the help of a friend: sixth-grade Levi. I learned through counseling that Little Levi needed my help—and that I needed his help too. He has given me compassion for others as they seek to make sense of the hardships they've faced.

He has helped me have compassion for you.

At some point a traumatic moment barreled into your story—violently and without invitation. You were thrust into confusion and pain, extremes you didn't know how to manage or navigate. You instinctively looked for things that might help you, and it always turned out they couldn't.

Little Levi gives me the courage to tell you this: You're not crazy. What you have had to endure *is* hard and scary. I'm sorry you have had to face those things. And it makes sense to me that those hurts drove you to the things they did.

If you are like me, you will be tempted to find a coping mechanism to protect yourself. Numbing might give temporary relief from your feelings. But not feeling is not the same as healing, and it will only stunt your progress to get high, stoned, drunk, or full of fast food. Or to spend a hundred dollars on Amazon.

NOT FEELING IS NOT THE SAME AS HEALING, AND IT WILL ONLY STUNT YOUR PROGRESS.

Another temptation will be to ignore the hard things and their impact on you. That won't work long-term either.

Far better to acknowledge those difficult things and feel them so you can move forward. Yes, it will be unpleasant and will take a super long time. But it is only when you choose to dredge all that to the surface that you can be in a place to receive what you desperately need: the unconditional love of a perfect Parent. It's not something a human or any experience can give. It comes only from God.

The psalmist said there was *one* thing he asked from the Lord, *one* thing he sought. What was it? "That I may dwell in the house of the LORD all the days of my life, to behold the beauty of the LORD and to inquire in His temple" (Psalm 27:4). They say never meet your heroes because they can't live up to the hype. But guess what? God can. You can gaze on Him forever and never see a flaw. And believe it or not, He loves you perfectly.

I learned the hard way that no one—not my earthly mom, not porn, no leader, not even my wife—will ever give me the comfort God can. The more I look at Him, the more there is to see. It's incredible.

He is holy. Holy. Holy.

And He is love.

Look down. Do you see the ring on your finger? The robe on your shoulders? Do you hear that? It's music. It's for you. Your Father is throwing a feast for you because you, His child, are invited home. You have a seat at the King's table! You belong here. And I am honored to have a seat next to you. Pass the peach cobbler!

If you have been striving for freedom from shame, for validation and worth, for acceptance and love, listen closely: In Christ you already have all those things. Let there be an end to all your hard, bone-wearying effort. All that's left to do is curl up on His couch and find rest in His arms.

I pray that after spotting your shadow, connecting the dots on how it got there, and putting two and two together on how it impacts you, you will learn to use the Enemy's energy against him. It can become like jujitsu. Instead of worrying one second longer about the person who left your life or hurt you at a significant moment of development, you can learn to pivot and put your focus somewhere else.

You can ask yourself, *Who can I show kindness to right now? Who can I send an encouraging text to or open the door for?* We all want to be seen, but the greatest blessings come when we choose to *do* the seeing.

It's much like what 1 Corinthians 13:11 (paraphrased) tells us: When we were children, we talked like children, thought like children, and reasoned like children. But when we grew up and became men and women, we put away those childish behaviors—including only seeing the world in terms of what it can give us.

You are not the only one fighting a difficult battle! I have these words written on my mirror, and I look at them every day. It

YOU ARE NOT THE ONLY ONE FIGHTING A DIFFICULT BATTLE!

makes me want to be gentler and more curious with my fellow humans because it is a hard thing to be human, and you never know what heavy burdens those around you are struggling to carry.

CHAPTER 6

ON TAMING YOUR SHADOW

ALEXANDER THE GREAT hit a wall in his thirties.

He had been running and gunning all the way across the ancient world, with battles to win and Greek culture to spread. But eventually he ran thin on soldiers, space on the map, and deputies to install in territories he conquered. After striving to establish a realm to reign over as king of kings, he ultimately found himself weeping—despite all his success, he was disappointed.

Alexander is reported to have said, "Have I not . . . good cause to weep, that being as there are an infinite number of worlds, I am not yet the lord of one?"

Jesus wept in his thirties too—not for Himself, but for us. He did not see a world He longed to conquer with a sword and spear

75

but one He was willing to give His own flesh and blood to save. Though he was the Lord of infinite worlds, He was prepared to give His life for this one.

"My kingdom is not of this world," Jesus explained to Pontius Pilate. "If My kingdom were of this world, My servants would fight, so that I should not be delivered to the Jews."

Pilate was baffled. He thought the way Alexander had: You grab what you want, chase worldly accomplishments, and find validation in them.

"Are You a king then?" Pilate inquired.

"You say rightly that I am a king," Jesus answered. "For this cause I was born, and for this cause I have come into the world, that I should bear witness to the truth."

Jesus influenced the world not by demanding service but by stooping to serve, and His reign would go on to last throughout the ages and have no end.

At the time of his death at age thirty-two, Alexander had named twenty conquered cities after himself in a desperate bid for immortality. He required his subjects to fall at his feet, worshiping him as the "son of god." He had wives, concubines and rumored boyfriends; plus actors, artists, and dancing boys for entertainment, but as time went on, he took less and less joy from life.

He died badly. While preparing for another gargantuan invasion, some accounts* say that he developed pneumonia after getting

---

* Unlike the life and death of Jesus, it is difficult to pin down with ultimate certainty all the events of Alexander's life and death because so few manuscripts detail them, and there are four hundred years between the original and the copies. Consider this: The majority of the New Testament was finished by about seventy years after Christ's resurrection and there are more than five thousand manuscript copies that are 99 percent identical, not diverging on one doctrinal issue of significance, to attest to the bloody death and resurrection of Jesus Christ.

drenched amid one of his drunken orgies. He grew sicker and sicker over a period of ten days.

Jesus, the true King of kings and actual Son of God, also died in a brutal way—not on accident, but while on mission and living with kingdom purpose.

The mighty King Darius once offered to surrender to Alexander and give him half his kingdom in exchange for a truce. Alexander shot back, "Heaven cannot support two suns, nor earth two masters."

He was right.

We get to choose what we do with our brief time on this planet. Will we try to be another Alexander, looking only for what we can take for ourselves? Or will we make Jesus the center of our solar system and, in humbling ourselves, tap into true greatness?

> WHAT MAKES YOU DAMAGED ALSO CAN MAKE YOU DANGEROUS TO DARKNESS.

Once you understand the darker sides of your nature that have driven you into dysfunction, you can begin to envision harnessing them in service to others. To put it bluntly, what makes you damaged also can make you dangerous to darkness. Wherever you were at your darkest can be the same place you shine the brightest.

STEWARD YOUR SHADOW

There is one story of Alexander that always stirs my soul—the tale of the day he and his storied steed, Bucephalus, chose each other. They would go on to fight in battles all the way from northern Greece to India. A horse of legendary proportions, Bucephalus had breathtaking beauty and, before he met Alexander, was known to be unbreakable.

One day when Alexander was a teen, his father, Philip II of Macedon, was standing with his court as a horse trader presented animals for purchase. When Alexander saw Bucephalus, he knew they had a destiny together. He asked his father to buy the horse, but the price was astronomical.

Hearing the trader say that the unbroken horse was unrideable, Philip constructed a challenge he thought was in his favor. "If you can ride him, I will buy him for you," he told his son.

Alexander readily accepted and cautiously approached the horse.

The beast bucked, hopped, and stamped with fury boiling out of his nostrils, like a volcano ready to blow. Alexander paused and watched the horse's movements for a few minutes. Suddenly his eyes lit up. He walked over, cautiously took the reins, turned the horse ever so slightly, then calmly and confidently leapt onto his back. The two rode away from the stunned audience and into the annals of history.

Philip coughed up the dough for Bucephalus and asked Alexander how he'd managed to tame the horse.

"Simple," Alexander explained. "I could tell that Bucephalus wasn't mad. He was afraid."

"Afraid of what?" Philip pressed.

"His shadow. When I turned him to face the sun, he was no longer scared."

Indeed. When we have our backs to the sun, our shadows stretch out before us, seeming bigger and longer than they really are. Those shadows can terrify and dominate us, causing all sorts of unwanted behaviors and conflict. But if we simply turn one hundred eighty degrees and face the sun, our perspective will change. Our shadows will still be there, but we will be unable to see and focus on them.

We aren't talking about Alexander the Great anymore, are we?

No, we are not. We are talking about where our eyes are focused. Jesus said in Matthew 6:22–23 that if our eyes are good, our whole bodies will be good. If our eyes are evil, it will infect all our lives.

Hear me on this: Our goal isn't for our shadow to go away. It is to steward our shadow.

Formed in the cauldron of pain, sin, and heredity, our shadow will be a part of us until we reach heaven. And unless we accept and acknowledge it, it will be able to hold sway in the background. The key is to see it for what it is and imagine how it can be harnessed for good.

Consider how the flip side of a virtue is a vice.

The charismatic can be manipulative.

The organized can become controlling.

The passionate can be domineering.

Excessive humility can lead to insecurity and self-loathing.

Unguarded strength can become a double curse.

In the same way, we all have unique gifts, abilities, and hurts that have formed us. They can become our superpower when we are healed and productive, or they can remain in the shadows pulling levers, driving us toward more darkness.

Which direction you go has everything to do with the amount of sunshine you let in. If you allow the light of God to shine onto your life so you can see yourself as you actually are, not as you wish you were, you can begin to experience healing and wholeness, walking in His plan through every season.

A shadow formed in our adolescence and twenties, if undealt with, will begin to poke its head into our thirties and be catastrophic in our forties and beyond. Too often it looks like clothes that are too tight, chest hair that's too exposed, a gold chain that's too obvious. A car that's too flashy, a gambling hobby growing a little too reckless, or a second marriage to someone too young. It's a tale told so many times it is predictable yet still heartbreaking. At the core there is disappointment at what life hasn't been like. Anger, despair, and perhaps self-loathing.

Some people experience none of these common stereotypes; they instead may have a smoldering apathy and disinterest in things that used to give them passion and put light in their eyes. This was my experience.

You probably have heard of *prolonged adolescence*, when someone is a teenager living in a grown person's body. There is also *delayed old age*, when someone over the hill is seeking to live like aging isn't happening.

Ronald Rolheiser has said that "as we go through the seasons of our lives the challenges we meet there can just as easily embitter and harden the soul as mellow it."

Wow. Let that sink in as you think of the people who are old in an angry, jealous, and bitter way, not a wise, sweet, seasoned way. It's an advertisement for the story you don't want to be yours! No one sets out to be a bitter person; it happens gradually through one nursed grudge at a time.

Here's the truth: Resentfulness is lethal. In his book *Sacred Fire*, Rolheiser unpacks this principle allegorically using two well-known stories in Scripture: the Prodigal Son, and Mary and Martha.

THE PRODIGAL SON
AND HIS OLDER BROTHER

Let's begin with the two brothers in the parable of the prodigal son and consider them representatives of the seasons we encounter between birth and death.

The youngest brother, aka the Prodigal Son, can be used as an illustration of the first half of life. He is caught up in the fire-in-the-belly energy of youth and is struggling with the devil's overt temptations. The older brother, illustrating the second half of life, struggles instead with resentment, anger, and jealousy and is wrestling with God.

In the first half of our lives, we are struggling to establish an identity, and success and achievement can help us establish a healthy sense of self-worth. In our later years, we need to let go of the sense of self-worth we get through success and achievement. Our tendency, though, is to use the scoreboard we used in the first half to rack up more points in the second half—not knowing it won't have the same meaning. Why? Because we are supposed to be at a new stage of development.

Success still feels good in the second half of life; it just has very little to teach us, Rolheiser posited. The new metrics aren't about success; they're about significance, impact, legacy, and becoming more like Jesus. It's a season when we should be more mindful about what people will say about us at our funerals than what looks good on a LinkedIn profile or an Instagram feed.

This means confronting your shadow, not trying to bury it under a mountain of accomplishments, purchases, hobbies, trips, or addictions. None of that will ever be enough; we will be like the older brother who had everything the father owned but complained he didn't get a goat. He was trying to build a kingdom like Alexander.

When we instead understand our wounds, acknowledge why we operate the way we do, and keep aware of which direction the steering wheel is pulling us, we can find ourselves in a meaningful story. We will still feel the weight, but it will not have the same power over us.

Life is different facing the sunshine.

What would it mean for you to orient your life in a way where your shadow no longer controlled the show? Envision a version of yourself where you are aware of your shadow's pull on you and you do the work of developing your tools so it's not your boss. Day by day, it loses its power.

WHAT WOULD IT MEAN FOR YOU TO ORIENT YOUR LIFE IN A WAY WHERE YOUR SHADOW NO LONGER CONTROLLED THE SHOW?

The trouble is, it stings to abandon your empire, make Jesus the center of your solar system, and take a seat at the feast the Father is throwing for you. It is tough medicine to swallow for those who want to earn their own way. That's the tricky thing about grace; once it's merited, it's no longer grace.

Hold that thought as we turn to the next set of siblings.

MARY AND MARTHA

In contrast to the last pair, these two really lived. Mary and Martha were two sisters from Bethany in close relationship with Jesus.

On a day Mary and Martha were hosting a party in their home,

Jesus was at the table teaching. Mary sat at His feet while Martha worked hard in the kitchen, frustrated that Mary wasn't helping. Martha had the audacity to interrupt Jesus mid-message and order Him to command Mary to help her with the pots and pans. This scene tells us a lot about each of their personalities.

Martha was a gifted, hard-working, type-A, never-say-die individual. You really pity the fool who ended up between her and an objective. Martha was not someone you would want to go on a road trip with unless you enjoy taking pee breaks every 175 miles, no more and no less. And she wouldn't allow you to eat in her car.

I respect and admire Martha's focus and drive, but the shadow of a gift this big is double the size.

Mary, on the other hand, seemed free-spirited, full of love, and unencumbered by things like schedules, responsibilities, or the day's agenda. She was in the moment, completely present and content with whatever came her way. Mary would be as happy going on a spontaneous adventure in the woods and watching the sunset as she would be staying in bed all day and missing both. As delightful as Mary was, she had her own version of a shadow too.

Whether you skew Mary or slant Martha, Jesus will meet you where you are.

YOUR SHADOW IS SHOWING

The beauty of the biblical narrative is that it's filled with stories that help us see ourselves—and how God sees our uniqueness and works with us.

When Lazarus, Mary and Martha's brother and Jesus' friend, became ill and died, Jesus showed up later than Mary and Martha had hoped. They had sent Him word that Lazarus needed Him, but He stayed where He was until Laz was dead and buried. He had a mind-blowing, God-sized alternate plan.

When Jesus finally arrived, who was there waiting to give Him a piece of her mind?

"If You had been here, my brother would not have died" (John 11:21). Martha said these words first, then Mary did.

Jesus responded differently to each of them. He used reassurance with Martha. And He sat with Mary and cried. He responded to them where they were, not where they should have been or where someone else was.

He does the same for you. He doesn't wish you were more like your sister, or as tall as your brother. He is not embarrassed, ashamed, or impatient with you. He made you, loves you, and wants to develop you into a better version of yourself, not a copy of someone else or an amalgamation of what you think success looks like. God's goal for you is not a Mr. or Mrs. Potato Head. You are His poem, a masterpiece He has been dreaming about since before the foundation of the world. You bring Him great pleasure! But you need to let Him help you bring your shadow into the light, otherwise it will cause you to miss out on the abundant life He died for you to have.

HE MADE YOU, LOVES YOU, AND WANTS TO DEVELOP YOU INTO A BETTER VERSION OF YOURSELF.

Let's jump back to the party at Mary and Martha's home again for a minute.

When Martha was standing in the doorway, her shadow was showing. Picture her with flour in her hair and stains on her apron, pointing a wooden spoon at her sister. Her leadership gifts flipped to a controlling, domineering presence;

she actually started lecturing the Messiah mid-sermon. Jesus tenderly but firmly corrected her, saying, "Mary has chosen the better part. It will not be taken from her" (Luke 10:42, paraphrased).

When you try to serve God without being fueled by time spent with God, you start to act like you're God. The things Martha did for Jesus were an idol. This is the dark side of being driven. Maybe checking off all the rides on the amusement park checklist becomes more important than how everyone in the family is doing. If so, I get you. Other people and even God can become barriers to your to-do list getting accomplished.

BEYOND WHAT YOU DO

Don't be discouraged: It is possible to thrive in your soul and in your calling. Ask John the Apostle, whom Jesus loved.

All the way to the end of his life, John remained blown away that Jesus loved him. He pastored in some important places, led some significant churches, wrote what would later become amazing books of the Bible; and, according to tradition, he survived being boiled in hot oil, sort of envisioned and described the end of the world—and yet he never lost touch with Jesus. In fact, he had some pretty incredible experiences with Jesus on the island where he got banished.

People can take everything away from you except your spiritual freedom—that is, if you don't let what you accomplish get in the way of the One you worship.

This is what Jesus was pointing Martha to—prioritizing significance, not just success. He wasn't suggesting she shouldn't serve; she just needed to face the sunshine so her shadow wouldn't get in the way. Once she sat to worship, she could stand to work.

When you tap into this level of devotion-inspired service, you become unstoppable. Only when you kneel like a lamb can you rise like a lion.

Paul and Silas knew this too. It is how they were able to spend the night in jail—with their backs beaten and bloodied, chains on their wrists and feet, and trouble looming over them—and sing praise songs to God in the morning. God answered them with an earthquake that set them free. In the ensuing chaos the prison warden got saved, a church got planted, and we got Acts 16.

Here's a huge epiphany: Worship that hurts like hell heals like heaven. It's fine if you can praise God in the sunshine; I don't think heaven rejects such celebrating. And you should, because turning blessings into praise is one of the best ways to keep prosperity from turning into idolatry. But if you get your power cut off and you can still sing in the dark? Heaven leans in, and Satan is terrified. To paraphrase C. S. Lewis, if a person can look around the universe and see not even a trace of evidence that God cares about them and yet still worships Him, the devil's case is lost.

Regardless of the shape our shadows take, once we are facing the sunshine, they will no longer be controlling us subconsciously. And we will have no occasion to shed tears like Alexander the Great when we come to the end of our "run of the map" because we weren't defined by

- the quality of the dinner parties we got to throw,
- the communities we got to lead,
- the waves we got to catch,
- the vacations we got to take,
- the success at work we got to see,
- the stocks we got to trade,

- the children we got to raise, or
- our record on the pickleball court.

All those things are fine and a part of our story, and we ought to approach them with all our hearts unto Christ—as long as He sees fit to fire our hearts with a calling and our bodies with the ability to do such things. Because they are not who we are. You and I are more than what we do. Facing the sunshine makes us less driven to appear successful and more aware of what truly matters.

Maybe your shadow side is different from Martha's or mine; perhaps it pulls you to unworthiness, shame, or self-sabotage. It's possible you are a people pleaser and it is difficult for you to assert your opinion. For years you've focused on reading what others want and becoming a chameleon so as not to rock the boat. But once you face the sunshine, you can use those people skills in ways that don't come at your expense or serve ulterior motives.

If ambition was once your only gear, it can be stripped of its ruthlessness and become an unstoppable drive. Paul was no less determined as a church-planter than as a Pharisee; he just learned how to control those parts of his personality that used to control him.

David's shadow side got him swept up in strong emotions, and it got him into trouble with Bathsheba, and with Uriah, but when he stewarded that same passion, he wrote brilliant songs.

The bigger the gift, the longer the shadow, and the more you need to learn to harness the ability lest it destroy you and hurt others. Just ask Samson.

In his super strength, he believed he was invincible, and like Alexander, became reckless. He was forbidden to touch dead things, so he got as close as possible, touching a dead lion with a stick to

THE BIGGER THE GIFT, THE LONGER THE SHADOW, AND THE MORE YOU NEED TO LEARN TO HARNESS THE ABILITY LEST IT DESTROY YOU AND HURT OTHERS.

get honey. He couldn't drink wine, so he would take walks in vineyards. He was addicted to the adrenaline rush and dopamine hit of putting his life on the line, and it ultimately cost him his hair, his eyes, and his life. Despite all Samson did, I think it was only a glimmer of what could have been accomplished had he faced the sunshine and learned to steward his shadow side instead of being ruled by it.

A LONG, HARD LOOK IN THE MIRROR

It's time to take a close look at your shadow side and really get to know it for what it is. Can you get specific in naming it? In describing the version of you that you don't want to be so it can't claim you? Spend some time journaling and reflecting.

Also enlist the help of a few key people in your life. Ask them questions like these:

- What are some of the ways my personality, skills, gifts, and pain work together to sabotage me?
- Does my strong leadership gift [for example] make me manipulative when unchecked?
- Does my sense of justice pull me to a victim mentality?
- When I help others, can it slip into unhealthiness and result in people walking all over me?

Where do the dots I established from the pain points in my journey triangulate the origin of some of these things for you? For instance, perhaps you became a peacemaker not by accident but because you walked on eggshells for fear of rocking the boat and setting off the temper of a parent with anger issues.

Through prayer, reflection, and wise counsel, you can get a bead on what the sunshine needs to assist you in stewarding.

Keep in mind that pattern recognition is huge. Once you learn to spot some of your tendencies, you can simultaneously develop the tools you need to arrest them early. You will still "hear the phone ringing" when your shadow is calling for your attention, but it will dawn on you that you are under new management now that Christ lives inside of you! You are not at the mercy of your shadow side.

You will be able to identify problem people and places that make it harder to be who God wants you to be. While at the helm of your life, setting boundaries will make it easier for you to be the grounded, healthy person you are capable of being. That's what Paul meant when he taught us not to make any provision for the flesh to fulfill its lusts, but to put on the Lord Jesus Christ. You can't get rid of sin until heaven; there will still be a pull until that day, but you don't have to be a travel agent for it, booking it a room and renting it a car!

Your worship, prayer, and membership in a faith community will be massively helpful as you make your way on this therapeutic journey. The world directs you to a path without any assistance from the Holy Ghost: *Hug your inner child but call on no power from on high.* But without God's power, all you are left with is willpower, and Romans 7 says that results in us doing what we don't want to do and not doing what we want to do. That will leave you weak like Samson with a buzz cut; you will know what needs to change but not be able to live it out. But when you have God's energy inside you, His Word setting the pace for the renewal of your mind, and some of the tools therapy offers, it is a powerful combination. You will be able to run and not grow weary, walk and not faint, and mount up with wings like an eagle. If I had written Isaiah 40, I would've started with walking, then talked about running, and climaxed with the eagle's wings, but I believe it was written as anti-climactic intentionally. Why? Because through the seasons of life, there will be times when we get to fly, opportunities to run, but walking with God? That we get to do forever.

We began this chapter by talking about Alexander and his despair. The key to not weeping like Alexander is to keep your eyes on Jesus. Tap into the purpose He has for you. Identify and see your shadow side for what it is, and then stop letting it control you and terrify you and provoke your bad behavior. Do what the apostle John did—never lose touch with the One who came to live and die for you. Be marked by His love. Stare at the Son; all else will fade away and become strangely dim.

THOUGH YOU MIGHT FEEL OVERWHELMED BY THE WORK OF LEARNING TO STEWARD YOUR SHADOW, IN GOD'S LOVE YOU ARE SAFE.

Once you finish reading this chapter, I want you to pick your favorite worship song that pulls you into God's love and find somewhere you can play it—and sing with it. As weird as that might feel, turn it up loud enough that hearing your voice doesn't bother you and really belt it.

I once heard a counselor say that singing can serve as a hard reset for your emotional state and has a powerful effect on your amygdala, even more so than simply reading Scripture, because normally you sing only when you're safe. It sort of tricks the panicking mind to slow down. And though you might feel overwhelmed by the work of learning to steward your shadow, in God's love you are safe. So sing, and you will feel what you truly are.

When the song ends, don't put another one on. Hit pause and sit like Mary did. Linger longer. Enjoy His sunshine on your face and reflect on your plan to keep your shadow where it belongs, not terrifying or controlling you but instead under your feet and on the ground.

CHAPTER 7

MONUMENTS VERSUS MOMENTS

A CONSISTENT FEATURE of Disney movies is the rigid line between villains and heroes. Scar is a monster; Mufasa can do no wrong. Jafar has a blackened heart; Aladdin's is golden. But in real life, people are too complicated to categorize as "good guys" or "bad guys." Every human has light and shadow, good days and bad days, victories and failures.

When we read the Bible, we often subconsciously do the same thing and identify with the "good" guys or gals. Especially when we go through a hardship or a storm, we see ourselves as the protagonist of the stories. We are always Ruth, never Orpah. Joseph, not his brothers. I'm obviously Esther, and if you are opposing me, that makes you Haman. If I'm suffering unfair opposition, I am Daniel, and the people against me are the ones trying to throw me into the lions' den.

I frequently have wanted to see myself as David and my critics as Saul, the crazy, spear-throwing monarch. On more occasions than I care to admit, I probably have not been. We can't all be David.

But let's hope that doesn't mean we become Saul.

Saul is endlessly both terrifying and fascinating to me. The first of the kings of Israel, he stood head and shoulders above everyone else, physically and metaphorically. He appeared to have humility in his earlier years—like when he hid among the equipment during his coronation ceremony—but that diminished over time.

When the prophet Samuel told Saul that his kingdom would be taken away from him and given to his neighbor (not remain in his family), Samuel shared an insight that stings me even now as I think of it: "Had you remained small in your own eyes, God would have continued to use you and established His work through you."

Saul had not remained small in his own eyes; gradually he began to see himself as a big deal. He was the nation. Above the law. Above the rules. A nation unto himself. The taller he saw himself, the smaller God became to him and the less he felt he needed to abide by God's word.

When he stopped submitting to God's authority, he lost the ability to remain in authority. As the late Adrian Rogers wrote, "We will never be over those things that God has set under us until we learn to be under those things that God has placed over us."

There is strength in surrender.

Oof. This principle can be seen all throughout the storylines of Scripture. We see it in Adam and Eve when they took what God told them not to touch and in turn lost access to what God wanted them to enjoy. We see it in Lucifer when he stopped covering God's throne with praise and began to covet God's throne for himself.

IT STARTS SMALL

When you refuse to be under God's leadership, you disqualify yourself from being in leadership. When you are too big to serve, you become too small to lead.

Saul's transformation began in small ways. Little concessions to his ego. He ignored God's instruction to wait until the prophet Samuel arrived to start a prebattle chapel service. He dismissed the details of how God said to steward the spoils of war. His shadow was showing.

The real crisis began after he heard he wouldn't be able to keep his throne. Previously, he had known he didn't deserve it—but it had quickly infiltrated his identity. So he dug his claws in deep, trying to keep hold of what God was tearing from his hands.

Contrast this to the moment when David learned that Solomon would build the temple. Though he'd longed for that privilege, David immediately pivoted and spent the final season of his life setting Solomon up to be successful. He made the switch from warrior to father to elder to sage. These are the four seasons of life with the first half being primarily about vitality and the second half being more about wisdom (stages we'll discuss further in chapter 8).

Henri Nouwen observed that "at a certain point of our lives, the real question is no longer: What can I still do so that my life makes a contribution? Rather, the question becomes: How can I now live so that my death will be an optimal blessing for my family, my church, and the world?" He was saying we shouldn't wait until it's too late to do what Inigo Montoya from *The Princess Bride* said to the Six-Fingered Man—"Prepare to die." It's not that you won't have battles to fight; it's that your battles must change.

WHEN YOU REFUSE TO BE UNDER GOD'S LEADERSHIP, YOU DISQUALIFY YOURSELF FROM BEING IN LEADERSHIP.

We all get to choose how we respond to the realization that we have "peaked." We can accept it and chalk it up as a success, grieve the end of the accomplishment, and move on by embarking on a new mountain called Significance. Or we can choose denial, refuse to accept the fleeting nature of mountaineering, and dig in on top of our summit, making a pathetic attempt to continue doing what was never meant to be permanent.

David responded to his disappointment gracefully, and as a result, he was willing to die to himself and live humbly, accepting whatever God wanted for him with an open hand. It is easy for God to bless someone who has a heart like that.

Not so with Saul. God told him straight up, "I am giving your crown to someone better than you. It will not be your son who sits on the throne, either; it will be someone else."

Saul's attitude was *You can have my crown when you rip it from my cold, dead fingers.* And in his manic pursuit to keep what wasn't his to hold on to in the first place, he destroyed everyone and everything in his life.

He never got his bearings.

He refused to learn to steward his shadow.

And he wasn't prepared to leave his spot at the top.

But he had to. And it went badly.

His mutilated corpse hung from the walls of the city of his rivals. His technical cause of death was suicide, because when he sustained life-ending wounds on the battlefield, he chose to die more quickly by his own hand.

The truth is, Saul had been killing himself slowly for decades.

Unlike the man in Matthew 13 who discovered the treasure in the field and sold everything to buy it, Saul was like the formerly rich, once young, used-to-be ruler who was unwilling to let go of what was in his hand, thinking it was better than what God had to offer. A case study in a midlife spiral gone wrong.

I can relate.

Saul could have yielded, humbled himself, and remembered the kingdom was the Lord's, as is the earth and everything in it. He could have repented, submitted, and given himself over to the season of life he was in, devoting himself to preparing David for what was next.

Instead, his eyes were clouded with jealousy and rage. Saul wasn't about to let anyone call him Grandpa. He still saw himself as the quarterback and was dug in firmly on the first half of life. It reminds me of Woody from *Toy Story* when Buzz Lightyear arrived. He was driven to madness while trying to keep his spot on the bed as Andy's favorite toy and ended up knocking Buzz out the window. Saul had the same mentality. He didn't want to stop being a warrior to be a father, and he definitely wasn't ready to be the elder or sage.

Think how different it would have been if Saul had remembered that both the one who sows and the one who reaps share in the harvest. He would have known the powerful truth that everything David did could be considered fruit to his account. How differently he would have reacted to the song being sung in Israel: "Saul has slain his thousands, and David his ten thousands" (1 Samuel 29:5). Saul hated that song. It was at the top of all the Spotify charts. I think he really hated the country-and-western remix: "Saul shot a rabbit, but David shot a buck. Saul drove a hybrid; David got himself a truck." It was the last straw.

Ironically, since they were on the same team, David's wins were Saul's wins. Saul should have been happy, but his shadow wouldn't let him. He didn't see things with a kingdom mentality of *we* and *ours*; he saw things only in terms of *me* and *mine*.

You and I will always be limited, stunted, and miserable when we are focused on our personal glory. Ronald Reagan kept a plaque on his desk that read, "There is no limit to what a man can do or where he can go if he doesn't mind who gets the credit." And I would say that there is no telling what God can do through someone who doesn't care who gets the credit.

But Saul wanted the credit. He didn't just want Israel to win; he wanted the win personally.

This is a slow death.

You can see this early on in Saul's life when, after a battle, he built a monument to himself. But to seek one's own glory is not glory.

In a conversation about the soul's need for transcendent meaning and purpose, even if you reject God, comedian Jimmy Carr essentially said fame has replaced heaven in a secular world. If people don't believe in heaven or an afterlife, fame is the closest thing to immortality. Touché.

In the book of Ecclesiastes, Solomon described looking to a long list of things to bring his life purpose and significance—and then proclaimed them all meaningless: pleasure and sex; alcohol and animals; work, wealth, and wisdom; fame and human empires. In each pursuit he was happy for a little bit, then it wore off. Like trying to catch the wind, anything truly meaningful remained out of reach.

We see this in our own lives. We turn to so many things we hope will fill the emptiness inside. They never do, and yet, like lemmings, we keep heading for the cliff.

Jesus said that whoever tries to keep his life will lose it.

Saul lost his life, all right. After his death, his corpse was treated shamefully. People cut off his head and hung it outside the city of his enemies. Eventually the honorable men of Jabesh Gilead scaled the city walls to rescue Saul's remains and give them a proper burial. Early in his reign, Saul had come to their aid in battle, sending an army to join their fight, and they remained loyal to him until the end.

If only he'd stayed small in his own eyes and kept the sweet spirit he'd had back when he'd swing for the fences for others. Instead, once he had something to lose, he started consolidating his power and keeping it at all costs. He forgot why he had that power in the first place, which is the same reason God gives you or me influence: to help other people.

THE MONSTER IN ME

Here's where I need to re-up on my confession that I'm often more Saul than David on my journey.

It is often easier to take risks and hold nothing back when we start out with the fire of youth and have everything to gain. But when we get a mortgage, dependents, and other responsibilities, we might become more measured in our generosity of resources—whether that's our time, skills, emotional energy, money, or possessions. While it is right for us to be discerning, we cannot forget that love is irrational. It doesn't make sense. Living with purpose can be paradoxical: Greatness is serving, and giving leads to receiving. Try to keep our life and we will lose it; if we lay it down, we will find it. This is the upside-down kingdom.

Saul's maniacal attempt to cling to his power cost him not only the throne but also his closest relationships, including David.

David had been nothing but good to Saul—defeating the giant Goliath when no one else would even try, and fighting battle after battle as the head of Saul's armies. Even playing his harp when Saul was in a bad mood or couldn't sleep. Becoming like a son to Saul. Yet Saul viewed David with suspicion. His vision was clouded by envy.

Jesus said if your eye is bad, your whole body will be bad, and Saul is a picture of that.

Saul threw a spear at David multiple times and tried to pin him to the wall while David was playing music for him. Over and over, Saul drove David away and brought him harm. Jealousy is a poison. Ironically Saul was blind to the fact that he was destroying his credibility as he behaved unlike the king he so badly wanted to be.

This came to a point when Saul's son Jonathan told him David didn't deserve the bad rap, and Saul flew into a rage. He grabbed his spear and tried to pin Jonathan to the wall. His sound reasoning for this? He wanted Jonathan to be king, not David! Makes no sense. Precisely.

It reminds me of the TV show *Breaking Bad*. Walter White broke the law and built a meth empire. Why? Supposedly it was to get money for his family, but along the way, he destroyed the thing he was originally trying to save. Toward the end of the series, he admitted that none of it truly was for his family; rather, it was for *him*, because he liked it and was good at it. There is a self-destructiveness built into self-centeredness.

Anything we expect to fulfill and satisfy us will be unable to handle the weight we put on it. This will be true of a career, substance, person, paycheck, sport, or possession. Sometimes we end up doing this as part of our fight not to lose a temporary thing that has become critical to our identity. It's like trying to camp out on the mountaintop of Jesus' transfiguration instead of letting that mountain moment fuel you as you face what is next—whatever is waiting for you on the descent and in the coming adventure. When you try to make what is meant to be a season into something permanent, you will make mistakes and others will get hurt in the process. A thing is not beautiful because it lasts.

A THING IS NOT BEAUTIFUL BECAUSE IT LASTS.

IT'S NOT THE OUTSIDE BUT THE INSIDE THAT COUNTS

Whenever you feel panic over the thought that you've peaked, you need to say to yourself, *That means I summited—yay! Now I need to figure out what God has next for me.* Celebrate the win and move on. This is so much healthier than dreading irrelevance and obsolescence, or desperately attempting to stay at an address that was never meant to be permanent.

Again, this is easier said than done. And it is not a one-and-done thing. Remember: You have to deny yourself and pick up your cross and follow Him *daily*. Yes, it hurts, and it's hard, but it is much better than the pain of who you will become and how you will hurt those you love if you don't.

Saul didn't see that. He was blinded to his illogical, self-defeating behavior as he tried to kill his son Jonathan so Jonathan could be king after him. He also spiraled into hypocrisy at the end. Though he had made a career out of clearing out sorcery and witchcraft in Israel, he sought out a black-market witch shop and paid for a séance on the final evening of his life. It was a sad, misguided effort to speak to the prophet Samuel, whose advice he had neglected years earlier.

It reminds me of Jesus' words: "What will it profit a man if he gains the whole world, and loses his own soul?" (Mark 8:36).

On the other hand, the story of David illustrates how, counterintuitively, you will gain your life when you are willing to lose it.

CALLING ALL THE HUMBLE AND ORDINARY

David never sought the throne; he was just as happy caring for sheep as he was writing songs or fighting battles. He was anointed as the future king one moment and the next was dutifully delivering food to his brothers on the battlefield. He remained small in his own eyes no matter what big things God did in and through him. He most certainly made mistakes, but he (mostly) remained humble.

This is huge! Why? Because "God opposes the proud but gives grace to the humble" (James 4:6 NLT).

In his early years, David was the least of his family. When the prophet Samuel came to his family home in Bethlehem to anoint a new king, David's buff older brothers got everyone's attention initially. And Samuel tried to anoint one of them, but God said to him, "Negative, Ghost Rider; the pattern is full. Do not look at him like man does, because I see the heart, not just the outward appearance." To the human eye, David looked nothing like a king, but the most important qualities needed for the job were invisible.

The same is true when we consider our calling. God doesn't require us to be exceptional. He uses the foolish things of this world to confound the mighty; He delights in using ordinary people to do extraordinary things. If you feel ultraordinary, take heart! God has a huge plan to use you too!

The challenge, as Saul illustrates, is to *remain* humble as you live out your calling. How you finish is more important than how you begin. David did remain humble— imperfectly, yet consistently. He never saw himself as deserving of what God did through him; instead he continued to see himself as a shepherd, servant, and psalmist more than as a sovereign and noble, worthy of what God had chosen him for.

HE DELIGHTS IN USING ORDINARY PEOPLE TO DO EXTRAORDINARY THINGS.

After Samuel anointed him as king, David went back to the sheep and to the leadership of his father. He didn't get all high and mighty and act like he shouldn't have to do small things like deliver food. He was still over what was under him and under what was over him.

Throughout the next twenty years of his life, David continued to serve Saul, even when Saul behaved like a tyrant and a psycho. David never retaliated. He sincerely sought Saul's best interests and never sought to take the throne. When he became king after Saul's death, he even took in Saul's one living descendant, Mephibosheth, to be lavishly and lovingly treated as one of his own sons.

We even see David's humility in his old age when his son Absalom staged a coup and drove David from the city. David accepted that it might be from the Lord and didn't cling to the throne. He didn't nurse the hurt. He was willing to live on the run, just as he had back when Saul was chasing him down. Or to live on the land taking care of sheep, as he had back before Samuel ever named him king.

The key is to accept whatever God puts into your hand and to use it to glorify Him with all your might, but not let it become your identity. Let it be what you do, not who you are. That will reduce the sting when it is taken away. Will it be easy? Heck no. But the best things never are. And with the Holy Spirit's help, you can find the blessing even in the seasons when you are spiraling.

> THE KEY IS TO ACCEPT WHATEVER GOD PUTS INTO YOUR HAND AND TO USE IT TO GLORIFY HIM WITH ALL YOUR MIGHT, BUT NOT LET IT BECOME YOUR IDENTITY.

David was a son of God, and that wouldn't be taken away. What he did fluctuated; who he was did not.

There was one specific chapter of David's life when he *did* violate his sonship, and it became the darkest time of his life. A season of spiritual cancer and poison both to himself and to those around him. I'm of course talking about the Bathsheba and Uriah fiasco, when David took himself out from under what was over him—God's authority. It was in that season that David acted like the one person he had never before resembled: King Saul.

WASH ME CLEAN

It is so scary how easy it is for me to become small and selfish and mean. It doesn't take much for me to go from praising God to losing my temper and coming close to blowing my witness. Just today someone in traffic cut me off, then flung a very unkind gesture at me. My response wasn't to pray for God's blessing on him; I was livid, self-righteous, and fuming. If I'd had the power to call down fire from heaven or grizzly bears from the woods, I would have. I often feel like I'm the worst pastor ever and barely resemble a Christian some days. It's frightening how quickly sin's temptation can gain power over me, pulling me to lust, jealousy, despair, or self-pity if I let my guard down—even though I have been walking with Jesus and pointing people to Him for many years. Just when you think you have grown and made some progress, there is the humbling realization that he "who thinks he stands" must "take heed lest he fall" (1 Corinthians 10:12).

The Uriah–Bathsheba tragedy was quite the fall, one of David's lowest moments. He exercised a lapse in his characteristic humility and arrogantly took himself out from under God's authority. And he paid for it dearly. But he also repented of it. It's not just how we fail that defines a life but how we respond to that failure.

IT'S NOT JUST HOW WE FAIL THAT DEFINES A LIFE BUT HOW WE RESPOND TO THAT FAILURE.

Psalm 51 is one of the Bible's most powerful psalms. It's where David opens his heart and pleads for mercy. I encourage you to read these well-traveled lines that millions of fellow pilgrims have journeyed through on the way to their own repentance and wholeness. I know personally that there is nothing in the world quite like what Psalm 51 contains for those "Romans 7 moments"—when you have done what you didn't want to do and not done what you wanted to do. They are a shower for your soul. A car wash for your heart.

The introduction to this psalm tells us David wrote it after "the time Nathan the prophet came to him after David had committed adultery with Bathsheba" (Psalm 51:1 NLT).

Here are a few of my favorite lines:

- "Because of your great compassion, blot out the stain of my sins. Wash me clean from my guilt. . . . For I recognize my rebellion; it haunts me day and night" (vv. 1–3).
- "Against you, and you alone, have I sinned; I have done what is evil in your sight" (v. 4).
- "Purify me from my sins, and I will be clean; wash me, and I will be whiter than snow" (v. 7).
- "Create in me a clean heart, O God. Renew a loyal spirit within me. Do not banish me from your presence, and don't take your Holy Spirit from me. Restore to me the joy of your salvation and make me willing to obey you" (vv. 10–12).
- "The sacrifice you desire is a broken spirit. You will not reject a broken and repentant heart, O God" (v. 17).

If there is any unconfessed sin in your heart, I invite you to take this chance, right here and now, to allow God's mercy and grace to flood into the chasm of your soul with a time of refreshment.

David, of course, still had to reckon with the consequences of his actions, and others suffered as a result too. There is always fallout. But God forgave him, and David's humility paved the way for him to walk with God through those consequences.

Saul had the opportunity to have such a spirit after each of his trainwreck decisions, but over and over again he rejected it.

WILL THE REAL MAIN CHARACTER PLEASE STAND UP?

Here is the lesson for you and for me: Yield. That's it. It's the difference between being a David and being a Saul. Those who will not bend will be broken. If you won't humble yourself, life will do the job for you.

Stay humble. Stay small in your own eyes. Be a person after God's heart who is focused on doing His will. And don't quit until you arrive at the distant shores of heaven.

And here's the best part about the whole good guys/bad guys thing when we read ourselves into the stories in the Bible: The Bible isn't about us. It's about Jesus. There are plenty of lessons in the Bible for us to learn from, either positively or negatively, and Romans 15:4 says we can and should take the examples to heart so we can have hope. But at the end of the day, Jesus is the fulfillment of everything even David couldn't be. He is greater than David; He never fell. And He won't fail you as you rely on Him to choose the life that feels like death in the moment.

He is with you now, ready to help you with your Saul moments, your David ones, and the stuff in between too. He is there for you as you courageously face the season in front of you, even if you have to creatively strain to find the blessing in it. His name is Jesus, and He always leads us in triumph!

LIVE FROM YOUR
GOD-GIVEN
IDENTITY,
FOCUS ON
TRUE TREASURE,
AND PREPARE
TO END WELL

PART TWO

CHAPTER 8

BECOME YODA

THERE'S A PARTICULAR pattern in most stories, and once you see it, you can't unsee it. It's everywhere—in Harry Potter, *The Matrix*, The Lord of the Rings, and even children's movies like *Moana* or *Aladdin*. It's a universal narrative structure called the hero's journey, which Joseph Campbell famously introduced in his book *The Hero with a Thousand Faces*. It resonates across cultures and appears in the story arcs of countless novels, movies, and myths.

The hero's journey framework can vary ever so slightly but consistently contains five basic movements, which I'll explain through *The Lion King* story:

- **Call to Adventure:** Simba is forced to leave home after his dad's death.
- **Meeting the Mentor:** While comfortable and complacent with Timon and Pumbaa, Simba comes to his senses after Rafiki guides him.
- **Crossing the Threshold:** Simba decides to face his past, returning to Pride Rock.
- **Ordeal:** Simba confronts Scar and faces the truth about Mufasa's death.
- **Return with the Elixir:** Simba drives out the hyenas and takes his rightful place, restoring order.

Star Wars is another clear example of this storyline—in fact, George Lucas blatantly utilized it to develop Luke Skywalker's journey.

My favorite character in those classic movies set in a galaxy far, far away is the mentor Yoda, who lives in the Dagobah system. Like Morpheus, Gandalf, and Rafiki with their pupils, Yoda guides Skywalker in his path.

Now, what I'll say next is based not on my love for the adorable green guy with hairy ears but on what I believe is true wisdom: You and I need to *become* Yoda. I'll be making a case for it in this chapter.

Being the young warrior is fine, but when you learn to see yourself as a mom or dad, then an elder, and finally a wise sage who focuses on mentoring those in need of direction, you can exponentially increase the impact you have in life. Because while it's easy to be impressed with the flashy light-saber-wielding warrior in the arena (and the platform and influence that come with it), you can easily miss a sage's deep value and wide reach at first glance. An old hermit living in a cave who spends their time training younglings hardly seems worthy of celebration or emulation, but when it comes to Yoda, there is more than meets the eye.

"TRULY WONDERFUL, THE MIND OF A CHILD IS"

A spiritual return to infancy was an underlying principle Jesus helped Nicodemus grasp when he was baffled by Jesus' saying, "Unless one is born again, he cannot see the kingdom of God" (John 3:3).

Nicodemus was much older than Jesus, but he came to Jesus as a student after scratching his head about something. He found Jesus' comment as bizarre as the cryptic messages Yoda gave to Skywalker. *Crawl back into their mother's womb and start again, who can?* he thought.

Jesus explained, "That which is born of the flesh is flesh, and that which is born of the Spirit is spirit" (v. 6). Meaning, the new birth is not by way of water in the birth canal; it is of the Spirit. The "pneuma" wind, not the amniotic fluid. You can be born out of your mother's womb into a family, a nation, or money, but not into the kingdom of God. That takes a second spiritual baptism by the Holy Ghost, something not visible in the physical realm.

When you are reborn from above, what happens next is amazing. Though your body continues to decline, each day, in every way, your spirit does the opposite—it is revitalized.

This is what Paul referenced in 2 Corinthians 4:16–18 when he wrote,

> We do not lose heart. Even though our outward man is perishing, yet the inward man is being renewed day by day. For our

light affliction, which is but for a moment, is working for us a far more exceeding and eternal weight of glory, while we do not look at the things which are seen, but at the things which are not seen. For the things which are seen are temporary, but the things which are not seen are eternal.

I can picture Paul looking at himself in the mirror later in life. He has crow's feet, wrinkles across his forehead, a few extra chins, sunspots, and scars from all his battle wounds. I see my own deepening furrows, scars, and hands that are looking increasingly old-man-ish holding the steering wheel. You probably have your own version of this. It can be discouraging. We have an earthly problem that stems from an earthly perspective.

If all your eggs are in this life's basket, that is an absolute crisis. What can you do besides nip, tuck, fill, backfill, and inject Botox? Not that there is anything inherently wrong with cosmetic procedures. But if this life is all you get, the perishing of the outward man is a calamity. Instead, like Paul, you should know that the mirror is only telling part of the story, and the least important part at that. As Eugene Peterson put it, "Reality is mostly made up of what we cannot see."

At some point every human will struggle with aging. Maybe you are wrestling with it super hard right now. But knowing we've been reborn of the Spirit and that there is so much more to us than meets the eye will guide us in wisdom! And this idea obviously has application far beyond the crisis of old age.

There is hope in the promise of future glory to sink your teeth into when you are grieving, dealing with medical setbacks, suffering from depression, or spiraling through any trial. The resurrection of Jesus and its implications will help you see wildflowers in your tornado. According to the New Testament, it is *the* emphatic answer to the question of whether our lives matter. If Christ is risen, our labor is not in vain! Since He is alive, your life on this earth matters—every bit of it!

And when, like Paul, you have been reborn spiritually and find yourself on the other side of the hill, you can find especially great comfort in knowing you are on the way to an eternity of glory. Between now and then, your spirit will be "reverse aging" like Benjamin Button (only less creepy than a baby version of Brad Pitt). You won't need to despair at the prospect of aging, because, in all the ways that count, you are getting better with time, not worse. To grow in maturity is to become more like Christ.

> YOU WON'T NEED TO DESPAIR AT THE PROSPECT OF AGING, BECAUSE, IN ALL THE WAYS THAT COUNT, YOU ARE GETTING BETTER WITH TIME, NOT WORSE.

You mustn't rely on what you can see with the naked eye.

Trials are temporary; triumph is forever. Ironically, part of how we become like Christ involves becoming like a child. G. K. Chesterton wrote, "We have sinned and grown old, and our Father is younger than we." Obviously, we are not to be childish and foolish; we instead are to be childlike and free.

Think about it this way: Children are naked and unashamed; they don't know or care about social standing. They practice imagination and whimsy; they wear bathing suits and cowboy boots. It's grand to be like a child! We may dismiss it, but as Jesus said, "Of such is the kingdom of heaven" (Matthew 19:14).

C. S. Lewis once wrote, "When I was ten, I read fairy tales in secret and would have been ashamed if I had been found doing so.

Now that I am fifty I read them openly. When I became a man I put away childish things, including the fear of childishness and the desire to be very grown up."

As we grow up in our faith, we trust God with that childlike dependence that can move mountains, even amid the trials we face in this life. This includes the aches and pains of aging—the stiff joints, circulation issues, hair loss, cloudy memory, and trouble doing simple tasks like tying our shoes. All of these can be opportunities for God to work something glorious in us. The more nicks, sagginess, bruises, bumps, and blotches we accumulate, the more occasion we have to trust in Him and become more like Him. As we depend on Him along the way, we can become more patient, gentle, kind, and caring.

When you get to heaven, you will not have to rely on hearing aids, walkers with tennis balls, or heart medicine. You will, however, get to keep the grace that was produced in you while enduring such things.

Do you believe that you can get better with time, like a fine wine? If you don't, begin now, my friend, because it's 100 percent true.

And do you ever celebrate that your signs of aging mean you are headed somewhere better? Another new thing to start up. After you press into Christ through every trial and come to the end of this life—when it's ashes to ashes and dust to dust for your body—you will get to go to your Father's house. Paul wrote with full confidence, "We know that if our earthly house, this tent, is destroyed, we have a building from God, a house not made with hands, eternal in the heavens" (2 Corinthians 5:1). For the Christian, death is not leaving home; it's going home.

Life on earth is like a camping trip. Life in heaven, which will culminate in living on a recreated earth, is like our real house. The house has what the tent does not—including a permanent address.

In a very real sense, death means coming off the road, ditching the tent, and moving into our forever home, because life does not end when our physical body dies.

As I have said before, death either takes you to your treasure or away from it; it depends on where you keep it. And once you realize your treasure is not on this earth, you don't have to be terrified of leaving it.

Having this perspective flips our view of death, bringing it out of the "dread" category and into the "defeated foe" category, one that accomplishes God's will. Thus "precious in the sight of the LORD is the death of His saints" (Psalm 116:15). It is the vehicle by which we are brought home.

With this jujitsu firmly in mind, we not only are free from fearing aging but also can appreciate what God is seeking to do through us while we face it. It becomes like Black Panther's suit, where all the pain is converted to power. (So bring on the fiber, the early dinners, the reader glasses, and the bird-watching if they make us more like Christ. *Wakanda forever, yo!*)

We know that aging—and any kind of suffering, for that matter—is not for the faint of heart, but it doesn't have to be full of terror. Don't mishear me. I'm not being glib; I have looked into the faces of loved ones I have lost, and it is hard. But Paul said that to depart and be with Christ is far better than remaining in this body. The house has got what the tent does not. This is our living hope.

THE GREATEST TEACHER, FAILURE IS

While I was working on this book, and after a long, slow decline through Parkinson's, my friend Stew Adams went home to be with

Jesus. For many years Stew had been a part of our church community along with his wife, Debbie. He always had tears in his eyes and a great joy on his face when he would talk to me about Jesus, God's Word, or the excitement he had about people in our church experiencing God. One time when I visited him, he was disappointed he couldn't be more active, so he began doing bicep curls with his aluminum walker. He kept coming to the church until his last day, whenever he could be out of bed, even when he was feeble, shaking, and hardly able to put sentences together.

At one point toward the end, Debbie called me saying he thought he was dying. He had told her goodbye, not expecting to make it through the night. But the next morning, he was still alive, and I went to see him.

Stew was embarrassed by the false alarm, feeling as though he had been dramatic.

I grabbed his hand and told him, "Stew, you've never died before. How could you expect to be good at it? Do you remember the first time you tied your shoes? Without practice, there's no reason to think it won't be clumsy and that you might fail. It's not on you to be a pro. You can struggle and even be scared. I know Debbie will be. But when it happens, angels will bring you straight to your Savior. He will be in perfect and total control. You have never died before, but Jesus has! And He overcame it. Don't let your lack of experience scare you; Jesus is very good at this."

He found comfort in this and soon fell asleep with a nod.

It was ten days later that Stew closed his eyes for the last time on earth. But I know he opened them in heaven, where even today he is experiencing fullness of joy. I can't wait to see him again!

Stew went home to be with Jesus on a Tuesday night. On the following Sunday morning, Debbie was in church, alone. When I saw her there, weeping in worship, it reminded me of the woman Jesus healed at the synagogue in Luke 13.

For almost two decades, the woman had been stooped over, her chest parallel to the floor, unable to stand upright. She came to the synagogue on the Sabbath when Jesus was present, and He ended up completely changing her life. But what blows me away is that she had no idea she was going to receive a miracle when she showed up that day. Jesus didn't announce in advance who He would heal. Showing up to worship after eighteen years of suffering and not receiving a miracle was just what this woman did.

Great things come to those who handle hardship and disappointment well.

I dare you to view your challenges as opportunities to trust God in new ways. To believe that your hard times are not there to destroy you but to deepen you.

And if you do—and you keep on doing it for years—you will become a deep well for others.

> I DARE YOU TO VIEW YOUR CHALLENGES AS OPPORTUNITIES TO TRUST GOD IN NEW WAYS.

ALWAYS PASS ON WHAT YOU HAVE LEARNED

As you become a deep well, you are in the position to distill and share the lessons you have learned to those coming along after you. You get a new place in the tribe. From there, your focus must shift from chasing your own individual achievement to identifying what you have learned and can be shared.

Someone once said that every time an old person dies, it is like a library burns to the ground. Don't let that happen! Decide to be a mentor however and wherever you can. If you're in your later years, make a point of sharing all the wisdom and memories you can. If you have aging parents, make a point of interviewing them—even if it's as simple as hitting record on your smartphone and asking them questions. It is free, and you will never regret that you did it.

There are also amazing new services that will help you preserve memories from your parents' lives. For example, for a fee, a company called Storyworth will email your parents one question a week. At the end of the year, the company will combine all of the questions and answers and bind them in a beautiful hardcover book. It's brilliant!

Once you are in the "older and wiser" seat, you have the chance to help the next generation win by allowing your hindsight to be their foresight. George Santayana said, "Those who cannot remember the past are condemned to repeat it." Let's stop the insanity where possible and pay forward the things we've learned.

But sometimes I find it so hard to connect with young people, you might think. *It's like they speak a different language and were born with AirPods in their ears.*

I get it. But remember, it is much easier to be critical of young people than it is to be their ally and advocate. And also much less helpful. As *Ratatouille* taught us, being a critic is easy. You sit back and pass judgment on the one who is creating. You contribute nothing.

I for one want to do what I can to be a part of the solution. Young people didn't ask to be born with iPhones and TikTok and artificial intelligence. We don't get to pick what era we are born into. We can, however, choose to fight *for* and not just against the generations coming behind us.

MUCH TO LEARN, YOU STILL HAVE

I hope that, as you begin to see more of life's milestones passing—with knees wearing out, cholesterol increasing, vision dimming, and hearing fading—that your faith will be rising and you will yearn to get into the arena God has prepared from before the foundation of the earth for *this* time of your life. It's possible.

This is what God wants for you—to grow up but not check out. George Bernard Shaw encapsulated this power that purpose can give you when he said, "Life is no brief candle to me. It's a sort of splendid torch which I've got hold of for the moment, and I want to make it burn as brightly as possible before handing it on to the future generations."

That is a beautiful picture of a vision for mentorship during the second half of life. God's calling on our lives—as we get older and wiser and hopefully have more perspective—is that we would unlock the greatness in others.

This is what John Maxwell calls *explosive growth*, one of his irrefutable laws of leadership. It involves leading leaders instead of only developing followers. Those leaders will also then lead leaders, and compound interest kicks in as things grow exponentially. The math gets bigger when you think this way.

It is especially powerful to do this in our later years, because there is blessing to give in our weathered, increasingly old-looking hands—one that we didn't have when we were young. There is delight and not just dread in aging. I for one rejoice that my hands are going to get better and better at guiding young Luke Skywalkers on their quest to defeat Darth Vader.

In the book of Genesis, Jacob gathered his sons to his deathbed and, one by one, he prophesied over each of them before "he drew his feet up into the bed and breathed his last" (Genesis 49:33). I love the imagery used in this verse, and I see it teaching a principle we can live out over a larger stretch of time. Instead of occurring in a single, emotionally charged, farewell event, this type of interaction could become our focus over an entire season.

We see a version of it with David and Solomon. Yes, there was one Hallmark moment when David specifically charged his son to be strong, to be a man, and to follow the Lord; then he gave the blessing. But leading up to that moment, David did everything in his power to prepare what his son needed to win.

For years, David had longed to build a house for God—and he was rebuffed in his zeal. God told him he couldn't do it because there was blood on his hands; his son Solomon would do it instead.

There are not many things that will test your heart more than hearing what God will *not* allow you to do. David could have easily taken his ball and gone home. Instead, he resolved that not getting to do it would not stop him from serving the one who would. He spent the final act of his life selflessly stockpiling resources for the project he wouldn't personally be involved in. He would not have left the legacy he did had he focused only on what he got to do himself and put himself in the spotlight.

Do you want to energize and animate the second half of your life? What can you do now to supply those coming after you with building materials—philosophically, financially, wisely—so that they can do things that you would have loved to do yourself?

The next, deeper question for your heart would be, Can you take as much pleasure in their doing it as you would if you were doing it yourself?

Heaven is your home, and this earth is a mission. Though we face hard things, including aging, between heaven and earth, there is a purpose, a dignity, and an assignment. And if we'll seek heaven's vision for our life, though we leave the strength of youth behind, there is another stair—new strength we can tap into.

Hear me. There is glory in your current and your coming season just as much as there was in your prior one. You can make it a spring. And when you do, you go from glory to glory. From death to resurrection. It is no good to cry for what is past when you should be embracing the power of what is coming next. As a part of that journey, you can look forward to becoming Yoda. Don't get me wrong; Yoda is good in a battle. But he is *far more* valuable to the Resistance as a trainer of other Jedis.

HEAVEN IS YOUR HOME, AND THIS EARTH IS A MISSION.

Genius-makers are more valuable to an organization than a genius, according to Liz Wiseman in the book *Multipliers*. She sorts out leaders of all stripes into two categories: multipliers and diminishers. Multipliers use their intelligence to amplify the smarts and capabilities of the people around them. They don't worry about being outshined or upstaged. Multipliers want to open doors for people, letting their ceiling be the next generation's floor. Multipliers are legacy-minded.

Diminishers, on the other hand, are prima donnas and love being at the center of attention. They demand people's best thinking but end up only getting the safest ideas. They drain intelligence, monopolize, and micromanage because they need to be the smartest person in every room, the quarterback of every strategy.

The math is simple but powerful. Multipliers get, on average, twice the capability from someone they lead. When extrapolated across an average organization size of approximately fifty people, that's the equivalent of adding an additional fifty people. "Eighty people can either operate with the productivity of fifty or they can operate as though they were five hundred."

You can be the key that unlocks greatness in other people.

Nate Bargatze credits Joe Rogan as being the first person to open a door for him to do stand-up comedy. They had only known each other for one night when Joe put his reputation on the line vouching for Nate to get a spot on the roster for an open mic night in Los Angeles. All these years and sold-out arena tours later, Nate looks back on that evening and what Joe did to open a door for him with gratitude and appreciation. It cost Joe very little but to Nate it meant very much.

Someone who sees greatness in other people—that's the kind of person God wants you to become. Not one who sits around talking about all their glory days, but the one who helps other people tap into glory days of their own. And in so doing, you are more glorious than you could ever imagine you'd be.

Before you turn the page, take a moment to prayerfully jot down a few names of people you might be able to help. Maybe there's a threshold they need to cross or an ordeal they need to face. How could you play a role in their ultimate return with the elixir, in whatever way God is calling them? It could be someone from work, at church, or even in your family, a niece or nephew. Invite them to coffee and offer to help however you can. Tell them you can't promise to fill up their tank but, with God's help, you want to empty yours as you pour into them.

When you embrace the transition from warrior to father or mother, on the way to becoming an elder of your tribe you can eventually get to sage. Yes, aging is a little scary; that's understandable and okay. Remember, you've never been here before!

But becoming Yoda? It's awesome.

CHAPTER 9

WHAT A FRIEND I'VE FOUND

WHEN I WAS a freshman in high school and newly saved, I began to experience spiritual warfare in big, scary ways. I sensed dark, oppressive presences in my bedroom at night and felt like I was being told I would kill myself. These were not thoughts like, *I want to die,* but instead *I am* going to *die, and at my own hand.* These thoughts seemed to come out of nowhere, and the strangest part is that I wasn't even depressed. It was terrifying. The thief comes in the room only to steal, kill, and destroy; Jesus brings life, and life more abundantly. (If a voice ever tells you to harm yourself, it is not from God, no matter what peace is promised. Taking your life won't get rid of your pain; it will multiply it and transfer it to those who love you.)

BLESSED ARE THE SPIRALING

I did what I hope you will do if you are suffering—I picked up the phone and reached out to someone, in my case a youth pastor. She spoke life into me; gave me verses to cling to, specifically Isaiah 26:3 and Deuteronomy 30; and helped me understand the attacks were because of the devil's recognition of my following God. She also believed they were coming in especially hot because I had a call to ministry placed on my life.

Satan hates what is a threat to him and attacks what is significant, not insignificant. But when you are being attacked, it can make you feel like you are weak and doing something wrong—which can cause you to sink further into despair.

DARKNESS ATTACKS LIGHT BECAUSE IT IS LIGHT.

My family likes to play Catan and Monopoly together. When we suspect someone is getting too much momentum and poses a threat, we all team up to thwart their progress. I want you to begin to see spiritual attack as an indicator of being on the right track; instead of it discouraging you, let it embolden you. Darkness attacks light because it is light. Mortal combat with demons, and the struggle against their temptations and accusations, are an indication of the Spirit of God at work in your life. Don't fear! You matter! If you were no threat, the devil would leave you alone; he would not seek to devour you.

FIGHTING FIRE WITH WORSHIP

During that time, I learned to fight fire with worship. Simultaneous to these spiritual attacks, my parents' marriage was crumbling, which created tension in our home. When bedtime came, instability and spiritual warfare would descend like a black cloud. Worship music became a saving grace, especially one song.

It was the late '90s, and the British rock band Delirious? was disrupting worship music, bringing a U2-like rock-and-roll sound. The spirit of their songs was like water in a desert for my tortured soul. Their album *King of Fools* was my go-to by day, but there was one song that especially eased my suffering at night. It was on an album called *Live & In the Can*, ingeniously marketed with the CD being sold in a literal tin can. The song "What a Friend I've Found," a five-minute lullaby-like track, was the opposite of kryptonite for me. Every night I would put the disc in my silver boom box and hit repeat on track twelve. And in the healing lyrics and music, in Martin Smith's soothing, calming voice and priestly ministry, I was able to find refuge under the safe shelter of God's wings.

I have no idea how many times I turned to that song for refuge. Maybe hundreds.

Delirious? broke up at the height of their popularity and platform, and I never understood why. I had no insider information, but from what I could gather it wasn't like The Beatles; they didn't seem to have had any big fight. They just sensed it was time to walk away from sold-out tours around the world and endless opportunities to ride the wave of their usefulness and commercial success.

Over the next fourteen years, I heard people mention Martin Smith here and there. They'd describe how he cowrote a song, mentored someone, or led worship at an event, always with a spirit of genuine respect and awe—as though Yoda were doing a clinic on the Force.

Ask any prominent worship leader today about the musician and speaker Martin Smith, and they will talk about him with deference, admiration, and gratitude.

In 2009 I had the honor of meeting Martin very briefly. I'd hoped to have a chance to tell him what he meant to me, but the moment wasn't right. There were others waiting to talk to him, and the opportunity faded away.

More than a decade later, Jennie and I were speaking at an event in Nashville where Martin and his son were singing and ministering. I physically leapt when we bumped into each other backstage. I wasn't going to let this chance pass. I expressed my gratitude for the way he had helped change my life—even saving it. Then he smiled mischievously and said, "Let's talk tomorrow."

The next day, after our sessions were over, I looked for Martin backstage. But it seemed it wasn't meant to be, so Jennie and I settled into our dressing room to wait for our airport pickup that would arrive in a half hour. Suddenly there was a knock, and standing in the doorway was Martin and his son Levi.

Before I tell you about our visit, though, I want to describe what Jennie and I had just watched these two do on stage.

They led two songs. The first one was "Obsession," which reminds us how our hearts burn for God. (Bookmark it and throw it on sometime.) Before they moved into the second song, Martin invited people who needed the filling or refilling of the Holy Spirit to receive Him, to open their hearts and welcome Him. As I sat back in my chair and listened to the notes from Levi's guitar accompanied by Martin's somewhat haunting vocalizations, I immediately felt like a weighted antianxiety blanket was settling over me.

This is why Elisha knew to ask for a musician when he needed to prophesy; it unlocks something in *your* spirit and puts you in touch with *the* Spirit. That is why it is a mistake to treat the worship set at church like the previews before the movie—a time buffer so you can slide into your seat before the main event. I don't think there will be sermons in heaven, but there will be worship, so why shouldn't we start practicing now for eternity?

Martin continued singing, and I listened with my hands open and my palms up. For the next fifteen minutes (or was it fifteen days?), I felt the same calm I'd had as a fourteen-year-old, only it was a new mercy. No longer was I a boy facing the angst of a transition into adulthood, needing to have my spirit soothed. Now I was receiving the ministry for a second puberty, a new stairstep into the next season of my life as a father and, beyond that, hopefully a junior Yoda in the making.

So when Martin and Levi appeared in our doorway, I sensed in my spirit it was significant. *Kairos*, not *chronos*. (These are two words for time in Greek. *Chronos* is time generically, and *kairos* is time specifically or significantly.) For such a time as this.

WALKING WARRIOR ACADEMY

Martin and Jennie sat in the room's two chairs while Levi and I sat on the floor. Martin and I both took our shoes off. As I sat there at Martin's feet, my soul told me I was there to receive an impartation. We chatted, but quickly he asked what Jennie and I were facing that we needed to navigate.

It was Jedi.

I told him I was seeking to understand what former glories we needed to quit chasing so we could readily receive the future glory God had for us.

He received that instantly and began talking about his exodus from fame at the height of his career with the band. At the top of the wave, he had felt like he was supposed to drop down into darkness and obscurity; to be set apart and hidden so he could be home more for his kids during their growing-up years. Martin's kids needed to be raised somewhere other than the middle of rock stardom. He wanted something quieter for them and chose to walk away.

Martin said it was terrifying to discover the darkness in the trough, far from the limelight around the wave he had been riding.

"My flesh was screaming," he admitted. "But God was calling me to quietly serve and be hidden, to be obscure. The flesh wants to be seen. I'm now a nobody. You want to do what God calls you to do, but it's hard to separate who you are from what you do—until you step away from what you've been doing."

I nodded my head vigorously as he put language to what many of us feel and struggle to articulate.

Martin admitted what it was like to see others' success, to wrestle with the ego energy clamoring to have written some big song or big book. *Someone else is now the most visible and the newest big deal. Where do I stack up? Who am I without this? Am I still me if I don't do what has always made me be me?* Ultimately he came to see the purpose of a time of quiet transformation. He embraced the hidden beauty of it.

"How old are you two?" he asked us next.

"We both just entered our forties," I answered.

"Your forties are good," he said. "You have energy and some scars—so you have a little more wisdom. Your fifties are awesome. You don't really care anymore so you can just relax and enjoy things."

Then there was a knock at the door. It was time for Jennie and me to leave for the airport. The shoes went back on, and the holy ground transformed back into a normal greenroom. But I will never forget those moments in that little earthly holy of holies.

What a friend I've found, indeed.

Talking to Martin was an enormous gift. It struck me afterward that I literally and metaphorically had sat at his feet as we received this impartation from him. Jennie and I agreed that he was deep water and a man at peace. We also believed that his words held a lot of weight; he wasn't just a warrior, he was a walking warrior academy. A father and a sage. He had become Yoda.

As he chose not to do all those visible things, he was very much *not* out of sight, out of mind, or yesterday's news. Instead, he was even *more* valuable. It calmed me in so many ways. I have no doubt that a huge reason God had me at that conference was so I could listen to Martin and learn from him.

It's natural that we feel afraid at the process of leaving behind the season of being the young man or woman of the tribe for the new calling: to be a father or mother and then the eventual wise man or woman. There is a clumsiness to transition, and in between you end up sort of green, small, and Grogu-ish, a Yoda in training. But we don't have to fear, for there is a glory to that rebirth.

That is a part of the process of becoming a sage. It's worth it.

BE LIKE DAVE

One time, my daughter Daisy and I were waiting for a table at the Carnation Café, a restaurant in Disneyland, when we heard a couple make an unusual request. "Can we be seated in the section where Dave is working as the busboy?"

The hostess said she would check.

While she walked away, I asked them, "Who is Dave?" I had never heard of someone requesting a specific busboy.

"Oh, Dave has been working at Disneyland nonstop for fifty years!" the man exclaimed. "He has some stories to tell about this place!"

My curiosity piqued, I soon asked the hostess if there was another table in Dave's section.

Laughing, she said he was very popular and found us a table where Dave would be clearing dishes.

After Daisy and I ordered, I pulled out a Yahtzee pocket set, and we played a quick round with the dice. When our food came, Dave came over to our table and asked, "Do you two need any refills?"

"No, thank you," I answered. "But I have to say, I heard you have worked at Disneyland for fifty years! That's incredible."

He shrugged his shoulders, as though that wasn't an impressive feat.

"There is a guy in costuming named Vick—he's been here fifty-seven—and a chef who just retired had been here sixty-one. There are lots of other fifties." He said all this with a lightly dismissive tone, like, *Eh, no biggie.* "Besides," he went on, "I love this place."

I racked my brain for a fun trivia question to query him with.

"Hey, I know that before Neil Armstrong the astronaut died, he was here for the ribbon-cutting of Space Mountain when they reopened it. Did you get a chance to see him that day?" I asked.

"Oh yes!" he said. "He and Chip and Dale, along with Mickey Mouse, played a game of basketball on a secret court inside the Matterhorn mountain before the ceremony."

Incredible.

Without trying to monopolize his time we asked a few more

questions about his favorite ride, what it was like watching the park change over the decades, and where he has most enjoyed working. (He said he loved the restaurants because they gave him the most fun guest interactions.)

We left, vowing to return to that restaurant on our next visit—not for the food, though it was fine, but to get to talk to Dave again!

Speaking to him was like encountering a rare Disney treasure. His "low-visibility" position didn't make him less valuable, but more. His knowledge and experience were a gift to everyone around him. He was like a walking, talking, bussing piece of history.

Time in the wilderness is what it takes to transition into your next stage in the "tribe." So many people in Scripture had to endure fiery trials in wild places before they could become holy vessels fit to carry new wine.

The idea of being set apart, holy to the Lord, is very sexy. But do you still want to be set apart if it means being *set aside*? This is the difficult question we must answer if we are to follow the cloud of God's presence over the clout of this world.

Martin Smith's path to sage was not the same as Disney Dave's, and neither of their paths may resemble what God has for me or you to do. I have never been a rock star; I can't carry a tune. And I doubt I'll ever work at Disneyland, although one of my first jobs was a busboy at Chili's and I loved it. The point isn't ever to do exactly what someone else did but to learn from their experience and wisdom. Martin felt God wanted him to step out of the public eye until his kids graduated from school. He honored that commitment, so he is now beginning to lead at events again.

He is doing what he feels God wants him to do.

In the same way, the heaviest opinion in our lives needs to belong to God.

YOUR NUMBER ONE SPOT

I once came across a jarring, apocryphal story attributed to Warren Buffett. It goes like this:

The famed investor was once asked by his pilot how to set priorities. He told the pilot to make a list of the top twenty-five things he wanted out of life and then to arrange them in order of importance. The top five should be those around which he organized his time. The pilot expected Buffett to say that after doing those five, he should focus on the remaining twenty. Instead, he said the remaining twenty should be avoided at all costs because they were not important enough to form the core of his life, yet seductive enough to distract him from what matters most.

Wow. The good is the enemy of the best.

EVERYONE HAS A MASTER PASSION OR A CONTROLLING INTEREST. WE ALL SERVE SOMEBODY OR SOMETHING— WHETHER OR NOT WE REALIZE IT.

This is the kind of singular focus you need to have when it comes to following God's plan for your life. If you created that list today, what would be your number one goal? Would God make the top five?

If anything besides God sits in the number one spot in your life, you have identified a god.

Augustine was right when he said that there is no such thing as an atheist. Everyone has a master passion or a controlling interest. We all serve somebody or something—whether or not we realize it.

IT'S WORTH IT

The apostle Paul taught us the power of having God as number one. We find it in Philippians 3:13–14: "I do not count myself to have apprehended; but one thing I do, forgetting those things which are behind and reaching forward to those things which are ahead, I press toward the goal for the prize of the upward call of God in Christ Jesus."

The secret to concentration is elimination. The sun can start a fire only if it is focused by a lens.

To live with that kind of desire and motivation is to tap into the power of the focused life. As the words from Jeremiah 9 remind us, "Let not the wise man glory in his wisdom, let not the mighty man glory in his might, nor let the rich man glory in his riches; but let him who glories glory in this, that he understands and knows Me, that I am the LORD, exercising lovingkindness, judgment, and righteousness in the earth. For in these I delight" (vv. 23–24).

You want to be proud about something? Be proud of the fact that you know God! He takes your calls. The King of kings has *your* name written on the palm of His hand!

That is better than being an influencer, walking a red carpet, belonging to a country club, or owning a Jet Ski. What's more, this King died on a cross to save your soul and redeem your life from destruction.

The problem with looking to our résumés or net worth to define us is that our value goes up and down depending on our performance that day. You will feel like garbage eventually. But when it dawns on you, like it did for Paul, that in Christ you are the righteousness of God and that your value doesn't rise and fall like the stock market, you will consider all else garbage—dung, actually—compared to the excellence of knowing Him (Philippians 3:8).

When that rings true in your heart, then no matter what God is calling you to do, the answer will be yes, just as it was for Martin Smith. Though it may sting in the moment, you are reselling all you have for the Treasure of knowing Him, and in the process you are being conformed to His image. If following means walking away from something, or walking toward something, you will be willing to do it because He is the prize. It isn't what He does through you or how He blesses you. You just want Him.

It's worth it. He is the true Treasure that can make all other treasures look like trash.

If I am honest, sometimes I'm afraid of what God might call me to or want from me. Maybe you can relate. It is that primitive fear that if we say yes to God in an open-ended way, He is going to send us a one-way ticket to a foreign mission field. We mustn't be so narcissistic. God loves the people of whatever mission field we are dreading far too much to send someone with such a bad attitude to reach them.

If we remember that He is a good Father—that He only knows how to do good and only wants good things for us as His kids—we needn't be afraid. James 1:17 reminds us that God is the Father of lights and that every good and perfect gift comes from Him. Of course the path to those good things is often very hard and scary, sometimes even painful, but the end He has in mind is far better than we could ever imagine.

As Martin discovered, your flesh might scream at whatever Jesus is calling you to as you deny yourself, pick up your cross, and follow Him into the unknown, but it will be a death that leads to life. And according to Psalm 16:11, in His presence is fullness of joy, and at His right hand are pleasures evermore.

Before you close this chapter, I would love for you to go online and listen to Martin Smith's song "What a Friend I've Found" from his Delirious? band days. I pray that as you listen, preferably with your eyes closed and your hands open, you will go all in with Jesus again, or for the very first time. Let the Spirit of God fall afresh on you. Feel Him in your room with you. Settle in.

Sell all you have in your mind for the Treasure of knowing Him. And don't let anything else on your list, or in this world, seduce you out of seeing Him as the prize—the most important person in the room.

CHAPTER 10

LEAVE NO CLAW MARKS

ONE TIME WHEN I was visiting San Diego, I went for a run and passed a gorgeous mansion that was across from a golf course and steps from the beach. The location couldn't be beat! It was modern, sleek, and pristine. I imagined it had every amenity inside and a pool in the back. It struck me that it would be a hard place to leave. Maybe it was the fact that back home in Montana it was subzero with gusting winds and pelting snow that could sandblast paint off a wall. I had a sudden urge to move to San Diego permanently. Like, send for my family and we all can remain here in this sun-soaked paradise, preferably in this mansion.

Then it occurred to me how much harder you would have to

work to keep your heart set on heaven while living in such a place. How difficult would it be to live in this house and leave it? The owner of this gorgeous place will die one day, and when they do, they will have to say goodbye.

In truth, ownership is an illusion. On paper we own everything we have bought, earned, and been given. But one day a piece of paper will be generated that will end all that. It's called a death certificate.

I learned the hard way that those are mailed out. It was weeks after my daughter left this world that her death certificate arrived in a stack of mail. Nestled in between an ad, a bill, and an L.L.Bean catalog featuring fuzzy slippers was a piece of paper announcing, with finality, that her time being alive was in the past—on earth, anyway. She no longer was a person, a citizen, a living being in the eyes of the state. Everything she "owned" was now no longer hers.

That will one day be true for you and me.

As I continued my run and envisioned playing soccer with my son in the backyard of the San Diego mansion (I don't even play soccer, but naturally I would surely take up the sport if I could afford to live in this mansion), I found myself asking an important question. *If this place were mine, would I leave fingernail marks on it when it came time to leave it?*

The extent to which we are not ready to leave this life, we are not ready to live this life. When Paul was staring down an execution sentence, the Philippian church was praying for his release. Paul almost wanted to talk them out of it, because he longed to be with Christ—even while acknowledging that believers would benefit from his remaining on earth. Ultimately he decided that, if he had his choice, he would just get on with it and go home to be with Jesus, because it was vastly superior to this broken planet.

How did he know that? Uh, because he had been there one time. No biggie. Some say it took place in Lystra when Paul got stoned. (With rocks, not weed.) He had been preaching, and members of an angry mob, who just ten minutes prior were trying to sacrifice to him because they thought he was a god, turned on him when he wouldn't allow them to adulate him.*

Right after Paul was stoned to death and dragged outside the city, he lay for a little while. Then he got up, dusted himself off, and went classic Paul—right back to preaching. Many believe that it was in the midst of this ordeal that he was caught up to the third heaven—the first being where the birds fly; the second being what we call space, which begins just past the Kármán line; and the third being what he got to see. And apparently it was so much better that even San Diego couldn't have captivated his attention.

WHAT ARE WE SUPPOSED TO DO?

You might be thinking, *Levi, are you advocating monasticism? Should we give all we have to the poor and live in a commune?*

The problem is, you can only do that once. And unless God calls you to specifically do that, you will likely end up in a situation the Thessalonians found themselves in. Paul chided them for sitting idly by, waiting for Jesus to come back instead of working with their hands so that they would have something to bless other people

---

* The truth is that we aren't nearly as good as those who look at us with rosy hero worship, nor are we as bad as those who have been let down by our shadows. We are somewhere in between: mere mortals with strengths and weaknesses, pluses and minuses, brightness and shadow. This was a massive counseling revelation during my crisis, and it helped me see myself and others accurately. And off the pedestal.

with. Besides, the Acts 2 communal living experiment didn't turn out so hot and the Macedonians ended up having to foot the bill for their expenses.

Most people are called to work jobs, earn money, enjoy God's blessings, and be generous. There are exceptions, and if that's you, you should absolutely follow the leading of the Holy Spirit. The rest of us need to work so we can support those who are the tip of the spear in missions and ministry.

Paul gave Timothy, a young pastor, advice on how to equip those with means in his church and guide them toward dying without leaving their claw marks on their fancy houses by the sea. It's a crash course on the secret to prosperity without idolatry, which is possible, but not without a strategy.

If you are going to have money in your hands and not let it into your heart, then check out Paul's dos and don'ts for the rich, based on 1 Timothy 6:17–19:

- Don't be haughty.
- Don't trust in money but in the living God, who gives richly all things to enjoy.
- Do good by being ready to give and willing to share.
- People who do these things will store up for themselves a good foundation for the time to come, that they may lay hold on eternal life.

Notice that Paul did not chastise anyone for being rich or say they should divest themselves of all their resources. The key issues are about heart attitude and how you use what is within your reach.

If you have the humility to be trained in this wisdom, you will find the power you need to protect yourself from great heartache and regret. You also will become ready to leave this life, so you are truly ready to live it.

Did Paul have any words for the poor? He sure did.

> Those who desire to be rich fall into temptation and a snare, and into many foolish and harmful lusts which drown men in destruction and perdition. For the love of money is a root of all kinds of evil, for which some have strayed from the faith in their greediness, and pierced themselves through with many sorrows. (1 Timothy 6:9–10)

Interestingly, this admonishment for the poor is harsher than the guidance for the higher tax bracket folks. The key issue here is about learning contentment.

WHAT HAS YOU?

You might think that the love of money is specifically a problem for those with lots of it, but Paul was saying it can often strike the hearts of those without it. That means it isn't always the guy in the San Diego mansion who struggles with greed. He could be generous and practice phenomenal stewardship while the person out front, running by, who has less financially, can actually be the greedy one in love with money he doesn't possess.

It's not about what you have but what has you.

You can be proud about not having wealth, thinking poverty is virtuous. But your bank account doesn't dictate your character. You can be righteous and rich—or be pious and broke. And no matter how much you have, you can pierce yourself through with many sorrows trying to get more.

One of my earliest memories as a child is being in a carpool. Though our family cars weren't exactly luxury vehicles, they were late model and clean. Another family in our carpool drove a rather old and run-down station wagon. As early as first grade, I remember feeling embarrassed when I would get out of their car at drop-off. As we'd pull up to the school, I'd sink low in the seat and feel my face grow hot, knowing other kids would see me getting out of the beater, which would make me look poor. Even at that young age I sensed guilt over how it made me feel. I was making the mistake of deriving my identity from material things—a track that can only lead to sorrow.

Why? Because more will never be enough.

There is a classic, probably fictitious parable about a Mexican fisherman who was approached at the dock by a visiting American investment banker. It goes like this:

Complimenting him on the quality of the fish in his boat, the businessman asked how long it took to catch them.

The fisherman said he worked only a few hours per day; he spent most of his daytime hours with his wife and children, then at night strolled into the village, where he sipped wine and played guitar with his friends.

The American told him that if the fisherman worked harder, took fewer breaks, and applied time-management principles to his life, he could scale things and make them much bigger. Invest his profits in more boats and build a fleet. Hire others to do the fishing. Leave the small coastal fishing village and move to the big city, where he could run his expanding business. In fifteen or twenty years, he could be making millions and eventually sell the company.

"What would I do then?" the fisherman asked.

"You would retire!" the businessman replied. "You could move to a small coastal village where you could fish, spend most of your time with your wife and kids, and stroll into the village each night to sip wine and play guitar with your friends!"

What does it profit to gain the world and lose your life in the process?

Such is the great illusion of chasing the wind. You have to ask: *Is more for more's sake actually going to lead to more peace?*

More time with loved ones?

More growth in your relationship with God?

Is it going to lead to a longer résumé or a better eulogy at your funeral?

Your kids won't remember how much money you had. But they will never forget how much time you spent with them, the way you made them feel, and the values you lived out along the way.

THE HEARSE WITH A U-HAUL

No matter what you manage to acquire, you will leave it all behind at the end of your four thousand weeks on earth (that'd be the count if you live to age seventy-six). You and I brought nothing into this world. Babies don't have iPads, Rolexes, or backpacks when they come from the womb. Naked are we born; naked we return.

As the saying goes, you never see a hearse pulling a U-Haul.

Except one day my family and I actually did see one! We were at Taco Bell. (I, by the way, love Taco Bell. Chalupa Supreme and a Doritos Locos Taco with a Diet Baja Blast—because it makes me feel better about myself to say "diet" right at the end of that calorie bomb.) We laughed and wondered why on earth that person would be traveling to the afterlife with all those possessions. Then we realized it was a band, and they were using the trailer to carry their musical gear.

We saw the anomaly. At first it freaked us out, then it prompted a great conversation about having a light touch so we can live with a full heart. It actually might have gone a little far, because it introduced Lennox to the concept of inheritance, and afterward he kept asking me questions like, "Dad, when you die, can I have your fishing pole?"

"Yes, buddy."

"Dad, when you die, can I have your boots?"

"Yes, buddy."

TO DERIVE YOUR IDENTITY FROM ANYTHING THAT IS TEMPORARY IS TO GUARANTEE UNPLEASANT FEELINGS WHEN THAT THING IS TORN FROM YOUR HANDS.

As shocking as it was, the answer was yes to all of it, because I can't take any of it with me.

The Egyptians essentially tried to do that, burying their kings with all their earthly goods.

But hundreds and thousands of years later, when the vandals and archaeologists opened the vaults, none of the possessions had been touched by the original owners.

To derive your identity from anything that is temporary is to guarantee unpleasant feelings when that thing is torn from your hands. If, however, you can learn to have things without things having you, you can enjoy them knowing they are only on loan and you are truly a steward, not an owner.

Generosity drives a stake through the heart of idolatry and reminds us that the things we have are not who we are. They are tools, something to enjoy and use to worship God, not idols to be worshiped. The mistake is to be rich on this earth but poor toward God. What we keep is all we get, but what we give away is ours to enjoy forever.

THE RICHEST PERSON

What do the seasons of life have to do with the nature of true prosperity? Everything. If we begin with the thesis that, in the end, we keep only what we invest in eternity, it will change our relationship with our possessions and belongings.

Imagine today is the last day of your life. Now picture the liquidation sale that would follow—the "everything must go" moment when loved ones take what they want, then lug the rest to Goodwill or the dump.

Envisioning this can, and should, alter your relationship with those things.

Since you know seasons change—winter *will* arrive, like it or not—your goal is to bring some of winter's clarity into today's reality. Accept the inevitable truth now, when you are in autumn, spring, or summer. Claw marks are optional. You can hold things with a light touch, or not.

It was rumored that Queen Elizabeth I, who died owning two

thousand costly dresses, said on her deathbed, "All my possessions for a moment of time." What is that, if not truth seen too late?

One of the gnarliest parables Jesus told involved a man who made a huge financial mistake: He invested only in this life and neglected his eternal portfolio, which was empty when he died. Read it and let it put the fear of God in your finances.

> The farm of a certain rich man produced a terrific crop. He talked to himself: "What can I do? My barn isn't big enough for this harvest." Then he said, "Here's what I'll do: I'll tear down my barns and build bigger ones. Then I'll gather in all my grain and goods, and I'll say to myself, Self, you've done well! You've got it made and can now retire. Take it easy and have the time of your life!" Just then God showed up and said, "Fool! Tonight you die. And your barnful of goods—who gets it?" That's what happens when you fill your barn with Self and not with God. (Luke 12:16–21 MSG)

The goal isn't to be the richest or the buffest or the most traveled or accomplished person in the cemetery, but to have given your life away and tapped into true significance.

If you knew you were staying in a hotel for only one weekend, would you paint the room? Upgrade the TV? Buy a rug? Of course not. Your mentality changes when you know you are somewhere temporarily.

You are on this planet temporarily. At some point, you—just like everyone else—will have to exit stage left from this planet and then face the music.

Reminding yourself of that all throughout your sojourning will keep you from getting lulled into complacency and dormancy. It will give you clarity when you're spiraling, bringing what matters most into sharp focus. And it will keep you from agony when the illusion of permanency is disrupted and you must leave.

Did you know that, if you are wise with earthly treasure, you can expect people in eternity to want to invite you over to their homes to thank you for how your generosity helped them get to heaven? This does not mean you don't have wealth or nice things; it means you realize they are not true Treasures. And it means you understand that the purpose of those things is to accomplish God's will.

Joseph of Arimathea used his wealth to give Jesus a burial spot in a tomb.

Mary Magdalene used her financial prowess to bankroll the ministry of Jesus, and she encouraged her friends to do the same.

Lydia, a seller of purple dye from the city of Thyatira, supported the ministry of Paul and invited the church in Philippi—the first Christian church in Europe—to meet in her home (one of several she owned).

Joanna, the wife of Chuza, the steward of Herod, gave generously to the earthly ministry of Jesus using money that wicked Herod paid them. How's that for using what the devil meant for evil to accomplish good?

There is a rich tradition of wealthy people who have used their financial savvy to invest in heavenly currency. For example, when William Colgate started a cosmetics company in New York in the early 1800s, a Christian friend gave him sound advice: Be sure to make the best product he could, be honest, and give God one-tenth of his earnings. So that's what he did.

From making laundry soap, Colgate eventually branched out into other products. And as he gave to God, God entrusted him with even more. Colgate started out giving one-tenth of his earnings, then

20 percent, and then 30 percent. The more he gave, the more God blessed him. Eventually he gave one-half of what he earned.

Throughout our marriage, Jennie and I have done our best to increase our percentage of giving. As we have been able to give to God, it has been a blessing to us. I don't tell you this to brag but to hopefully encourage you by example. It was very difficult when we were young and strapped financially, but it has been a keystone habit in our life and, honestly, a key to how we endured the grief of death striking our home. It was easier to handle having a daughter in heaven since our heart was already going there through our treasure.

It is so tempting to think you will be generous one day in the future, when this or that happens. But that's a mistake. You won't.

Consider this. In 2017 Derek Carr signed a contract extension that made him the highest-paid player in NFL history. He was quick to declare that one of his top priorities was, yep, you guessed it—tithing. "The first thing I'll do is I'll pay my tithe like I have since I was in college getting $700 on a scholarship check," he said.

John Rockefeller, who was the richest person in the world at one point, said, "If I had not tithed the first dollar I made, I would not have tithed the first million dollars I made."

What we give we keep forever, but what we keep we lose forever. That's life in this upside-down kingdom, where the way up is down and the way to be great is to be the servant of all.

THE THREE PHASES OF LIFE AND THE ILLUSIONS OF OWNERSHIP

I've heard it said that there are three phases to life: In the first phase, you build a container. In the second, you decide what to put in that container. And in the third, as you approach the end of life, you prepare to give your container and everything in it away. You can visualize this sequence through Lightning McQueen's metamorphosis in the three movies of Pixar's *Cars* trilogy. In the first film, he has all the fiery horsepower of youth—he's hungry, selfish, and focused on a container: the Piston Cup, which he thinks will bring meaning to his life. In the second film, despite his global success, he discovers how hollow it is to have a massive container if it comes at the expense of the relationships in his life, and he begins to prioritize his friendships with Mater and Sally.

In the final film, he is no longer young and resents being viewed as the elder statesman by younger, faster race cars. He is forced to grapple with big questions of identity and purpose after his retirement. In the end he chooses to jump the curve, embracing a new season of life as pit chief for Cruz Ramirez, taking delight in giving his wisdom to her and discovering the joy of seeing her go faster than he ever had. Like Doc Hudson before him, he tapped into the surprising delight of giving his container and everything in it away. Now that's what I call *kachow*.

I can't help but wonder how often the despair people feel comes from wrongly diagnosing their season of life. Perhaps they are trying to build a bigger container when they should be filling it with precious things, or they're finally getting around to filling it when it's really time to prepare to give it all away.

Jesus said it is more blessed to give than to receive. What season of life are you in? Is the company or your platform getting bigger and bigger, but your container is looking pretty empty? And what can you do to begin to prepare to give it all away? At the end of life, everything must go. The real power comes when you start seeing yourself as a steward and caretaker, not an owner. Augustine said that asking yourself *What do I want to be remembered for?* is the beginning of adulthood.

As a wise and generous steward, what could you do with what is within your oversight to maximize your legacy?

And what enormous good might come from whatever is yours whenever you die? If you don't have a will, go ahead and set one up. If you have one, consider what you might update and how you might consider ministry impact in your estate. Like Samson, your last day on earth might trigger massive kingdom impact.

Maybe there is a way your estate could bless people in the world who don't have access to the gospel. Or fund a Bible translation. Or support disaster relief through a Christian organization that would also help spread the good news of Jesus. What priceless ways might you allow God to continue to work through your legacy long after you are in heaven? Imagine sitting by the sea of glass, having a Slurpee, and getting an epic one-up sound effect as a Mario-style coin flashes above your head, indicating God's use of your life from beyond the grave. You can even consider making your church part of your eternal legacy through planned estate giving.

WHEN WE SEE WHO GOD CREATED US TO BE, AND THAT HE DESIGNED LIFE AS A QUEST TO GIVE, NOT TO GET, IT CHANGES EVERYTHING.

Where I live in Montana, the bald eagles need a PR agent to help them realize their worth. We often see them eating roadkill or pecking away at trash in the landfill, and I always want to stop and tell them, "Do you know what you are? What you represent? You are a symbol of liberty, freedom, and majesty the world over!"

I think the same principle applies to us. When we see who God created us to be, and that He designed life as a quest to give, not to get, it changes everything. Don't sit by the side of the road eating out of a deer carcass when you were meant to soar. Never forget your true identity. You are an ambassador of the kingdom of heaven! You are here to serve as His royal representative, putting His generous love on display so a weary world can rejoice!

CHAPTER 11

CREATE OPEN SPACE

I HAVE TOO much stuff. It overwhelms me.

The natural tendency over time is toward complexity, not simplicity. It's been said that "aging is the aggressive pursuit of comfort"—that's how most of us experience it. We come to believe we need lots of particular things as we try to make our lives as comfortable as possible. And we need to fight against it.

The average home in America in 1950 was 983 square feet. Today it is 2,480 square feet. The largest soda you could buy when McDonald's first opened was five ounces. Today there is a thirty-ounce option. Do we really need a Swiss Army pocketknife with a hundred different accessories when three will do? Washing machines that can tweet? Or microwaves that are controlled by Alexa?

Matthew McConaughey, in his book *Greenlights*, reflected on the day when he knew he had arrived. He had someone who not only did his laundry but also ironed his jeans. When he bragged about this to a friend, she punctured his braggadocio and sobered him up with a simple observation: "That's great, Matthew, if you want your jeans pressed."

The truth was, he did not. The point is, just because you *can* doesn't mean you should. As a rule, additions don't tend to make our lives better; they just make them more complex. It's easy to think your family will be better off if you are financially better off, but you must weigh in the opportunity costs. The Notorious B.I.G. astutely identified the problem with his song "Mo Money Mo Problems." Deep down, your kids might not be craving fancier things but more present parents.

A FRUITFUL VS. STRESSFUL LIFE

In one of His parables, Jesus talked about different ways the growth of wheat—a symbol for a fruitful life and our response to His Word—can be thwarted.

Some seeds are eaten by birds, symbolic of Satan.

Other seeds are planted on rocky ground. When the plant springs up, it has no root because the topsoil is thin. All it takes is one day of scorching sun for it to wither. This illustrates the person who has zeal but no foundation to rely on during hard times.

There are seeds sown among thorns, symbolizing the cares of this world—the deceitfulness of riches, wanting more, more, more.

They choke out the spiritual life of many people. I know this first-hand; it has happened to me.

Last, there are seeds sown in *good soil*, which yields a gigantic harvest—sometimes thirty times what was sown, or sixty, or one hundred!

The parable might prompt you to question, *Which kind of ground am I?* Or, *I know I'm in the good-soil category. Is my life showing a harvest of a thirty, sixty, or one hundred increase?*

I believe we don't strictly fit into only one category of ground. And we can end up with a thirty-time increase when we are meant to have one hundred in an area of our lives, because we were a little influenced by thorns. Or we might start out in good ground early in life, then drift toward rocky ground in our later years. It's not black and white; you are not completely one or another. You might be living in good ground for a while, then some birds show up or thorns creep in; perhaps that's what keeps you from a one hundred increase and leaves you with sixty or thirty.

I have seen thorns choke out my fruitfulness and stunt my growth—the thorns of the hypnotic siren song of materialism and the compulsive addition of *more* over time. If the goal in life were simply to acquire, this would be great. But all of life is preparation for eternal life. So the more we accumulate and stockpile, the less prepared we are to die. And the more of a headache our departure will be for those we leave behind.

Not only that, but simplicity is far more enjoyable than complexity. The more you have, the more you are divided in your mind as you manage it all. There will be less of you to be present and enjoy what is in front of you. If you are getting Ring notifications from your multiple properties, or hearing that a pipe has burst and water is damaging a house a few states away, how can

A CROWDED HEART IS THE ENEMY OF A FRUITFUL LIFE.

you give your energy to what's in front of you like you are meant to?

A crowded heart is the enemy of a fruitful life. The smothering effect of "too much" is stress and worry.

Jesus once asked His followers how many of them could add a day to their life by worrying. The answer, of course, was none of them. Same goes for you and me. In fact, we *shorten* the time we will spend on earth by stressing.

The average person spends 116 minutes in a sixteen-hour day in negative thinking and dealing with intrusive thoughts. And a raft of medical issues are caused and exacerbated by worry.

Theologian and philosopher Søren Kierkegaard once said, "If I were a physician and someone asked me 'What do you think should be done [about the present state of the world]?' I would answer, '[C]reate silence . . . ; God's Word cannot be heard, and if . . . it must be shouted deafeningly with noisy instruments, then it is not God's Word; create silence!'"

So why do we automatically think we will be happier in a bigger house or with more toys? It starts with the messages we receive from our culture.

In a lifetime, the average person will spend 140,000 hours watching TV. That doesn't factor in screen time on mobile devices. We see commercials for new products, always with new features, shiny bells and whistles, and extremely happy people enjoying them. We form a subconscious picture of happiness in our heads—a *telos*, meaning ultimate object or aim. We are given the mental model of the good life, and, subliminally, we pursue it.

But this *telos* we have is not true. We can't purchase happiness. It doesn't happen with a new truck, a successful workout routine, or a trip to the Amalfi Coast. I have a friend who sold several companies for more money than he ever could have fathomed, and—even though he and his family would never again have financial worries—he soon became the most miserable he had ever been. There is a pervasive hollowness to anything that we expect will do what only God can do. That's why Solomon described materialism as chasing after the wind or trying to catch oil in your hand.

THE WRONG PUZZLE PICTURE

All of us have a vision of what, if achieved, it will feel like snapping the final piece into place on a million-piece puzzle. The problem is, we are terrifically bad at predicting what will bring about that happiness.

Put another way, the top of the puzzle box, the image we are building the puzzle after, determines how we handle the individual pieces.

This is your *telos*. The vision you are striving for.

If the *telos* you are shooting for is wrong, it won't feel right even if you get it.

Mark Manson experienced "this profound kind of emptiness" once he'd achieved all of his life goals after the release of his explosively successful book (with *The Subtle Art* in the title). "The worst thing about that type of depression," he said, "is nobody wants to hear you talk about it." He got zero sympathy from his friends on the emptiness of selling millions of books. After his dreams had come true, he found himself asking, "What do I do now? How do I follow this up?"

Celebrated author Seth Godin has spoken about the disappointment he experienced when he achieved his lifelong goal of hitting the *New York Times* Best Sellers list. He cried. He didn't shed tears because he was happy; he cried because he felt nothing.

We think that the picture on the box, once assembled, will bring happiness, but in fact it is incompatible with true flourishing. Even as Christians we can become more oriented around earthly ideals than heavenly ones. More crazed with indulgence than forming Christ-like character. More interested in comfort than seeing the Spirit work through us to ease suffering and shine light in dark places. So we end up putting pieces into place that will help us avoid pain, inconvenience, or discomfort—anything incompatible with the photo of happiness we think we need in order to thrive.

Again, the glaring problem is that we are really, *really* bad at accurately determining what exactly will bring about a positive outcome.

HURTS So GooD

We hear a lot about post-traumatic stress disorder (PTSD). Honestly perhaps a bit too much. People are using anxiousness from crowds to get front-of-line passes at Disneyland. Others are getting emotional support peacocks. (Google it.) I know I will ruffle some feathers here, but I believe it is important to address. The problem with overusing and abusing real psychological terms and therapeutic language is that it cheapens them for those who truly have clinical issues, like a soldier who has PTSD from war or a person who has been abused.

I once listened to an interview where a popular pastor talked about the trauma of leading his church through the pandemic. He kept using the phrase *PTSD* and describing how deeply, emotionally taxing it was. As it turns out, he is no longer leading his church but is now one of a growing segment of consultants who will (for the right price) advise those still in the arena. "Here's how you too can survive the grueling, taxing, and no doubt emotionally jarring rigors of life in the church."

While listening to him discuss the trauma of getting angry emails from people in his church and being unfollowed on social media by those who didn't appreciate how he led, it *did* remind me of a disorienting season in my own ministry. But I also kept thinking, *Are you kidding me?! Paul endured shipwrecks, snakebites, beatings with rods, and imprisonment; plus, he was stoned and left for dead. And that was all before breakfast!* How did Paul describe it? As a small and inconvenient setback on the way to a joyful eternity.

I don't see much language in Scripture about how traumatic it was for Paul. And I don't say this to shame people who have genuinely been through difficult circumstances—very few have the bandwidth that Paul did for the kind of suffering he endured. But, as Charles Spurgeon said, "Many men owe the grandeur of their lives to their tremendous difficulties."

Post-traumatic stress isn't the only clinical response to pain; there is also post-traumatic growth. In fact, almost all people who go through grueling medical ordeals like burns, serious illnesses, and amputations come through their experiences more grateful, joyful, and grounded. Some even look back on their brushes with death with thankful hearts. Cancer survivors tend to have a higher level of happiness than before their diagnosis.

Contrast all of this with lottery winners, who seldom come away from the experience better; the common report is that suddenly getting loads of money did not improve their lives.

Would you rather win the lottery or get cancer? It's something to really think about.

Professional athletes are often broke or in financial distress within a few years of walking off the field or court. That's different from how we think about what it takes to build a life of love and happiness.

And what about being famous? Do the bright lights of Hollywood tend to make marriages thrive? Provide a setup for a life of better inner health? Help people steer clear of the abuse of substances? Lead to lower or higher rates of narcissism? There are plenty of sweet, deep, genuine people in Hollywood, the music industry, and in professional sports, so it is unfair to lump any industry all together as one. That said, it seems the marriages with longevity and lives of simplicity and well-being tend to be outliers. And it is an uphill battle for all of them.

So why do we have an image on the puzzle box that is getting us nowhere? We keep secretly finding ourselves steering toward that *telos* one Apple Pay transaction at a time. Deep down, we wish we would be discovered, go viral, or be able to afford anything we want. We often imagine ourselves rich and famous when we picture ourselves truly happy—when those things almost never bring about joy. Why don't we fantasize about being pulled from the burning wreckage of a Humvee on fire in a battle? Or watching drops of poison drip into our veins only to emerge aware of the preciousness of life?

Here's why.

There is an invisible battle raging all around us. The serpent still slithers, causing us to think we need what we don't have and trying to keep us from realizing and appreciating all that is ours. When Eve was thriving in the garden of Eden before there was sin, she had everything she needed, but the serpent made her think something was missing. "Take and eat, and your eyes will be opened. You will be like God."

Uh, hello. Eve, sister, you were made in the image and likeness of God; you can't be more *like* God than you already are. You are His image bearer!

Some have posited that the prohibition against graven images in the Old Testament existed because you and I already are.

The devil offers a picture of a life that, once obtained, will lead to pleasure. It's called the lust of the flesh, the lust of the eyes, and the pride of life. The kingdoms of this world. Angels catching you by the foot as you BASE-jump down the side of a cliff in a squirrel suit. Going viral on TikTok or becoming a YouTube influencer like MrBeast, Marques Brownlee, or Logan Paul. The endorsement deals will start coming and the promo codes will drop from the sky. Products will show up on your doorstep, and you will make bank just for being seen using them.

The problem is, there is no end. You will trade jealousy with hundreds of thousands for millions of thousands and finally with millions of billions. This is as true of streams and views as it is of followers and dollars. There is no pot of gold at the end of that rainbow, just ash. Again, naked were you born, and naked you will return. The one who dies with the most toys still dies. And along the way you miss out on the chance to get true Treasure.

THERE IS AN INVISIBLE BATTLE RAGING ALL AROUND US.

DEATH-PROOF YOUR TREASURE

Jesus has investing advice for all of us: Don't keep your true worth, treasure, and identity in a place that is vulnerable to invasion. Matthew 6:19–20 says it this way: "Do not lay up for yourselves treasures on earth, where moth and rust destroy and where thieves break in and steal; but lay up for yourselves treasures in heaven."

Your value is vulnerable if it is bloated with earthly focus or caught up in trivial trinkets of temporal importance. The litmus test of the puzzle we are building is, Can it survive the valley of the shadow of death?

I'm reminded of 2 Corinthians 4:18, which says, "The things which are seen are temporary, but the things which are not seen are eternal." If the vision of what we need in our lives to make us happy is shaped by the things that will only be in this world, we are setting ourselves up for misery. This is why it is so crucial that we challenge the love that we are allowing to dominate our lives.

"Do not love the world or the things in the world," 1 John 2:15 reminds us. John didn't mean don't love the people in the world; he was saying not to allow anything in this life alone to become the image on your puzzle box. No possession, person, project, or pursuit. It won't work.

But what is the natural course in our culture? To constantly upgrade the car or the house, even when we can't afford it. To get a dryer that can be controlled by Siri. Meanwhile, according to C. S. Lewis, the little luxuries you surround your heart with threaten to knit your heart to this world. Far from making your life complete, they just make it crowded. Soon there is no oxygen for the best things; they have been crowded out, choked to death by the weeds that crept in. It happens gradually, slowly, imperceptibly, right under your nose. It's possible that it's happening right now.

"So," you are saying, "what am I to do about it?"

"Garage sale time! Let's get rid of stuff!"

Maybe, but hold on. Let's give it a second before we rush to extremes, because we need to realize the very human urge to hack at leaves instead of getting to the root of things.

PICTURING THE PATH TO TRUE DELIGHT

It is within us to go all Sons of Thunder and flare up with a big show of energy that will last only as long as we are inspired. Call down fire from heaven, take a vow of poverty, book a two-week stay at a monastery, never drink alcohol again! And then of course post judgmental remarks on Instagram about the evils of consumerism. Report how, from now on, you will only purchase clothing made from ethically sourced cotton woven on looms that contain no ivory. Also, for good measure, get baptized in tiger's blood. We instead need to attack this at the level of the heart and not just through a short-lived, impulsive show of emotion. Extreme self-deprivations—especially when they're rash, knee-jerk decisions—are often precursors to binges.

Back to the puzzle box top.

One reason the pull and allure of this world is so hypnotic and influential is that it is in front of us so often. YouTube videos, Instagram carousels, commercials between videos, and outfits of the day (OOTDs) on TikTok—they all present an image of what the good life looks like. If we do nothing else, this will, by default, become what we chase.

But we have said they are lies, and we combat lies with truth—which is why God's Word is called the sword of the Spirit. Like Jesus, we must both offensively and defensively utilize Scripture to paint a sensual image of the good life that we run to and reinforce.

Psalm 1 says, "Of the blessed man we all want to be, his delight is in the law of the LORD, and in His law he meditates day and night" (vv. 1–2, paraphrased).

We need to constantly, methodically, and aggressively engrave this picture into our minds. What does the good life actually look like? God's Word is waiting to paint the proper picture into our spiritual imagination. It is not temporary, carnal pleasures, nor is it a herculean show of spiritual power on your part. It is the cross that Jesus died on and that we are invited to pick up and carry. It's a death that leads to resurrection, a spiraling that leads to blessing. Round and round, tighter and tighter; closer to the center. When it gets taken away, we must replace it. This is the *telos* we are aiming to reproduce as we snap our puzzle pieces into place.

This is living.

You must often tell yourself, *What seems to satisfy brings only a counterfeit kind of pleasure, but what God has for me is the path to true delight.*

This is not to say that the earth is bad, or that the answer is stoicism, denying pain and seeing pleasure as an enemy. This is godless secularism, and it is rampant today as people tap into the journals of Roman emperor Marcus Aurelius, for example, looking for answers. There is what the theologians call common grace (leftover goodness from before the fall spoiled things) in a good meal or a well-designed product. In the simple pleasures of a sunny day, a good book, and a cup of tea. God has given us richly all things to enjoy.

But at their absolute best, these things only hint at true eternal pleasure. To paraphrase Teresa of Ávila, one kiss from the mouth of the Father at the gates of heaven will make a thousand lifetimes of suffering seem like a night in a bad motel. His presence is fullness of joy, and at His right hand are pleasures evermore. Until we get to heaven, we can enjoy blessings while simultaneously accepting their limitations, knowing they offer a fleeting echo of that eternal coming joy, not the final substance. They are not the basis or cause of our contentment. We are able to be abased and abound.

So, again, placing scriptural truths and pictures at the forefront of your mind at the beginning of the day is vital! It marks you as you go out into a world of temptation and rival pleasures with your palate already conditioned to look to ultimate joy and not see only surface froth. Never let your desire for heaven get snowed under or choked out. Regularly fan it into flame. Hide God's Word in your heart that you might not sin against him.

FEASTING THROUGH FASTING

Another tool to enhance your spiritual senses is fasting. More and more, God has been opening my eyes to the grace He gives through it.

Before Adam and Eve sinned in the garden of Eden, part of how they honored God was connected to what they ate and didn't eat. They spent time with God in the evening, at sunset, resting their souls through a devotional time, then they rested their bodies through sleep. When they woke, they'd eat certain things and abstain from one specific thing.

The way we eat is connected to what we worship.

This is huge! We are now living post-fall, and Jesus, our bridge back to Eden's joy, is in heaven, where we will one day sit at His table and feast. We will be able to walk with God again in person and eat from the Tree of Life. But until that day, one of the most underutilized and significant ways to boost heaven's reception and live with a greater perception of the way things truly are is through fasting.

The Pharisees once asked Jesus, "Why don't your disciples fast?"

"Because I'm here," He answered. "They will fast when I am taken."

He was saying that one of the things fasting does is strengthen our connection to Jesus. The disciples walked by His side; in His absence, fasting would draw them closer to that experience. When we fast, it enhances our spiritual senses and our awareness of needing God. It doesn't make us weak; it makes us strong. After all, "Man shall not live by bread alone, but by every word of God" (Luke 4:4).

Fasting also helps us keep a pilgrim spirit, not getting too comfortable here. Daniel 1 describes Shadrach, Meshach, and Abednego faithfully abstaining from eating delicacies with great purpose: to remind themselves of their true home. Even as they were living in Babylon as exiles, they fixed their gaze on God's land for them and emerged stronger than anyone around them. Jesus fasted in the desert while being tempted, resisting turning rocks into bread to satisfy His hunger. Moses, Esther, Elijah, and Mordecai fasted; so did Peter, Paul, Daniel, and John.

There is something powerful that happens when you pray while you are hungry. It steers you away from living with your belly as your god, which Philippians 3:19 says is the alternative to living focused on the cross. I believe God has an easier time accessing your spirit.

Perhaps one or two days a week, you could benefit from skipping breakfast and lunch and just eating dinner, allowing the time between dinners to foster greater dependence on God. Spend time with Him, waging war on whatever is pulling your focus and heart away from Him and stunting your growth.

CUT AND RUN

Hebrews 12:1 tells us to throw off any weight that hinders us, any sin that slows us down. What unnecessary features of life have crept in for you? For Matthew McConaughey, it was having his jeans ironed. What in your life isn't adding value but is taking up space?

Incorporating fasting, prayer, Scripture, and worship as regular rhythms of life brings regular reminders that life is brief and eternity is coming. Subtracting things from your life ensures there is proper space for the good things to breathe. Remember, just because you can doesn't mean you should. So take inventory of your life and what is choking away your passion. Assess what has power over you. Then reassess and reassess some more.

"All things are lawful for me," Paul said, "but not necessarily profitable" (1 Corinthians 6:12, paraphrased).

I refuse to be under the power of any of it.

Perhaps there is something in your life that, in essence, isn't necessarily a bad thing—but it has turned into a bigger thing than it should. It could be spending, drinking, ZYN packets, shopping, loading up on entertainment or desserts, or even something you do for God.

I once sensed God impressing on me to spend a Lent season abstaining from speaking at events away from Fresh Life Church.

OUR LIVES WILL
INEVITABLY
SUFFER IF WE
LOAD UP EVERY
AVAILABLE SPACE
WITH THINGS
WE SHOULD HAVE
SAID NO TO.

Doing this helped me see myself without those experiences entangled with my identity and acknowledge that one day I won't be asked or be physically able to go. It also reminded me that sometimes saying no is what makes room for fruitfulness.

Our lives will inevitably suffer if we load up every available space with things we should have said no to. Thomas Merton wrote that all you really need is in your life already. He called it "the hidden wholeness."

The slithering serpent wants you to chase what is already yours. Don't look outside of yourself to find fulfillment; the kingdom of heaven is within.

What things are you allowing to have space in your life? Should they all be there?

Don't forget—every act of subtraction is also an addition. You are adding negative space. Breathing room. Margin. The opposite of an opportunity cost.

You don't have to write all the way up to the edge of the page.

You don't have to always get the new phone.

"No, thank you" is just as vital as "Yes, please."

You can politely decline.

Go without a meal.

Change your mind.

RSVP no with regrets.

Redefine your relationship with alcohol or purchases or travel.

Your soul will thank you.

Free yourself with open space.

CHAPTER 12

SEE THE NORTHERN LIGHTS

IF YOU HAVE flown on a plane, you might have heard the pilot directing you to see the Grand Canyon on the left, or that those on the right side of the plane should look as you are passing Mount Rushmore. It's the universal signal to do whatever it takes to crane your neck to see something cool.

My wife, Jennie, was on a plane when she glanced out the window and, to her amazement, noticed that the northern lights were visible in the sky over Minnesota. At first she thought her eyes were playing tricks on her because she hadn't heard the pilot say a word about it. But no, there they were, dancing and streaking and shaking across the sky in all their shimmering, glowing, glorious wonder. It took her breath away! She pulled out her phone to take a picture, and the photo was even more amazing than what she saw with the naked eye. Somehow the photo sensor detected even more of the light spectrum that her eyes couldn't catch.

Still stunned, she turned in her seat to look around the plane but didn't see a single person with their window shades open. Row after row, they all were staring at their six-inch screens, their faces glowing in the reflection of the devices they were absorbed in. She sat there gazing at the incredible light show all by herself, then wanted to run up and down the aisles screaming about the heavenly display that was unfolding outside the window.

How ironic is it to be glued to inflight entertainment when, if you just lifted up a flimsy piece of plastic, you could be enraptured by the aurora borealis? It's a staggering sight, something people fly all the way to Nova Scotia, or stay up all night in national parks, simply hoping to capture a glimpse of. If only these people knew they were settling for a microwavable frozen White Castle burger when Michelin star–caliber delicacies were right in front of them.

Those passengers didn't miss out on the heavenly show because they were evil but because they were oblivious.

The devil doesn't just destroy us with trials; he distracts us with diversions. It has been well said that if he can't make us bad, he'll settle for busy. We can't be awed by what we are unaware of.

I remember the first time I experienced God in a way that shook me. It happened at a prayer meeting in high school. I felt warmth and heaviness. Time stood still. It was like that verse in the Psalms about a day being like a thousand years. Nothing I had ever experienced, no drug-induced high, pornographic ecstasy, or praise of man could hold a candle to sensing the God of creation in His glory and splendor.

Holy. Holy. Holy.

I would rather scrub floors in His castle than spend a thousand years lying on sun-soaked Greek beaches without Him.

I want to jump from the pages of this book and shake you into snapping out of whatever distracts you so you will lift up the sunshade and behold the Lamb!

Don't.

Waste.

Your.

Life.

You are going to hate the rest of this book if all you want is comfort and control. I am inviting you to go where the wild things are.

The gods of this world have mouths but don't speak. They have eyes but can't see. They have hands but don't touch. In 1 Samuel 5 the god Dagon fell on the ground before the ark of the Lord over and over, finally breaking off his head and hands. He couldn't take care of himself, much less his followers.

Why would you spend your life on what won't satisfy?

Why would you put your wages into a purse with holes in it?

Why settle for being defined by how many square feet your home is or how many epic spots you have camped at in your dirt-bagging van?

Many things we pursue aren't wrong; they are just not big enough to fill up our soul and give our life the true significance we crave.

Don't chase clout or the attention and praise of people. Chase the cloud of God's presence, what the Bible calls the *shekinah* glory of God that is waiting to woe you.

WHY WOULD YOU SPEND YOUR LIFE ON WHAT WON'T SATISFY?

I hit a point when I realized that the success of the things I did for God could be tainted if I hoped they would do for me what they couldn't. If I preach or write without being grounded and focused on serving God, I am essentially staring at a tiny screen, closing myself off from the northern lights. I can't give out of emptiness. I don't want to try to serve out of some deficiency I am trying to make up for; I want to serve out of the overflow of an encounter with God.

A prophet once told King Ahab a fictitious story to illustrate that the king had failed to obey God and fulfill his calling. It's found in 1 Kings 20. Allow me to paraphrase.

A man checked a prisoner of war into the custody of a soldier. "Keep him under close supervision and guard him," he ordered the soldier. "No matter what happens, do not let this prisoner escape." If the soldier did let him go, he'd take on the prisoner's punishment himself.

This soldier had one job. Yet due to negligence, he let his guard down, and the prisoner escaped.

So, *when* did it happen? That is the worst part—he didn't even know. "While your servant was busy here and there, the man escaped." It would almost have been better if it had happened in some epic way. Dynamite smuggled inside of a cake or an elaborate prison break involving a hot air balloon like in *Paddington 2*. But he couldn't even be sure when it had happened, much less how.

While I was busy here and there.

How does passion erode? How does vision leak? How does integrity unravel and backsliding happen? When do morals slide and motives become tainted?

Slowly. Gradually. When you are not paying attention. Next thing you know you are absorbed in episode three of season four of some unspectacular show while the heavens dance outside your closed window. Soon you are sixty and depressed or angry and not even sure why.

King Ahab wasn't the only one meant to see himself in that parable. You and I should too. In this life you have one person to watch over: yourself. The Trinity has been compared to a dance, with the Father, Son, and Holy Spirit all joyously cascading about in a frenzy, a symphony, a waterfall of love and glory. And you are invited to join in. To live a story that can't be explained or contained. To dance the dance of God. Your job is to keep yourself in the love of God, to watch over that one person. If you let them go, you lose. You must fight the good fight, keep the faith, guard your heart with all diligence, run your race, and keep wonder alive like a little child.

God is seeking those who will worship Him in spirit and in truth, so seek Him with all your heart. And whatever you do, don't ever close the window shade! Turn your eyes to Him when you wake. View Him as the prize. Not what you do for Him or the blessings you receive from Him. Just Him. In all His radiance, like the sun, riding on the wind, having died and taken back His life, reigning forever in splendor. You will never reach the end of the beginning of who He is.

Consider this: The northern lights are just flecks in His eyes!

What can you specifically do to keep the window open in your life and wonder alive in your heart? Here are three ideas to consider.

1. Go Outside

There was a sharp uptick in depression and anxiety (disproportionately for teenage girls) after two things broke loose in our world:

Facebook's acquisition of Instagram and the improved front-facing camera on the iPhone. People used to stand *behind* a camera when they took pictures. But now we take a selfie in *front* of the lens. What happens? We don't linger in the visual splendor of a landscape. The Grand Canyon is in the background, small and insignificant, and our faces are in the foreground, huge and the focal point.

Author John Eldredge believes humans have an unrecognized appetite for beauty. He has described moments of seeing God's creation and whispering, "I receive it into my soul," acknowledging that his soul was hungry for the vista before him—and sensing a profound change in himself. We don't just need food, water, prayer, and human contact. In his book *Get Your Life Back*, Eldredge postulates that we also have an unacknowledged hunger for sunrises, mountain streams, lightning storms, and rainbows.

Research has shown that experiencing awe leads to a greater sense of well-being, vitality, and creativity. Studies prove that awe—defined by what you feel while looking at art and nature, or in religious experiences—increases empathy and generosity, makes you less likely to cheat, and reduces stress and inflammation.

We weren't meant to rank ourselves based on what we are doing and seeing but rather by refreshing ourselves with time in the great outdoors.

There are so many instances in the book of Psalms where creation and worship are linked.

"Deep calls unto deep at the noise of Your waterfalls" (Psalm 42:7).

"As the deer pants for the water brooks, so pants my soul for You, O God" (Psalm 42:1).

"When I consider Your heavens, the work of Your fingers, the moon and the stars, which You have ordained . . ." (Psalm 8:3).

"The heavens declare the glory of God; and the firmament shows His handiwork" (Psalm 19:1).

"Day unto day utters speech, and night unto night reveals knowledge" (Psalm 19:2).

It bears repeating that we'll need to guard against using creation to worship ourselves with a spirit of, *Hey, look at me! Look where I've been, how great I am!* Experiencing the forces of nature is not supposed to be a vehicle for flexing but for feasting on the glory of God. We become right-sized when we look up and see mountains, stars, and eagles. So we defeat the whole point of it when we continually brag about our time in Grand Teton National Park or a trip to the Great Barrier Reef. Those constant posts (which I have definitely been guilty of) never give us what we are hoping they will. Sure, momentarily we might get attention and validation and make people jealous—but none of that will fill our internal deficiencies.

We also miss the chance to be filled with what we so badly need from the experience: the fear of the Lord.

A challenging experiment would be to seek out encounters in nature that you don't post about. Or maybe you don't take pictures at all. You just let those moments be for your soul.

Also try looking for ways to experience both nature and animals. Consider, for example, the often quoted aphorism, "There is nothing better for the inside of a man than the outside of a horse." There is a reason that horses are used for therapy. Being around big, majestic animals touches some core part of us that is no doubt connected to the garden of Eden.

2. Be Playful in Your Work

Deadlines and the pressure of doing any task well can rob you of the insight that comes from working in a relaxed state. One of the best ways to ideate and problem solve comes from not forcing a solution, which only strips gears and constipates creativity. For instance, I'm writing this book on a device that has no internet browser. I cannot play games, check the news, or get email. It literally can do just one thing—type words. On writing days I love to put down my smartphone, grab my internet-free device, and feel the freedom of letting myself wander.

In his book *Deep Work*, Cal Newport explained how to develop the skills needed to focus at an optimum level so you can reach peak productivity. He pointed out that you can unlock deep work when you are *not* in the "shallows" dealing with the attention residue that comes from flitting back and forth between social media and your job, then back again, then back again.

Returning to this writing project, there is no pressure involved because I am not contracted to create it; my publisher and agent don't even know I am working on it. I could easily throw it away or simply never tell anyone about it. It literally takes away all of the pressure. In fact, when people ask me about writing, I recommend that they allow it to be playful. If you try to create outside of a relaxed, whimsical, freewheeling state, in my opinion, it turns off creativity and can pollute the well.

Depending on what you do for work or for a hobby, this may not be easy. Especially when it comes to hobbies that begin as an outlet, then become a side hustle, and then become full-time work—you lose the life-giving playgrounds you once had.

Hello, Etsy.

For me, it would be the prospect of focusing solely on writing books would suck the life out of it for me. I don't know that I could ever write again! The fact that I don't have to write frees me to write—again, not because I must but because I like it and want to play with words.

Whatever work you do, you might consider beginning on a project far out from a deadline so you have the luxury of dreaming up unique concepts and out-of-the-box solutions. You might be surprised by what ideas start flowing when you are not under pressure, straining to produce and deliver.

People have tried all sorts of things to freshen up their approach to work. One creative would take naps with a key in his hand. The moment he fell asleep he would drop the key and it would wake him. This would often lead to a flash of insight that would overwhelm the creative log-jam he was feeling.

Another person would utilize a *nappuccino*, which is drinking a coffee and taking a power nap, then rising from the nap just as the caffeine hits your system. He said this was better than groggily looking for caffeine post-nap and having the additional delay before it hit him.

For me, going for a walk while remaining light and free or taking a shower while letting the project simmer in the background seems to help.

All of these allow the inner self to remain playful. They can even lead to breakthrough moments of genius when God can work through you.

Seth Godin, in his groundbreaking book *Linchpin*, shifted the definition of a genius from having rare intelligence to unlocking the unique potential within. Meaning, everyone has the ability to become a genius. This thinking is in line with Scripture's promise of spiritual gifts to all who are in the body of Christ. Each gift is different, yet all are powerful.

You don't have to have one specific gift to be special. All are needed. Whether you are a teacher, a firefighter, or a manager at a gym, you have the opportunity to contribute something important. You might be the one to stumble upon a stunning idea for a human resource problem, marketing plan, new classroom, or team dynamic.

These things will emerge not just when you need them to but as you remain relaxed and playful. Even childlike. Perhaps this is part of why Jesus said that to become great in His kingdom we must become like little children.

3. Shake It Up with New Things

Challenge yourself through God-given vocation and outreach. Step out in faith on mission trips, service projects, and new challenges. Get out of your comfort zone.

My dad is a great example of this to me. He is seventy and still has a Caleb spirit. If you don't know or remember, Caleb was one of the spies who Moses sent into the promised land to scout it out. You can read about it in Numbers 13 and 14, how twelve men were sent out and ten came back talking about how daunting it would be. They saw giants! They were freakishly tall and insanely intimidating. Most of the Israelite spies backed out and decided that the promised land wasn't it. They were discouraged and in turn discouraged the nation.

Only the remaining two, the minority report, were positive. Caleb and Joshua focused on how fruitful the land of milk and honey was. They didn't deny the presence of the giants; they just chose to dwell on the size of their God instead of the height of those giants.

Every day you and I must choose if we are going to be more

focused on the obstacles or the opportunities that God has set before us. The more we focus on God, the smaller our problems will seem. And vice versa.

Multiple times the Bible records that Joshua and Caleb had a different spirit in them. How funny that we so often resist standing out, especially in middle school and high school. Wanting to wear what the cool kids wear, we forget the power that comes from being different. Peter said that we are meant to be peculiar people. Weird is the point! Especially when we live in an age of cancel culture, criticism, and acidic YouTube comments and Reddit posts. All you have to do to stand out is focus on finding the good in people and believing the best about situations. Let's be that kind of different.

> EVERY DAY YOU AND I MUST CHOOSE IF WE ARE GOING TO BE MORE FOCUSED ON THE OBSTACLES OR THE OPPORTUNITIES THAT GOD HAS SET BEFORE US.

As a result of the nation listening to the ten spies who were cynical and jaded, the entire adult generation that came out from Egypt would perish in the wilderness; only their children would get to enter. Except Joshua and Caleb. They were the only ones of those original Israelites who left Egypt who got to go in. The perks of being different.

Years later when Caleb was considered old, he had Yoda-like status and was still ready to take new territory. He was as young in his heart as he ever was, Caleb told Joshua, and he still had battles to fight and giants to drive out. "Now therefore," he continued, "give me this mountain of which the LORD spoke in that day" (Joshua 14:12).

There was still awe and fight in his heart. He would not go

quietly in the night or gently without a fight. He would whack some Canaanite giants with his walker before he would drive a camper around the United States or spend his life golfing.

Last year my dad took time off work to travel through Macedonia and Croatia. He used his expertise in media to help other pastors and ministry leaders understand the tremendous tool that radio, television, and internet can be in the spreading of the good news. As I write this book, he is planning a trip to Africa to tell people about Jesus and is so excited about it.

This, I believe, is supposed to be how we keep seeing God do glorious aurora borealis–type things in our souls. We weren't meant to function on autopilot, daily doting on our grandkids and hunkering down in our armchairs after a 4:30 p.m. dinner, not realizing we have a major part to play in God's plans. He wants to keep using us to reach the lost, touch the world, and establish His kingdom on earth as it is in heaven.

TAKING STOCK

What is God saying to you today?

Do you need some more serious boundaries in your life to keep you off your phone? Are there other things you can do in your spare time that bring meaning and purpose?

Is it time to plan a "staycation" approach to a mission trip, serving in a soup kitchen or food bank? Maybe you volunteer through a Big Brothers Big Sisters–type organization, mentoring an at-risk youth or someone who has aged out of the foster system.

Do you need to get out to the woods more regularly to live deliberately and Thoreau-like, to leave the phone behind or switched to Do Not Disturb in your backpack? It wasn't that long ago that we didn't have them, so it shouldn't be that we allow our lives to be controlled by them.

Could you take up a hobby or be intentional about remaining playful at work? Envision the fireworks exploding in your creative endeavors, not by gripping tightly but by holding your pencil loosely.

My friend Peb Jackson,* another Caleb, told me to keep my hands open when invoking God's name before my quiet time. He went home to heaven at seventy-eight, but before that—actually the second-to-last time I spent time with him—I slept on the floor of his hotel room in a sleeping bag. And I am so glad I did.

Peb loved to talk about what he called "the nature fix," which is exactly what it sounds like—letting God use nature as a cure for aches and pains your soul accumulates when you are cooped up for too long. Incorporating intentional time in nature truly helped me through my midlife spiral. Fly-fishing, which Peb ordered me to pick up, gave me a wonderful distraction from the cares of this world and a chance to blow off steam while standing in a stream.

I still picture him, the last time we ate dinner together, licking his fingers to smooth out his eyebrows. Mischievous, childlike, and joyful, always quick with a book recommendation or an encouragement, he would watch me preach and give me feedback. The last time we spoke was during the height of COVID-19, when he was in a cancer ward and no visitors were allowed. Over the phone we

---

* Peb Jackson frequently used an expression that became a key phrase for me during my midlife crisis and is the title of this section: *taking stock*. He told me about a G. Harvey statue of a cowboy surveying his herd with his hand on the saddle horn and told me prophetically the crisis was a chance to sit back and take stock of my life.

prayed together, and I got to tell him how much he had influenced my inner life. I can't wait to hang out with my friend Peb in heaven.

As the saying goes, most people die at twenty-five but don't get buried until they're seventy-five. But this haunting statement doesn't need to be your story.

Wonder is waiting.

WHAT IF THE DARKNESS YOU ARE FACING ISN'T A BARRIER TO GLORY BUT THE PREPARATION FOR IT?

What's that you say? It's so dark where you are that it's hard to imagine wonder being possible? I get it; the darkness of pain and suffering can smother imagination. But Isaiah 45:3 says that God gives "treasures of darkness and hidden riches of secret places."

What if the darkness you are facing isn't a barrier to glory but the preparation for it? I've never seen the northern lights in the daytime. If God has allowed you to be plunged into darkness, do not fear. There are Treasures and secrets He will show you if you let Him.

CHAPTER 13

YOU DON'T HAVE TO BE A RANCHER

THERE WAS A man in our church in Montana who worked as a rancher and, at the age of thirty-nine, realized he hated ranching. The problem was, it was all he had ever known. He had grown up on a ranch, which was the family business, and as an adult, he joined it full-time. His children likely would end up doing the same. But then came the epiphany: He did not want to ranch.

There's a big question for you to ask if you dare. It's an especially important one when you feel like your world is spinning at a big transition moment: *Am I doing what God wants me to do?*

This man hit a wall and felt disoriented. It became a midlife crisis of sorts, but he ultimately saw it as the chance to take a step in his personal progress. *What is the calling on my life?* he asked himself, more earnestly than ever. He had not chosen ranching because of a passion God had ignited in his heart; it was simply the expectation of others. It was what one did in his family.

He previously had heard me say, "Five years is a long enough period of time to completely change your life."

When was the last time you considered completely changing your life?

If you took a step of faith, what would you do?

STRATEGIC, LITTLE-BY-LITTLE CHANGE

We all tend to underestimate what we can do in the long term and overestimate what we can do in the short term. But five years is a long enough stretch of the calendar to get some serious things done. It's long enough to read through the Bible five times, begin to learn a new language, pay down debt, save up to buy a home, read sixty books, or learn a new trade by going to night school. After all, you could get a degree and still have a year of buffer.

I shared this with our church one Sunday in 2018, then asked, "Who do you want to be by 2023?"

That was enough for the soon-to-be-former rancher. When his wife told him to either do something about it or stop whining about needing a change, he heard himself say, "I'm ready."

She blinked. "What do you want to do?"

That's when a light bulb went on over his head. "The only thing I could see myself doing is to become an electrician," he said.

So he applied himself in studying and eventually mastered the trade. Five years later he was working full-time as an electrician.

It is amazing what we can do when we take small steps toward accomplishing something big, all while not being deterred by the smallness of our progress. Sometimes this means chipping away at training for a new job over several years; other times it means forming mini habits that, little by little, change your daily routine—and change you in the process.

By design, mini habits should be "too small to fail." Placing one puzzle piece. Reading one page. Maybe not even working out but simply going to the gym. Chances are, once you start, you will place a second puzzle piece, read two pages, and maybe even use the water fountain at the gym. Perhaps if you are feeling frisky you might attempt to use one machine at the gym, which would be extra credit! You end up doing it because you want to, not because you are required to.

The easiest thing in the world is to get discouraged by how daunting a goal is and how pathetic your progress seems to be. But, like Bob Wiley learned in the classic movie *What About Bob?*, it's all about baby steps.

Let's go back to that big question: *Am I doing what God wants me to do?*

IT IS AMAZING WHAT WE CAN DO WHEN WE TAKE SMALL STEPS TOWARD ACCOMPLISHING SOMETHING BIG, ALL WHILE NOT BEING DETERRED BY THE SMALLNESS OF OUR PROGRESS.

Or are you living out of the script someone else wrote for you?

God's way is not allowing other people to determine what we do with our lives and then living under the power of their expectations. Paul wrote to the churches in Galatia telling them he was an apostle not by the will of man but by the will of God.

If you're not doing what God called you to do, what are you willing to do about it?

Perhaps God has called you to take a step of faith and go on a short-term mission trip. Could it be time to take on more responsibility at a nonprofit, or learn a musical instrument and join the worship team at your church? Maybe He wants you to begin the journey of foster care or start your own business.

I can already hear you objecting, "Levi, I am too old and have responsibilities and obligations. I can't begin again. It's too late for me to reinvent myself."

Well, if you say so. As Henry Ford reportedly said, "Whether you believe you can do a thing or not, you are right."

I'm not saying making a change will be easy. Not by any stretch of the imagination. But neither will sustaining continual improvement in any career past a certain point.

As Harvard professor Arthur Brooks put it, "The biggest mistake professionally successful people make is attempting to sustain peak accomplishment indefinitely." There are exceptions to this, of course, notably in the fields of teaching and writing, which tend to be more immune. But, for the most part, breakthrough is a young person's game, as we've discussed before.

This makes sense because of what is taking place in the aging process. But there is good news.

JUMPING THE CURVE

Scientists have pointed out that, as we hit midlife, we begin to fade in what is called fluid intelligence. In the early 1940s, Raymond

Cattell expanded on the work of Donald Hebb, categorizing two distinct streams of intelligence: fluid intelligence and crystallized intelligence.

Fluid intelligence is, as I understand it, raw, computing intelligence horsepower, and it peaks startlingly early in adulthood. Think the founders of Google, or Bill Gates, or Steve Jobs, all in their twenties, seeing the world differently.

Crystallized intelligence comes in handy when dispensing a stockpiled knowledge that has been accumulated in the past. So while fluid intelligence is basically raw smarts, crystallized intelligence is the seasoned wisdom of older age.

It's sort of cruel when you think about it. You have all the energy, ideas, and (for the most part) health when you have the least time, wisdom, and money. By the time you actually have room in your schedule, a little money, and insights from life knocking you off your high horse, you no longer have any idea what to do with it, feel exhausted, and might even be sick.

Brutal. But it shows why we need each other.

Proverbs 20:29 gives us insight: "The glory of young men is their strength, and the splendor of old men is their gray head." In God's kingdom He highlights the insight of the young and the wisdom of the old. The trick is to gracefully jump from the first part of this verse to the second, making it up the spiral staircase without a catastrophic crisis.

And therein lies the delight.

It has been called "jumping the curve," pivoting from what you can't hang on to if you try (fluid intelligence) and learning how to play to your strengths (unleashing your crystallized intelligence). I think it's one of the reasons this book is in your hands right now. God wants you to bend your legs and prepare to jump. With God's strength, you can leap over the wall of development that you smacked your nose into.

As with the rancher-turned-electrician, this *can* mean a brand-new endeavor. After all, if we get twenty years of improvement by embarking on a new journey, we buy ourselves two more decades before we find ourselves plateauing. But we also get to bring the crystallized intelligence we've accumulated from our previous life to the new venture.

Consider the founder of Orangetheory Fitness (OTF). As a fitness instructor, Ellen Latham trained celebrities privately for twenty years, learning what worked and what didn't, what motivated people and what turned them off. After detecting patterns over all those years, she perfected the formula for doing the least amount of work for the maximum effect. And with the wisdom people have in their fifties, Latham unleashed her crystallized intelligence before it waned. Then *bam!* OTF became a global phenomenon.

Latham jumped the curve. And she is by no means alone.

Millions know Ridley Scott's movies, like *Gladiator*, *Black Hawk Down*, and *Blade Runner*, but did you know that Scott didn't release his first feature film until he was forty?

There are tons more examples:

- John Pemberton invented Coca-Cola at age fifty-five;
- John Glenn flew into orbit on the space shuttle *Discovery* at age seventy-seven;
- Noah Webster completed his *American Dictionary of the English Language* at age sixty-six;
- Peter Roget published his thesaurus at age seventy-three, after working on it for fifty years;

You Don't Have to Be a Rancher

- Colonel Sanders opened his first Kentucky Fried Chicken (KFC) franchise at age sixty-two;
- Benjamin Franklin signed the Declaration of Independence at age seventy;
- Ronald Reagan entered politics as a candidate for governor of California at age fifty-five; and
- Nelson Mandela was elected president of South Africa at age seventy-five.

Many people in the Bible began their best work while advanced in years. Abraham was seventy-five when God first called him to leave his homeland; Moses was eighty when God called him to lead the Israelites out of Egypt. And Noah? Well, he beats us all at five hundred years of age when he began to build the ark. (Go Noah!)

One survey asked if participants wanted to live to reach their one-hundredth birthday. I was stunned to discover that only 54 percent of Americans answered yes. Almost half of us would rather be dead than old?

As I have said, old age is not something to be dreaded, avoided, or dishonored. It has a unique strength that is to be respectfully received with gratitude, then stewarded and unleashed. It is something we will give an account for—whether we faced it well or poorly.

What if today you decide that, five years from now, you are supposed to be at a different spot—and you chipped away at it in between now and then? How do you eat an elephant? One bite at a time.

Maybe you feel like you really want to write a novel or a screenplay, and you have been thinking about it and putting it off forever because you don't know how you will find the time to get away and focus on it.

So many have this image of a writing retreat or a cabin in the woods where you stay up all night, like Sylvester Stallone writing *Rocky*. If that is how you work, more power to you. My approach is different. Books are composed of sentences, and a sentence can be written in a very small period of time. So all I need to do is steal enough moments to get some sentences strung together, and, eventually, *voilà!* I have a book.

In the book *The One Thing*, Gary Keller says habits are hard only in the beginning. Over time, the habit you're after becomes easier and easier to sustain. It's true. Habits require much less energy and effort to maintain than to begin. Put up with the discipline long enough to turn it into a habit, and the journey feels different.

You can do this with any project you are undertaking, whether it's fitness, financial, creative, home remodeling, or something else. You just need to shrink it down so it's manageable and come back to it consistently over time. It's powerful.

So many things start out gradually. King David's affair didn't begin when he was on the rooftop gazing at a naked woman; it began when he stayed home from battle and let someone else go in his stead. Kings become fools when they stop going out to battle. Few people enlisted as soldiers get caught up with the affairs of everyday life; they only want to please their commanding officers. In the same way, you don't need to end up like David did in your crisis. Just keep going out to battle. There is protection in purpose.

What is the war God intends for you to go out to?

REFLECT ON WHAT MAKES YOU YOU

When I was a young boy, my dad, a pastor who also worked a full-time job, known as a bi-vocational minister, would study in the den, a little room off our living room in our house in Falcon, Colorado. I loved opening the pocket door that slid into the wall leading to this den.

Hold the phone . . . I just realized it was probably for this exact reason that when I designed my current study I included a pocket door. I have always liked the way a pocket door opens and closes, how the mechanism pops out when you push the lever, and how it slides into the wall. It is simply satisfying. And now I realize why I subconsciously wanted that setup.

Don't mind me, I'm just connecting some dots over here on how I was shaped in a positive way in a developmentally crucial time by something I witnessed. Hopefully you're doing that as well as we walk through this together. It's important to celebrate the positive associations we have with our childhood formation and core memories because God knows we love to run up the flagpole all the negative ways we have been shaped in a painful or damaging way. (Note to self: Call Dad and tell him about this pocket door revelation and the way you see that as an emblem of studying as a pastor to preach, and how thankful you are for his example in your life.)

When my dad studied for sermons, it would be after working a full day at his other job. I'd see light glowing under his door and

---

* I did call my dad driving home from work on this day and talked to him about the pocket door connection. We had a great chat about how grateful I am for the positive associations I have from watching him study, and I was able to thank him for being such a great role model.

leave my siblings and the board game or Nintendo we were playing; then, as quietly as possible, I'd open the door and sit on the floor with my back against the wall. I was fascinated to see his Bibles, books, and yellow legal pads filled with scribbly handwriting and watch him work. Sometimes he would let me sit on his lap and would show me what he was doing. Occasionally he would hand me his big, green *Strong's Exhaustive Concordance of the Bible* for me to look up cross-references for him as he would use the Bible to interpret the Bible. I loved flipping through this ten-pound monster of a book calling out the references that my dad would then look up.

I was only in the second or third grade, but in these moments, I can now see the formation of lifelong skills and admiration for my dad as a man of God, and a respect for the hard work it takes to faithfully preach the Word.

As I now have a son who likes to open the pocket door of my office and pretend to type on the keyboard, it feels very symbolic and full circle. He, too, often tells me that he wants to be a pastor and an author and to be just like me. No kidding, this week, at the age of five, he went up on our stage and preached his first "sermon." He chose as his text Moses striking the rock instead of speaking to it and the consequence Moses suffered as a result, forfeiting the chance to personally lead the children of Israel into the promised land, and how instead it would be Joshua because Moses would die on Mount Nebo.

Run, Lennox, run!*

What are some positive, formative moments in your life that

---

* The boy also has a sense of humor. I was recently speaking at our annual youth conference, and he asked me what I was going to talk about. I told him "How Jesus is the Good Shepherd." He thought about it for a moment, then shook his head no and explained, "Dad, it's been done." Wow. Tough crowd.

stand out in your memory? Could it be that any of them could give inspiration for what you are called to do today? There are often clues in our origin stories we can use as a footpath to where we are called to go. Peter was raised to be a fisherman, and he used that know-how to fish for men. Jacob was a sneak, but, once redeemed, that same cunning was harnessed for the kingdom. Moses' dual citizenship as a Hebrew raised by Egyptians gave him the political savvy to lead the Hebrews out of Egypt. Once you let Jesus make your heart sing, He can run roughshod through the halls of your life on a shopping spree, making every mundane or difficult detail spring to life with eternal redemption.

YOU NEED A CAUSE

If you look at your mortality and realize that your life is a vapor, and you have precious little life to live, you can come back on the field at half time and play differently.

Chariots of Fire, a movie that tells the story of sprinter Eric Liddell, includes the famous line, "I believe God made me for a purpose, but He also made me fast. And when I run, I feel His pleasure." This is the place God intends for you to arrive. Start making your way there by examining your path and assessing your trajectory. It might not be a completely new career; it could be a different approach to your current one.

For me it has been a renewed and invigorated approach to the same old work. I am still a pastor and author, but, more than ever, I am focused on our youth. It's the battle I feel God has called me to fight as I answer the question, Who can I reach that might play a hand in ministering to and reaching our grandchildren for Christ?

I felt God calling me to plow up the back pasture of our property, like Kevin Costner's character in *Field of Dreams* did, only ours didn't involve baseball. We launched an outdoor national youth conference—in a rodeo arena of all places. It's kind of a cross between *Yellowstone* and a Passion Conference. Youth groups and family groups camp out, worship, and study the Bible under the big Montana sky. I felt God tell me that if we built it, they would come. And they have. From all over the country.

The calling I will give my life for is to reach young people so that they can walk in God's vision for their life. This is how I have jumped the curve and become Baby Yoda. I've focused less on using my fluid intelligence and more on unleashing my crystallized intelligence.

This has involved some intentional changes in how I use my time. I say no more often, and I try to say yes to what's best. I prioritize investing in our church's leadership, college students, residents, and interns. I speak at events that allow me to reach young people and other leaders God is raising up to do the same. And I am more protective of self-care and family time.

I'll share the specifics of what positively impacted my jumping the curve in the hopes that something here could help you, too, as you get a new lease on life.

1. Prioritize your soul so you are at your best and able to do the things God has you focusing on in this season.

Learning rhythms of sustainability is huge. We all have to push through times when the candle gets burned at both ends, but we must rest beforehand and afterward. Don't let too many spikes on your adrenaline needle happen without intentionally bringing yourself down from that state of heightened arousal. This is how you perform at peak levels and avoid everything in your life becoming like Tetris pieces piling up at the top of the screen. Do that too much for too long, and it's game over. *Smack.*

Look at the calendar as a series of sprints and recoveries, remembering that there are times your soul needs silence and your body needs movement. Block out some time and put yourself in a solitary place where you can reflect, pray, and recover. Schedule in activities that invigorate you. For me, these have been tennis, hiking, fly-fishing, road biking, and uphill snowboarding with a splitboard. (Yes, it's a thing.)

Remember there is *nothing* selfish about taking care of yourself, and it will take trial and error to decipher what will help you to be at *your* best.

2. Love your people well.

Who are the most important humans for you to love on the planet? Maybe it is your family or your close friends—the family you choose—or both.

If you are married, make sure you are giving your spouse the currency of time and focus. When Jennie and I are together, I put my energy into paying attention to her; she needs that more than shiny objects and fancy clothes. Have you considered whether your spouse's love language is one you are fluent in? If not, can you dip into a little intentional Duolingo to brush up on what makes them blush?

One thing that has been helpful for us is writing notes in a journal we share. It has our initials on the cover, and we take turns writing to each other in it and then leaving it somewhere the other will find it. It's like a message in a bottle back and forth, and, when it is filled up, it will be a bound volume of our story together. We share funny moments, prayers for each other, apologies, and our raw thoughts on what is going on in life. It has been really special.

If you have kids, see how you can be intentional about having one-on-one time with each of them consistently.

And in any important relationship, whether you're with a family member or friend, work at being a dutiful listener. A hack that has been helpful for me has been allowing this time to be on their schedule, not mine—to make room for it when they seem to feel ready for it. A teen might not be chatty when I talk with them at times that are convenient for me. Alternatively, when she is open to gabbing, even if it is not a perfect time per my high-control schedule, I tell myself to go with it and embrace it, even if that means I get less sleep than I planned.

3. Address any bad habits that are holding you back.

What comes to mind for you?

My continual hang-up is texting while driving and being on my phone when I shouldn't be. Two things have helped me with this.

First, I have a Screen Time password that limits my social media use. Once the password is required, I have to stop. Only my wife knows the password, and I asked her not to tell me.

Second, for behind-the-wheel struggles, I bought a kSafe, a time-based vault that was on *Shark Tank*. When my phone goes in it, I can't get it out until whatever time I've set it to. I even use it when driving alone. I set it for twenty minutes, or however long my drive is. Then I set my Bluetooth to play something on the car speakers for the drive, and I just listen to music or a podcast or even take phone calls, but drive safely without touching my phone. It is awesome!

I say all of this to encourage you with some tools that have helped me. As the king or queen you are, there is more than one way to stay in the battle. When you go out to war, you don't want the things inside you to atrophy, nor do you want your precious, blood-bought life to be wasted—languishing and withering instead of thriving, especially into old age.

Yoda, remember?

Which of those three areas need the most realignment in your life? Do you know what it takes to be the version of you that you are destined to be? I know change is hard and staying the same is much easier, but when you begin to notice a difference, it will become addictive. So start small and keep going!

George Washington is revered in part because he had the courage to walk away from the presidency and lay down his power. His role model was Lucius Quinctius Cincinnatus, the namesake for the city of Cincinnati. He was a Roman statesman and military leader who walked away from power in favor of a simpler life. Washington did the same and is remembered as great because he wasn't afraid to walk away from the political power he could have kept because of his military success. Interestingly enough, both men knew they were supposed to be farmers later in life, and both were willing to disappoint their fans to stay true to their inner compass. King George III said that for relinquishing power GW should be considered the "greatest man in the world."

Great things happen when you don't let other people make your decisions for you. The electrician didn't just shed his farm life; he also faced down an alcohol addiction and, in the journey toward sobriety, saw God rescue his marriage.

> GREAT THINGS HAPPEN WHEN YOU DON'T LET OTHER PEOPLE MAKE YOUR DECISIONS FOR YOU.

Your spiraling is a gift because it can give you the grace and humility to listen to God. Listen carefully as, through it, He says, "Don't waste your life." You can, and should, use all of the energy of your crisis and channel it into something productive and life-giving. Then it won't be released in a way that is harmful to you and others and instead will propel you forward.

In case no one has ever told you, you don't have to be a rancher.

CHAPTER 14

ALBERT EINSTEIN'S DIRTY LITTLE SECRET

ALBERT EINSTEIN HAS been called "the patron saint of distracted school kids everywhere." As a child, he had so much trouble with language and remembering words that people thought he would never learn. He also disdained the rote learning and military-style teaching of the day and had a certain "cheeky rebelliousness" that set him at odds with his teachers. How ironic that a person who would go on to come up with $E = mc^2$ was considered a poor student. The word "Einstein" has gone down in history as a synonym for the very kind of a person Einstein never really was.

There is one episode of his life that is staggering to me. No, it does not involve his marriage to a cousin or his ten known extra-marital affairs. It is the catalyzing moment in his childhood that unlocked his curiosity—the curiosity that ultimately led to his fathoming light moving through the universe.

BE OPEN TO GOD

One day when young Albert was in bed, too sick to go to school, his father attempted to cheer him up with a gift: a compass.

Albert was mesmerized. No matter how he twisted and turned the wayfinding device, he couldn't trick it. The compass's needle always found its way north.

Years later, Albert identified this as the all-important moment his curiosity came to life. His eyes were opened to invisible forces he knew nothing about—forces that were all around him, even in his bedroom! If the magnetic force existed, what other forces might be out there in the universe?

Albert considered curiosity, not traditional education, to be responsible for his success; it's what led him to learn so much and stumble into success. His dirty little secret is that it was the size of his curiosity, not the size of his brain, that made him a genius.[*]

He is not unique in this respect.

Bill Gates was constantly curious and counted it as his most important trait. He attributed his success to having a high threshold for confusion and an ability to keep studying a new subject until he was not confused anymore.

---

[*] Studies of his brain postmortem have found it was on the lower end of average for humans.

To paraphrase Gates, for most adults, the minute they start getting confused, they're like, "Oh, this isn't for me. I'm not good at this. I must not belong." But confusion and curiosity kept Gates going, and that's how he changed the world.

Leonardo da Vinci, too, was an extremely curious person, doodling in his notebooks about the woodpecker's tongue, wondering why it was so extremely long. He never cracked the case but died curious about it.

Centuries later, a fascinating discovery proved that he was onto something: The woodpecker's "too long" tongue functions as a sort of airbag for its brain. The tongue protects the brain from the pecking forces that, while drilling holes in trees, are strong enough to kill the woodpecker many times over.

On paper it made no sense for da Vinci to be fussing about some random bird while he had the *Mona Lisa* to paint or *The Vitruvian Man* to design. But it was because these kinds of questions haunted him that he was so successful, not in spite of it.

Let me ask you: Are you curious? What are you curious about? What interests you? And what's your threshold for confusion when you are seeking to unlock that curiosity?

If you don't have a ready answer, spend time exploring and piquing your interest! Don't worry if it doesn't seem perfectly connected to your industry or life. Woodpeckers, remember? I believe that an enormous part of finding purpose in life involves being curious and open to God moving the needle of your compass. Then, you have to push through the confusion until there is clarity.

It's been said that the two most important days in your life are the day you are born and the day you discover why. When you get your bearings, an exhilarating sense of purpose and destiny will come, even during a disorienting season. Each morning you'll be able to plant your feet on the floor deliberately, because you aren't an accident. You were created "on purpose and for a purpose," as Tim Tebow likes to say.

BUILD A TOWER OR CLIMB A LADDER

Someone we read about in the Old Testament who had his own compass-moving moment with God that unlocked the power of curiosity in his life was the patriarch Jacob. It's safe to say he needed some new direction. He had been a sneaky cheat, a lousy brother, and a pampered son who'd made nothing of himself until a life-changing moment with God.

While trying to sleep on a stone as a makeshift pillow (clearly, he was not a good camper), Jacob encountered an invisible force. He'd thought he'd been alone, but then the heavens opened and a ladder dropped down, as if coming through a hidden trap door. God was with Jacob in that place—and upended everything about his life.

For years, Jacob had thought only about Jacob. But in this moment, wonder awakened in him. God showed him that what he had seen as the end of the line was in fact a fork in the road, an opportunity to begin again. Jacob walked away gripped by purpose and spent the rest of his life relying on the invisible force that pulled the needle of his soul, even through all the confusion he experienced.

In that holy moment, God told Jacob, "I am the LORD God of Abraham your father and the God of Isaac; the land on which you lie I will give to you and your descendants. Also your descendants . . . shall spread abroad to the west and the east, to the north and the south; and in you and in your seed all the families of the earth shall be blessed" (Genesis 28:13–14).

We're going to unpack the epic meaning of these words (which, to this day, cause nations to declare war against one another), but here's a snapshot of where we're headed: All his life Jacob had strived to be more than his brother, be enough for his father, and live up to the overbearing love of his mother. It had been a never-ending cycle, like the moving stairs on the exercise machine bearing his name (Jacob's Ladder). Then, in one fell swoop, Jacob saw a way to navigate his chaotic search for significance by not *climbing* a man-made ladder or tower but by giving his life to God, who would send His Son down to *be* our ladder.

LET'S BACK UP TO THE BEGINNING

To grasp the power of God's words to Jacob, we need to run it back to Genesis for a minute.

The first mention of the gospel in Scripture is in Genesis 3:15, when God told Adam and Eve that He would send His Son to be a substitute for their sins, crushing the head of the serpent. Then the glimmers of the coming salvation continue, page after page, until Jesus hangs on the cross and completes the deal.

Abraham received a ram on Mount Moriah to be a sacrifice in Isaac's place.

Noah and his family found safety in the ark, with God shutting the door personally, protecting them from wrath.

Joseph endured the betrayal of his brothers, then rose out of the pit to a seat of power.

David, an unimpressive shepherd from the root of Jesse, was born in Bethlehem, defeated Goliath of Gath, and went on to be a great king who would sit on an everlasting throne.

From beginning to end, the Bible is one story: God rescues us through His sacrificial love.

Someone had to die for our sins. As Scripture says, "The soul who sins shall die," and "the wages of sin is death" (Ezekiel 18:20; Romans 6:23). God vowed for His Son to die *instead of you and me*—if we will accept Him. For every person who believes and receives that gift will not perish but have everlasting life.

Sadly, though, after the bite into the forbidden fruit and the promise of a substitute sacrifice, a competing strain of religion emerged. Cain offered a gift to God with a heart of pride, not faith, focusing on the work of *his* hands. People at Babel devised their own approach to God, apart from the cross. It was the path of ignoring the gospel, the illusion of humans working their way to wholeness.

The devil would love for you to think that you can work your way to God. But you go to God to get to good, not the other way around.

The group at Babel was ignoring the command to "go forth into the world," to spread out and live by faith until the snake crusher arrived. They instead clumped together and sought to make a name for themselves—never mind living for the One with the name above all names. Then they started building a great tower reaching up to the heavens, attempting to create a gate into heaven.

It was a clear statement to God, and it's one we can find ourselves making too. The spirit of Babel is alive and well today.

We don't need You.
We don't need to live by faith.
We don't need Your Son's blood.
We will do it our way.

And now we turn back to Jacob with his comfy rock pillow and the peculiar vision floating before him.

It was in stark contrast to the Tower of Babel that God dropped a glorious ladder down from the sky, stretching *down to* Jacob, in all his inadequacies. "This is the gate of heaven!" Jacob marveled when he saw it.

He was saying, "Ah! So this is how heaven works! I can't possibly work my way up; heaven comes down to me. I was a nothing and a nobody and not even seeking Him. I hurt people, lied, and cared only about myself; still, heaven broke through and came down to earth. He sought me while I was a stranger."

As the famous hymn puts it, the gospel is this: "Nothing in my hand I bring, simply to the cross I cling. / Rock of Ages, cleft for me, let me hide myself in thee."

Jesus is the ladder who came down to us. God is the One who accomplishes our salvation; He gets the glory for it all!

This is powerful, Levi, you might be thinking, *but why are you telling me all of this?*

Because Jesus isn't just the gateway to salvation but also the door to wonder, purpose, significance, and life more abundant. You will never discover all that life holds until you come to the One who holds life itself in His nail-scarred hands.

Satan would love nothing more than to keep you climbing never-ending ladders of career, religion, keeping up with the

HE IS THE ONE PULLING THE NEEDLE ON YOUR COMPASS TO TRUE NORTH.

Joneses, and any other hopeless pursuit. Jesus wants to explode into your story with mercy flashing in His eyes and open you up to all joy, peace, and curiosity. He is the one pulling the needle on your compass to true north. And He has grace for the confusion that will follow as you follow Him. He didn't come to make your life better; He came to save your soul. But life is *much* better with a saved soul.

TRADING SUCCESS FOR SIGNIFICANCE

At the end of Genesis 28, Jacob propped up the rock he had slept on, turning it into a pillar, and poured oil on top of it, making a vow to tithe to God and follow Him as a pilgrim. It might not have been a very good pillow, but it served as an amazing altar. He told God that he would use whatever time he had to seek God and participate in what He had for him.

Jacob no longer saw life as a contest to win or a quest to accumulate or accomplish. He decreased, and God increased. He sought to live for God's glory and story and to treasure what couldn't be taken from him. He traded success for significance. Ironically, this is when God made Jacob more successful than he could ever have asked for—because Jacob was seeking God and not success.

The foot catcher had met the Foot Washer.

Jacob got his bearings and a new outlook on life, which launched him down a path of more encounters with God. Angelic activity and supernatural encounters became the norm for him.

God wrestled him to the ground, changed his name, and helped him sort out relational reconciliation with people he had hurt. Simply put, once Jacob reset, he had purpose to navigate life because of his spiraling. Tighter and tighter, closer and closer to the center, one revolution at a time.

The same can happen for you and me. The key is to trade the Tower of Babel for the ladder Jesus has lowered.

Religion and workaholism both say "Do."

Jesus says, "Done. It is finished."

The world says, "Find yourself. Prove yourself."

Jesus says, "Lose yourself. Take up your cross and follow Me, and you will find life."

Let the one who created the woodpecker and its astonishing tongue be your Master, and "you'll learn to live freely and lightly" (Matthew 11:30 MSG).

Maybe the reason for the chaotic search and sense of crisis you feel is that, like Jacob, you have spent time pursuing misery, one selfish and shallow day at a time, and now it's time to form a new plan. I believe the real reason these moments of breakdown come is because God, in His mercy, is giving us the opportunity to recalibrate. It's His way of moving the needle on the compass so we don't waste any more of our lives worshiping the creation instead of the Creator.

The goal in life isn't to be the richest, have skied the most vert, accumulated the most followers, or visited the most countries. At your funeral most people won't talk about accomplishments or sales records or square footage. They will remember kindness, generosity, and wisdom.

Focus more on what Jesus will say to you at the gates of heaven and less on what looks good on a job application, résumé, or Instagram post.

KEEP TURNING YOUR HEART TOWARD HIM

Jacob repeatedly came back to that place he'd seen the sky ladder, renewing his allegiance, going all in for the Treasure of knowing God. These visits became a special way to disrupt the magnetic interference of this world and home in on heaven's homing signal.

It's something we all need to do—not just once, but over and over and over again.

Is there a place you could turn into an "altar"? It could be a special chair, a spot in your yard, or a certain table at a café. Go there often and be refreshed. May He lift His countenance upon you and awaken your wonder. His face, which is like lightning, will strike your life with significance and meaning and give you strength for the confusing bits of your story. Time with Jesus will cure the despair you feel when pursuing your goals and agenda for your own sake, helping you focus on what is significant and less on appearing "successful," whatever that means.

Jacob went on to patch things up with his brother, who he had deceived, and to bless his sons with his dying breath. This is a glorious death.

Like Einstein, the distracted student, you will feel uninspired and listless pursuing your own happiness, pleasure, and status. But when you respond to the revelation that you are seen, known, loved, and included, you will want to prop up a pillar and pour out the oil. You will give whatever you have in pursuit of a God-given vision. And that will never go away; it will simply keep unrolling and unfurling, getting better and better. The nearer you get to the end of your life, you will discover you are not moving away from but toward your Treasure—the true north of that which pulls nobly on the strings of your soul.

There is incredible clarity and purpose in recognizing you are not alone. We see that in Einstein and in Jacob. A normal bedroom or a camping trip can become afire with the glory and presence of God. He is near enough to whisper. You shout across a room but whisper only when you are close. God speaks to you with a still, small voice. I know sometimes He feels distant in your feelings, but heaven whispers because Jesus is not far from you.

Knowing that you are never alone changes how you look at every situation. You always have the chance to play a part in the cosmic symphony of God reconciling all things to Himself.

Going to work and going to watch birds.

Making cookies and babysitting children.

Building a business and burying septic lines.

Any everyday thing can become a way for you to do what those at the Tower of Babel refused to do—live for His name instead of your own. Like the obscure bits of the Bible where Jesus' coming is foretold, every seemingly random detail of your life can take on importance that will last forever, even the load of laundry you need to rewash because you forgot to dry it and now it's got that funky smell from sitting wet too long.

> YOU ALWAYS HAVE THE CHANCE TO PLAY A PART IN THE COSMIC SYMPHONY OF GOD RECONCILING ALL THINGS TO HIMSELF.

USE WHAT YOU'VE GOT AND DON'T WAIT

Foster your curiosity, open yourself to your wonder, and ask, like da Vinci did, *Why, Lord, is that tongue the length it is? Why did You make me the way You did? You had to have a reason. What is my unique purpose, and how can I do it to the best of my ability with all my heart?*

You are His workmanship, created in Christ Jesus that you might do all the things He long ago destined you to do.

For Jacob, this meant carrying on the family lineage and stewardship over the promises God gave to Abraham, Jacob's grandfather. Jacob went on to have twelve sons who grew into tribes and became a nation, the one that Jesus—the ladder from heaven who carried the sins of the world on His holy shoulders—would come from. His family dwelled in the land to the north, south, east, and west and was a blessing to people everywhere.

When Jacob caught a glimpse of God's cosmic plan, he wanted to do anything he could to participate in it. The problem was he was penniless and had no influence. This is where many of us get paralyzed with inaction. We tell ourselves that one day we will get around to doing what God put us on the earth to do; we just can't do it yet. Because, you know, it's just not the right time. Or, we will have a better ability to do it when such-and-such lines up.

But that's a trap. You mustn't let what you can't do keep you from doing what you can.

When Jacob poured oil on that rock, it symbolized pouring out his life for a worthy cause. He wanted to ascend God's ladder, not by his good works but through God's undeserved grace. Jacob basically said, "I'm in. I refuse to miss out on that opportunity." He could have said, "One day I will do something." Instead, he decided to lay the first stone of Bethel, the house of God, on the spot. This is huge.

When you can't do the good you would, do the good you can.

Jacob couldn't build the entirety of God's house, which he

caught a glorious glimpse of, but he could lay the first stone. It was all he had, but that was all he needed to participate.

Table stakes for active participation in God's kingdom is whatever He has entrusted to you. He didn't make a mistake when He made you or called you. He was wise and deliberate when He gave you your talents, skills, and experiences, your physical stature, family of origin, and personality. Ditto for spiritual gifts, drive, common grace, saving faith, the Holy Spirit, and on and on. He doesn't wish you were richer, taller, buffer, smarter, or better with directions. He sees you as the Einstein of whatever He entrusted you with. There's no one like you!

That means that whatever you currently have in your hands is precisely what God wants you to use to play a vital role in the miraculous. He wasn't disappointed when the little boy had only five loaves, or embarrassed by David's slingshot. He didn't think to Himself *Ugh* when Nehemiah offered up the cup in his hand or roll His eyes when Mary said she had never known a man. These seemed to be limitations, but in God's eyes they were qualifications. He selects what man rejects.

That's just life in His upside-down kingdom, where dying leads to life, losing leads to winning, and serving is the precursor to ruling.

DON'T SLIP INTO COMPARISON

Part of Jacob's spiraling before his sky-ladder moment was perceiving his worth and success in relation to someone else. He got caught up in wanting to be better than his older brother, Esau, so he spent a lot of energy conniving and trying to get ahead.

Comparison is a distraction from what matters. And it always destroys joy.

Jacob's massive inferiority complex led to jealousy of Esau, and jealousy is a road that leads nowhere. It literally left Jacob by himself in the middle of nowhere. He wore a disguise to try to get a blessing.

When I've done a version of this, I've discovered that wearing a mask cuts me off from God's richest blessings and that He actually just wants to bless *who I am*. The same is true for you.

It was only when Jacob came to the end of himself and discovered that God loved him and wanted him in His story that he stopped chasing success and instead chased God. Jacob had wrestled with God and man and had prevailed. His walk was different from that day forward. It always is when you walk with God.

And, as we said earlier, success started chasing Jacob. He couldn't miss. Blessing overtook him. God mysteriously led him to the woman of his dreams. Jacob worked for her family for fourteen years, which seemed like only a few days because of the love he had for her. Children were added to the family like hotcakes. He married three other wives (though that is not recommended). His sheep had sheep, then those sheep had sheep.

Jacob kept on the righteous path, staying honest and not cutting corners. He went above and beyond in issues of integrity, absorbing losses and going out of his way to put others ahead of himself. For his selflessness he only excelled more.

Jacob illustrates what so many have discovered—you can't keep down the person walking in God's will. No one can oppose who God has decided to exalt. No one can shut doors He has decided to open. No pit of lions, demon of hell, or scheme of man can prevent God from blessing someone He has chosen to promote.

No longer focused on himself, Jacob had a compass focused on God's glory, and God saw fit for him to go down in history. God is proud to be the God of Abraham, Isaac, and Jacob. And guess what? Even though there are mistakes you have made, insecurities you struggle with, shameful moments you have faced, and painful wounds that have tried to wipe you out, He is proud to be the God of *you*.

TAKING STOCK

Before we end this chapter, let's consider a few powerful actions we can take to instill the message that Jesus is the Treasure to pursue. Then, when life sends you in a spiral, you can be assured that as you call on God He will lead you through the chaos and on to joy.

Take some time to think about the moments in your life when God has made Himself unmistakably clear, when you knew without a doubt He was trying to get your attention. Make a list of your "compass-moving moments." It could be when you were a kid and used to lie in bed, or when too many coincidences, like seeing a certain bird (a woodpecker?) or other special connection, kept showing up in your story and—maybe, just maybe—felt like a God wink. I have a friend who sees dragonflies as reminders of God's love for her. Maybe for you it is particular moments of worship or prayer. When has God made you feel super seen?

Next, thank Him for His relentless pursuit of you. Renew your commitment to Him and His kingdom. Renounce your agenda and status control, and embrace His glory, graciousness, and kindness to include you. Remember you are chasing the cloud, not the clout!

Then, do a couple tactile things to express how you might live this out. Grab a cup of water, go outside, and pour it out as a symbol of your renewed consecration in this season of your life. Regardless of what is behind you, determine to wholeheartedly pursue what God has for you in the future.

Find a piece of paper or a journal and doodle. Wonder. Ponder. Use your curiosity to think about what it is God wants you to create or focus on during the time you have left on earth.

Do you need to pivot from what you are currently engaged in, or can you do old things in new ways?

Imagine you are the person tasked with writing the eulogy they will read at your funeral. What do you want them to say?

What confusion do you need to persist in that you have run away from?

Are there some God dreams whispering below the surface that you know are where you should be pouring your energy into, but you have hesitated because of all the things you don't know and answers you don't have?

Perhaps today is the day to get uncomfortable. And what better way than, like Jacob, to turn a "rock pillow" into a pillar. Comfort zones won't keep your life safe; they will keep it small, and perhaps even keep you from your part in the vision in the sky God wants to show you.

CHAPTER 15

FAME OR FLAME?

IT'S HARD TO imagine, but there was a day when the same painting hung on the wall of almost every bar in the country. It was
a reproduced lithograph of the Battle of Little Bighorn, a skir-
mish between warriors of the Lakota Sioux, Northern Cheyenne,
and Arapaho tribes fighting men of the 7th Regiment of the US
Cavalry, along with their Crow and Arikara scouts in 1876. In the
scene, dead and dying soldiers are about to be scalped by a sea of
surrounding Native Americans who have defeated them in battle.
Google "Custer's Last Fight Budweiser" if you want to check it out.

In the middle of it all stands George Armstrong Custer with
his iconic wavy, flowing hair and his fringed buckskin clothing.

In one hand he grips the barrel of a revolver, positioned to be wielded like a club, and in the other he brandishes a sword above his head. Anheuser-Busch secured the rights to the painting and distributed a million copies to places across the nation that served their beer.

Imagine an entire generation coming out of both World Wars all the way through Vietnam and beyond, sitting at their favorite watering hole with this image of courageous greatness and masculine ideals before them. It mythologized the American West, implanting a narrative of good versus evil while conveniently pushing a dying-with-your-boots-on bravado Anheuser-Busch wanted people to associate with their beer.

The painting is riddled with historical inaccuracies, including the suggestion that it was a long, protracted battle. The reality is the Native American warriors were far superior in strength, and it was over in the amount of time it takes a hungry man to eat a meal. Battlefield legends say that Custer's enemies mutilated him in myriad ways. So much for a glorious death.

This is what people raised up as an ideal and said "Cheers" to while having drinks with a friend after work. It is shocking for a number of reasons, including:

- the atrociousness of the entire military campaign this represented;
- the awful way the settlers treated Native Americans, violating treaties with them, forcing them onto reservations, and wiping out the millions of buffalo they depended on;
- and the cruel order for Custer's army to force the Native Americans to either die or leave the rich land of the Dakotas when gold was discovered there.

Those issues notwithstanding, what troubles me about Custer is how much I see myself in him. His failure to control his ego. His desperate desire to be great. And the way those around him suffered for his inability to live up to the better angels of his nature. How did he end up there?

YOU CAN'T EAT FAME

George Custer was raised by a simple blacksmith and was not on track to make anything great of himself from a young age. He got into West Point because a girl he wanted to date had a congressman for a dad who wanted to get rid of him so he wouldn't be able to pursue his daughter. For this reason, the father wrote the letter of recommendation that got Custer into the prestigious military academy; it was the beginning of what has been called Custer's luck.

He graduated at the bottom of his class after racking up 726 demerits during his time there (the highest number in West Point history), mostly for little rebellions, slovenly behavior, and stupidity.

He was court-martialed for a dereliction of duty during his first posting as an officer when he failed to break up a fight; he instead watched it along with the mob that had formed. It should have jeopardized his career, but instead, he again got lucky and went unpunished.

After a gutsy performance at the First Battle of Bull Run, Custer got his dream posting in the US Cavalry. There he distinguished himself with his genuine strengths: boldness, daring, and throwing caution to the wind. His charismatic knack for rushing into a battlefield at the front, with his sword raised high and his blond locks flowing, inspired the men under him and endeared him to the men over him. He was involved in one crucial battle after another.

At age twenty-three, Custer and his men helped turn the tide at Gettysburg that won the engagement and kept the Union line from breaking. His young age, joined with his dashing, one-of-a-kind sense of style and flair, gave the impression that he was a cultural wunderkind, a cavalier rock star. As one of the youngest brigadier generals in the Union army, he was dubbed the Boy General.

Custer played to the cameras and knew how to work the media. He was ahead of his time—born for Instagram or TikTok. Today he would, for sure, be an influencer.

Custer's hardest moments came when the Civil War ended. As a man built for battle and with no battle to fight, he lost his sense of purpose. His greatest problem was becoming successful at a young age and liking the taste of it.

He was famous, but you can't eat fame.

Custer spent the rest of his life chasing the attention he'd gotten at the beginning. He became a glory hog, constantly looking for ways to distinguish himself, redefine himself, and achieve again the level of notoriety he'd once tasted. He rebranded himself several times—sportsman, grizzly hunter, gold miner—then reached his final iteration at age thirty-six: American Indian fighter. The problem was, it worked.

Yet again, the nation gobbled up the coverage of his exploits as all signs were pointing West. He was the man to do the dirty work of confronting the Plains Indians who were unwilling to abandon their ancestral homes and move to the reservations.

In the words of one historian, "All the attributes that made Custer great were traits of youth." Custer knew there was precious little time to do something with that opportunity, that the sand was falling through the hourglass above his head. If he didn't do something to cement his status, he would never get the chance. So he prepared to go for broke, to go for glory.

Custer made the monumentally foolish and ultimately fatal choice to lead two hundred men in taking on a far superior force at Little Bighorn, though he had been instructed to wait for reinforcements. Had it worked, he wouldn't have had to share the credit with any other units. But it did not work. It left him and all his men under his command dead, and his corpse mutilated in an awful way.

THE GAMBLE FOR GLORY

Custer failed his midlife spiral. He chose to gamble on status, and that gamble proved deadly. Matthew 16:25 reminds us, "For whoever desires to save his life will lose it, but whoever loses his life for My sake will find it." Custer did go down in history, but ultimately as an example of what not to do. Seeking one's own glory does not lead to true glory.

Again, I say all this not to pile on Custer but because there is Custer in me. He is a mirror for me to see where my shadow wants to take me if tendencies are left unchecked and not brought into the light. Pain is all that waits for me if I don't pick the flame of God's glory instead of the fame of this world.

What about you? In your desire to figure out how you stack up and where you stand in this world, how might you have inadvertently sought your value in the wrong places? Perhaps it is through people pleasing, name-dropping, networking in a forced way, or, in some other way, to quote the book of Haggai, putting your money in a bag with holes. It never works.

My family visited Little Bighorn Battlefield National Monument and bought a puzzle of the famous Custer's Last Stand with five hundred pieces and, to our dismay, there was one piece missing when we finished. The gaping hole in the scene spoke volumes of any attempt to make this world more than it is meant to be. Try as you might, there will always be a hole.

IN YOUR DESIRE TO FIGURE OUT HOW YOU STACK UP AND WHERE YOU STAND IN THIS WORLD, HOW MIGHT YOU HAVE INADVERTENTLY SOUGHT YOUR VALUE IN THE WRONG PLACES?

Maybe you have an underlying dread or overlying terror about the passing of time. *What if I become irrelevant and am no longer at the top of my game? What will that mean?* The fear of peaking and eventually declining is normal. The key is to avoid entering a state of desperation, because desperate people do foolish things.

You don't get to stay the Boy or Girl General forever. In every industry, sector, and sphere there are always going to be newer and younger models coming out. Traditionally you have a few choices for handling this.

1. **Dig in your heels and live in denial.** Blissfully pretend it isn't happening and you're still in your glory days.
2. **Reinvent yourself** and seek to become the king or queen of a different domain, like Custer did. The cycle will repeat, though, and you will have to keep getting zanier, gutsier, and riskier to keep the glory coming.

3. **Give up.** Accept irrelevance, sit on an ice floe, and wait to die. Jesus presents us with a fourth and much better option.

4. **Age gracefully.** Jump the curve. Accept the strengths and power of the new season. Integrate and mourn the one that you are closing out with celebration and sadness, then, equally as passionately, embrace the strengths of the new season. It's a death that leads to resurrection.

For the athlete who has been cut and "put out to pasture," there is no doubt some loss of identity alongside lingering addiction to the adrenaline and accolades of the spotlight. And there is no doubt some resentment at becoming the elder statesman of the sport banished to the island of ESPN commentating.

But my friend Tim Tebow has shown that there *can* be new battles to fight! After an epic football career, he now loves on and celebrates children with special needs, opens orphanages in developing countries, and fights human trafficking. Does some part of him wrestle with no longer being on the football or baseball field? I'm sure it does. But he has found beauty and purpose in the fields that are white for harvest, which can't be taken away. He jumped the curve, and so can you.

Let's say arthritis eventually takes you away from painting, woodworking, or something else you love. Instead of fighting against that grain, which will only give you splinters, ask God, "What do You have for me now?" Open yourself up to the unexpected blessing and invitation into something greater than the former things: the current glory of God present in your midst.

Our problem is that rather than embrace what is in front of us, it's easier to cling to the past, even if our rosy remembering of it is incomplete and inaccurate. Why? Because new things are scary.

And our sense of identity and security is typically wrapped up in the familiar.

HOLD ON TO WHAT IS PERMANENT

You will be able to let go of what can be taken away when you remember what can't go away.

Jesus promised, "I will never leave you nor forsake you" (Hebrews 13:5). Circumstances will inevitably change—but His presence with you never will.

He won't forsake you in your twenties when you are all skill and energy but light on wisdom.

He won't leave you when your beauty and strength fade but your perspective is richer because of your battle scars.

He won't leave you when you are full of wisdom and physically declining.

He won't leave you when you complete graduate work and feel alone and insecure as you venture into the job market.

He won't leave you when you are in the twilight of your life and those you love have died.

He won't leave you when your kids go to kindergarten and they aren't your young babies anymore.

He won't leave you on your deathbed; He will send His angels to collect your spirit and bring you from your body to paradise, where you'll await the resurrection of the dead at Christ's return.

He will be with you always in the new heavens and new earth, where you will serve Him, eat from the Tree of Life, and enjoy life to the full. You will forever be part of the flock of the Shepherd and Overseer of your soul. Your life is hidden with Christ in God, and when Christ appears, you will appear with Him in glory. Amen.

So, you don't have to be afraid of anything. Not irrelevance, or old age, or the phone no longer ringing. You don't have to fear the crushing weight of opportunity, which, as fun as it is while it lasts, also comes with unique pressures, challenges, temptations, and snares.

His love for you is an eternal, unchanging fact. It isn't based on how impressive you are; it's placed on you because of Jesus. There is nothing you can ever do to make God love you less or more. Breathe out a sigh of relief that your performance isn't keeping you on His radar.

God isn't in heaven with arms crossed saying, "What have you done for me lately?" He's saying, "I love you."

That is grounding for me. I hear Jesus whisper it to me in moments of fear over my worth. I'm not "trying out" for His love, and neither are you!

HIS LOVE FOR YOU IS AN ETERNAL, UNCHANGING FACT.

GET FIRM ON YOUR ETERNAL IDENTITY AND WORTH

He will be an anchor for our identity and worth through every season if we let Him.

We will be able to close a life chapter with a light touch, saying what the disciples were told to do when they did a great work: "Rejoice that your names are written in heaven."

Jesus had seen them flexing and posturing—confusing what

God did through them with who they were. "We told the demons to flee and they fled!" they bragged.

Jesus warned, "I saw Satan fall like lightning from heaven" (Luke 10:18).

Don't go around crowing and chanting, "Rufio! Rufio! Ru. Fi. Ooooooooooo!" as if you are a Lost Boy in the movie *Hook*. Don't glory in that; glory in the fact that your name is written in heaven.

Jesus is putting His nail-scarred hand on your shoulder today. The message for you may be, "Do not glory in your Mercedes even though you are able to afford it through the massive hard work flipping Airbnb properties or hustling in your job as a Realtor." Or, "Do not glory in your law degree even though you busted your butt to pass the bar."

Jesus invited you to heaven, and that is beyond all hype! That is the lead story. Beyond that, anything He does through you is playing with house money.

Look at it this way: Your worth and identity are fixed and cannot be adequately reflected in the status of your output, waistline, social media following, or "spiritual accomplishments." Nothing like that could ever contain who you are. So, fundamentally, you are not a banker, plumber, influencer, or college pastor. You are not a consultant, pageant winner, football star, or honor-student parent. You are not a CEO, tire salesman, or astronaut. Those are roles you have filled and actions you have taken, and they are seasonal.

You are a blood-bought, Spirit-filled child of the Most High God! You were entrusted with His image and called by His name. Your name is written in heaven, and, day by day, you are being invited to conform to His likeness.

You will never have less or more value than you do right now.

You will never be yesterday's news, because you were never the lead story. Jesus is. If people think the world of you, they are wrong. If they want to cancel you and make you a pariah, they are wrong. You are not God's gift to planet earth, nor are you as bad as your worst mistake. You are a human being God loves.

GET CLEAR AND GO LOW

This perspective will keep you from having your last stand, hanging on to your glory days in a tightfisted fight to the death. If you and I can serve God with our whole hearts during our "working years" without connecting *what we do* with *who we are*, we can take a different path than Custer did. We will bid adieu to being the Boy or Girl General with a few tears and fond memories from the closing season. We won't end up idolatrously dying at Little Bighorn River because we were reaching for a former glory a decade later.

If we are humble, we'll remember that God did not choose us because we were the best and brightest or the most wonderful. He sets His love on the weak and broken to prove His glory and strength. And there is no end to that if we give Him all the credit. That can continue no matter how unlovable we feel or long in the tooth we eventually get.

Any glory attached to our works is fleeting, and, if you and I are honest, we had more than our fair share of Custer's luck to add to our hard work. To have been born in a free country, to have a healthy body, to have not been born during the bubonic plague . . . all these are things you can claim no responsibility for. Besides, of our natural skill and spiritual giftings, how can we take credit for what was a gift? If we want to glory in something, we should glory in this: Our name is written in heaven!

Knowing this can snap us out of the puffed-up, high-horse, big-headed lunacy that may creep in when we feel like we nailed it. It is stabilizing to take a deep breath and say, "How fortunate am I that I got to see that victory? And better yet, my name is written in heaven!" And then with a shrug of the shoulders, it is off to the next thing—be that rest or the next battle. This will keep us from becoming like Custer; we'll think of ourselves rightly, not more highly or lowly than we should. Because if we are our work on our best day, then sadly we are our work on our worst. Our objective isn't to think more or less of ourselves than Jesus does but to simply think of ourselves less.

LET HUMILITY OPEN THE DOOR TO MORE

Here's the lesson: Great opportunities come and go, but none of them are big enough to define you. So anchor your worth in what remains no matter what!

> GREAT OPPORTUNITIES COME AND GO, BUT NONE OF THEM ARE BIG ENOUGH TO DEFINE YOU.

Interestingly enough, this makes the nicks, bruises, bumps, and wrinkles your allies and friends, not your enemies, because every one of them is an opportunity to deny yourself, pick up your cross, and follow Jesus. You get to say to yourself, "I have been crucified with Christ; it is no longer I who live, but Christ lives in me; and the life which I now live in the flesh I live by faith in the Son of God, who loved me and gave Himself for me" (Galatians 2:20).

I don't have to fear winter.

I am clothed in scarlet.

Come what may, I rejoice in what can't be taken away.

I belong to Jesus, and nothing—not cellulitis, not Alzheimer's, not cancer, not crow's-feet, not love handles, nor any other thing can wrestle me from His grip. And ironically, the more I die in that way, the more valuable I become in God's paradigm.

Dying is living.

Losing is keeping.

Serving is reigning.

Being buried is being planted.

So, the more you feel yourself fainting and you strengthen yourself in the Lord, the less you will need to have some dramatic, foolish last stand. And the more you will kneel before the Lamb. Instead of having less to offer, you suddenly will have more to give.

It's like the widow in the story with Elisha. The more she poured out of her pot, the more she had to offer. It kept flowing as long as she kept pouring. Our problem is that we tend to clam up and stop giving when we are no longer the ones on the field playing. But if we can graciously accept the role of third-base coach in God's kingdom just as happily as that of pitcher, eye has not seen nor ear heard what God has prepared to pour out through us.

Yoda is hotly desired for a reason, friend. Age, when paired with humility, is a powerful thing. Kurt Cobain believed the Custer lie: that it is better to burn out than fade away (as he wrote in his suicide note). That is a demonic trap the thief uses to steal and kill and destroy.

This is why we see some celebrities die deaths of despair, often just as their natural vigor starts to fade like the flower of the field. "Better to live fast, die young, and leave a beautiful corpse" is the deception that the enemy would have you swallow. "Hold on to greatness at all costs."

Jesus teaches us a better way!

Die to self and die to selfies. Serve and keep serving. If you can lead, then lead; if you can mentor, then mentor; if you can encourage, then encourage. If you can pray, then pray; if you can sing, then sing; and if you can love, then love. There is *always* a place for you in the body of Christ and in the kingdom of God.

I have a tattoo on my chest that says *memento mori*, which means "Remember you are mortal." It comes from the parades that kings would allow generals to have in the aftermath of a successful military campaign in the Roman Empire. The ruling caesars, who saw themselves as divine, would allow the general to ride in a chariot with a crown of leaves and with captured foes being dragged behind them as they made their way up the Via Sacra heading toward the Roman Forum.

Every time the crowd would raise a cheer for the general, a servant of the divine emperor would whisper "Memento mori" into the general's ear. The so-called god-man wanted this human instrument to not confuse who was who. In essence, he was saying, "You are being cheered today, but you are just a man." To me, this is a somewhat confused yet powerful reminder of how things really are.

Jesus is the God-Man who has defeated the Enemy and reigns over all. The resurrection triggered a victory parade that will consummate when the "already but not yet" is completed. On that day the last domino will fall, and the kingdoms of this world will become the kingdoms of our God.

This is all so certain that the New Testament speaks about it in the past tense. *Hello.*

When Jesus came to the city of Jerusalem and presented

Himself as King, however, He was riding a donkey. As Tim Keller put it, Jesus displayed "majesty but in meekness; strength but with weakness." No king would ride a donkey. Like Custer, they would want to be on a stallion with their saber flashing in the air. But Jesus, King of kings, stooped low.

In His upside-down kingdom He would never have you or me mistake what true greatness looks like. It is not grasping power or status, obsessing over our accomplishments, or beating ourselves up for the lack of fresh ones. Instead, He would have us memento mori, or remember we are mortal.

Don't flex your muscles; fix your eyes on His coming kingdom. You don't need some epic last stand. Jesus reigns in immortality, and when at last He stands on the earth, we will reign with Him. He will swiftly crush Satan under our feet.

Listen to me, friend: As a follower of Jesus, your worth is fixed and your future is certain. Your name is written in heaven!

JESUS REIGNS IN IMMORTALITY, AND WHEN AT LAST HE STANDS ON THE EARTH, WE WILL REIGN WITH HIM.

CHAPTER 16

THERE'S AN ANGEL ON MY PORCH SWING

THERE'S A SAYING that when the student is ready, the teacher will appear.

Can you think of a time that was true in your life? It is amazing how often God sends the right voices into our lives, when we are ready to listen. If you have ears to hear, there is a Yoda in the wings.

During the crucible that was my midlife spiral, God sent an angel to me. Her name is Lisa Harper. She sat with Jennie and me in one of the most draining, complex, and painful moments of my life and prayed over us as we wept for what felt like an hour.

It was during a visit at our home. The three of us were walking in the backyard when Lisa let Jennie and me know that she could tell we were carrying something heavy. The world, at the time, was in the thick of the pandemic and everyone was somewhat confused, so at first we both kind of laughed it off like, *Aren't we all?*

She wouldn't let us off that easy.

Sitting us down on our porch swing in front of the firepit, she placed herself in the middle of us and made it clear we weren't going anywhere until we opened up. Ready or not, we were about to have some serious back-porch theology in real time.

I went first.

ALL-OUT PANIC

I had started having panic attacks on the Sunday before Jennie's book *The Fight to Flourish* was released. I had preached from March until May without a break, but Jennie was going to do the next four Sundays. I was exhausted, relieved, and ready for a mental, emotional, and spiritual break.

Instead, what I experienced was a breakdown.

Jennie and I were lying in bed when it began. My heart must have hit 180 bpm or higher. (Note: A resting heart rate above 100 bpm is too fast for most people. My hands were sweaty. I started to picture myself hanging from the suspension training straps in my gym. Mind racing, arguing with myself, terrified, choking back tears, struggling to catch my breath . . . this was not the rest I was expecting. It felt like it was out of nowhere, but as I mentioned in an earlier chapter, it was really my body reacting to the pace I had been keeping for the previous seven or eight years. I was staying still long enough to finally feel some of what I needed to heal.

I felt like a ton of weight was sitting on my chest. Gasping, I grabbed my Bible from my nightstand and flipped on a light. Colossians, Ephesians, I needed a promise, an encouragement, something to comfort me. But nothing. All the words were blurred. It brought no comfort to me. I turned on a Louie Giglio sermon hoping for comfort but only felt fear. Ephesians *and* Louie weren't helping me. I was in big trouble.

It was truly terrifying.

Waking up Jennie, I almost told her to get our next-door neighbor, a police officer, to come over and put me in handcuffs so I couldn't accidentally hurt myself. Instead, I asked her, as calmly as possible, to please pray for me because something was happening and I was scared. She could hear the alarm in my voice and leapt into action, but there was nothing she knew to do that might help, except pray.

Jennie sat on the floor of the bathroom and prayed while I took a shower and tried to calm down.

Nothing worked. I was sweating in the shower under cold water.

I was so disoriented and perplexed. I found myself pacing in the shower, increasingly alarmed, because never had I experienced anything like this.

"Something is very, very wrong," I said.

After drying off I was still clammy and had to physically resist the urge to pace, to go run, to fight. But where could I go? I was thirty-eight years old and coming unglued at the seams like an inflatable toy left out in the sun too long.

Jennie downloaded an app that read Christian meditations

over peaceful music and played it for me while I tried to lie still, all while crying tears of liquid fear. I would doze off and wake up again with a fire alarm going off inside my brain, and the process would play out on repeat.

Aside from the initial weeks of grief following Lenya's going to heaven, this was the worst thing I had ever experienced. For most of my life, I had struggled with anxiousness, night terrors, and waking up sweaty after bad dreams, but this was like every scary moment from the past three decades of my life in a gallon jug distilled down to a six-ounce bottle.

How would I survive this?

The next morning, I talked to my counselor. With sheets of tears rolling down my face, I explained what was happening. We began to formulate a plan together.

I expressed how angry I was about the timing, how inconvenient and mean it was for this to intrude into our life when I was supposed to be taking time off.

She lovingly let me know that soldiers often don't fully experience what they have been through until they get home from the battlefield. It's sometimes not until then that their bodies allow them to feel what they have faced.

"In some ways it makes perfect sense that you would experience it now," she explained. "You told yourself there is no longer a big battle to rally yourself up for, so you are getting a sense of the miles you have put on your system."

That made sense but was no easier to accept. I was so bitter, and I honestly wrote it off as a fluke.

That is, until around nine p.m., when I started climbing the stairs to head to bed. I had a premonition that the panic and fire alarm in my body was about to start up again. It was like the tremors after an earthquake: aftershocks. Or more like the seismic activity before an earthquake that lets you know it is about to start. I got dizzy and lightheaded just thinking about entering our bedroom because I associated it with the panic. That made me even angrier because a safe space of intimacy, *selah*, and sanctity had been intruded upon and violated. It was like the Joker had set up camp in the Batcave.

I did not end up having another breakdown that night—but the cycle continued. Several days would go by with no episode, then another one would come. Afterward, I would be on edge expecting it to return, then I'd drop my guard only to have it show up.

Jennie was fighting a battle that involved her own crisis and inner turmoil at this time. Hers was different from mine and involved hormones and cycles, issues specific to female biology. It hit the fan at one point with us both needing the other and neither having anything to offer. We were both spiraling simultaneously and smacking into each other in the process.

This hadn't happened when Lenya left for heaven—not like this. For the most part we each had been strong when the other was weak; we took turns being the shoulder to cry on or keeping calm and carrying on for the other. Our journey through grief had been like tag-team wrestling.

During this visit to what felt like the seventh circle of hell, however, we both hit rock bottom multiple times without any spare bandwidth, compassion, or empathy to offer. That was the scariest thing of all, as it was without precedent in our (then) sixteen years of marriage.

As I mentioned, Jennie was carrying the preaching load at this time—for an entire month, which she had never done before. During this time, I was going to rest. And by *rest* I mean cry in the corner. Unbelievably, on Mother's Day, she broke her ankle tripping on a tennis ball while in the middle of a fight with her husband.

We had found a way for things to get worse.

CALLING ALL CARS

I visited my medical doctor on the advice of my counselor and was given an Rx for Xanax that I was to take during a panic attack or when I felt like one was coming on. It was to help take the edge off.

I had to get off my pre-workout drink and stop consuming any caffeine after lunch. The pre-workout drink was the equivalent of an entire pot of coffee, and I'd often been consuming it right after finishing a full French press. As it turns out, eight cups of coffee in two hours does not help with rapid heartbeat and feelings of nervousness. Which is what the label on the pre-workout drink container said would happen: "May cause feelings of irritability, anxiety, and in some people, panic."

I began making some seismic shifts in how I approached life. I had nothing to give to our staff and had pretty much ghosted everyone in that season as I was simply surviving. So I reached out to our board of directors at Fresh Life, the wise, stabilizing voices in my life, and walked them through what I was facing. I received their prayers and blessing to figure out what was happening to me.

Acting on one of their recommendations, I began to talk to a Christian psychologist, someone with a doctoral degree in clinical psychology, who could address different issues than my other counselor. He helped normalize what I was facing by explaining to me the mechanics of the autonomic nervous system, the arousal and fatigue on the system when there is not adequate rest between peaks of excitement and adrenaline. How eventually everything begins to spill over.

I have one vivid memory from that first month.

Jennie's *The Fight to Flourish* book release was on Cinco de Mayo, so we had a Mexican theme: the Fight to Flourish Fiesta. We bought different hot and spicy salsas to put on chicken wings and faced the gauntlet of tasting sauces that were off the Scoville scale charts. One after the other we ate the wings. It was comic gold on the livestream.

Then came the feelings of an approaching panic attack, triggered by a particularly nasty hot sauce called Da' Bomb Beyond Insanity (which is thirty-six times hotter than Tabasco). I fought back until the segment was over, then collapsed on my bathroom floor. I was sweating, crying, and struggling to compose myself. My mouth was on fire, my stomach was in knots, and I was crying my eyes out, feeling like I was about to die and then explode. I finally emerged and was grateful to blame it on the hot sauce when we sat down to interview our friends, Steven and Holly Furtick, because there was no hiding that I had been crying.

Two days later was my birthday. I turned thirty-eight.

The night before, I had experienced a temporary ceasefire in the fear camp, so I resolved to start doing something I'd wanted to do but felt terrified about: write a new book. Sitting in bed, I snagged my laptop and started typing what became *The Last Supper on the Moon*. It was the most ambitious writing project of my life and, in some ways, became a lifeline. There was no pressure because I told no one I was writing. There was no sense of "I have to write something," but rather a creative freedom in directing energy somewhere.

I could have never released that book and still smiled about it until I died. I wrote six days a week until it was finished. My psychologist also introduced me to breathing exercises that induced calm and performed a hard reset on my nervous system.

It worked.

I still have the bottle of Xanax I was originally prescribed. I ended up taking only half a tablet maybe six times. The bottle is now old and faded, the label illegible, but I appreciate knowing it is there.

Through writing, walking, playing tennis, and fishing, I have found calm and rhythms of rest and recovery that help to keep me from hitting high points of code red. I can still get keyed up for moments of having to perform at a high level; I just make sure that sprints are followed by plenty of time to come down.

A PRAYER FOR US

It was at the peak of this seismic fear that God sent Lisa into our backyard to give us a hug. After Jennie and I described all we had gone through in that season, she held us while we wept, and then she prayed. In the same way that we had been approaching it practically, medically, and psychologically, she helped us stay spiritually aware of God's presence.

There were three things in Lisa's prayer that I have held on to: the trees, Lennox's laugh, and my imagination (she prayed for Jennie, too, but those details are not mine to share).

First, Lisa prayed that the trees in our backyard would remind me that angels stand guard over our home. This caused me to lose it! My most violent panic attacks had taken place in our home and in my backstage prep room at church, where I pray before preaching. These two places are both so personal and intimate. My home is where I recover, enjoy family, and find solace in times of grief or worry. Backstage is where I get my heart right to minister. During the previous few months, I had felt like both places had turned on me and had, to some extent, been taken away.

Lenya also had lived in our house. Our family had bloomed within those walls. It felt like the Enemy had crossed over a crimson cord and snatched Rahab. It was a violation of the rules.

The trees in our yard are like my babies. I have watched them grow up from saplings to a height that stretches taller than our house. Every year I look forward to spring, when the buds first show up, and I love reading in the backyard. It is through these trees that I watch the sun rise, the snow fall, the birds come eat from the feeders, and where I hear the wind rustle through the leaves.

Lisa singling out those trees as a reminder of angel armies watching over us was a "woodpecker type of moment," a sort of God wink—she did not know what they have meant to me. It was as though, through that prayer, the Lord whispered to me that it was not just the angels who were standing guard above us but also He Himself. Nothing could get through to us that hadn't passed through Him first. We were safe in His arms.

It felt like flipping a switch, like when Kevin McCallister in *Home Alone* decides he is the man of the house and stops hiding under his bed. He proclaims he's not afraid anymore, that this is his house, and he will defend it. I decided then and there that the Lord's grace was over our home, so I wouldn't give another moment to fear.

The associations would change in time, but first I changed my mind.

They did. And I liked it.

This all came to a head one year later when my thirty-ninth birthday approached. It was also the one-year mark of that terribly dark season.

Never one to care much for birthdays, I course-corrected and threw myself a big party. I put on a special cowboy-print Hawaiian shirt and, in front of friends and family, talked about the hardship we had faced a year prior and how I longed to celebrate and mark the occasion of growth and progress. The party became an act of defiance and an opportunity to showcase the goodness of God who guarded our home.

NOTHING COULD GET THROUGH TO US THAT HADN'T PASSED THROUGH HIM FIRST.

This is one of the reasons you shouldn't skip over seemingly strange psalms, when David wrote things like, "I will both lie down in peace, and sleep; for You alone, O LORD, make me dwell in safety" (Psalm 4:8).

Maybe you haven't had panic attacks in your most personal, beloved places. Maybe, instead, the safe space of your car was violated through a sexual assault, or your home seems darkened by a divorce, or some other location you previously took shelter in is now stained by pain.

But in Jesus' name, darkness, fear, and anxiety have no stronghold that can't be broken! Shame has no grip that the hand of God can't pry open. And fear's icy fingers on your neck will be loosened and then broken by the Lion of the tribe of Judah.

Even if you're shaking, like I was in my Hawaiian cowboy shirt, you can come to a place where you no longer live in terror. Psalm 91:7 says, "A thousand may fall at your side, and ten thousand at your right hand; but it shall not come near you."

The Lord your God is your defender.

And whenever you hear the sound of trees rustling, I hope it reminds you of the chariots of angel armies sent by the Savior that keep you as you sleep, as you eat, and as you play and pray.

The devil can't have your bed, or your church, or your car, and he can't have an inch of your thought life. You belong to Jesus!

He also can't have your pain. Because when Jesus bought you, He bought all of you and He has a plan to use every dark thing in your story to accomplish good.

By the way, this is called exposure therapy. I didn't find out until much later that "running toward the roar" is actually a psychologically proven way to confront phobias! Whether it's elevators, death, or heights, how much better to face them than live in terror of them? We must not forget that "God has not given us a spirit of fear, but of power and of love and of a sound mind" (2 Timothy 1:7).

The second prayer Lisa prayed was one I was not expecting. She asked God that the laughter of our son, Lennox, would be a powerful flood of clean water washing away the residue of grief over the loss of Lenya from our hearts. At this point Jennie and I began shaking—with both sadness and joy. We didn't even realize how prophetically profound that was until the next time we heard him laugh. How cleansing his little laugh was!

Growing our family had been an extremely tender and scary subject for us after Lenya's death. I'd been scheduled to have a vasectomy when she was alive, but when she suddenly left for heaven, I canceled it. While I was scared to have more kids, I didn't have peace about ruling out the possibility.

Five years later, God surprised us when Jennie became pregnant—while on birth control! It very much felt like God had spoken.

Both Jennie and I had an *Oh no!* moment, as we knew there would be grief in it. And this child would be the only Lusko family member who had never known Lenya. What kinds of challenges would that bring? We didn't know then that this child would develop a strong relationship with Lenya, even though they never lived at the same time. In fact, in some ways, their connection in personality is uncanny. We also honored Lenya Avery Lusko by giving her initials, LAL, to her brother, Lennox Alexander Lusko.

After having four daughters, we were stunned to discover we were having a boy. I had been happily living on the set of the movie *Little Women* for years and honestly never expected a son. We knew it would no doubt be an adventure—but we had *no* idea. We needed to throw out our playbook, because raising a boy, especially this boy, was nothing like raising the four girls.

Already Lennox has squirted cleaning spray into the eyes of a babysitter who asked him to clean a mess he made off the floor. Then, when she was temporarily blinded, he punched her in the face. I didn't know whether I was more horrified or impressed by this and had to try really hard to keep a straight face when she told me the story. *Wow, what a move!* I thought. *That is straight Jason Bourne.*

Lisa surprised me by naming our wild and wonderful Lennox in her porch-swing prayer, but it makes perfect sense to me now. Lennox had been a help to our grief healing, not a barrier to it. And in that dark season, somewhere deep under the water, we clearly still had an ache needing medicine.

When Lisa said those words, the Holy Spirit impressed on me that there were perhaps a few more rough edges in need of His touch. I sensed His loving-kindness in sending this little boy to be an agent of that power.

While we always appreciated Lennox's rambunctious, hilarious, and somewhat destructive creative genius, I saw new meaning in it. I used to say, "It's amazing that he's here because had Lenya not gone home, we probably never would have had him."

But once when I said that, Alivia interrupted me. "Dad, that's not true. God could have found any way He wanted to bring Lennox into this world."

I realized that Lennox was in no way a replacement for his sister, nor was our love for him a betrayal of her. It was a part of how we would heal, and that connected him to her in a one-of-a-kind way.

Of all our kids, Lennox's and Lenya's voices have the most in common, both with a smoky, unmistakable rasp. So often when we hear Lennox laugh and talk, it reminds us of Lenya. Not in a negative way that makes us sad, but in a beautiful way that pings longing and heavenly hope.

The third prayer I'll only mention briefly, and it was for me to see myself as a little boy with wide-eyed imagination. These three prayers from Lisa were an essential spiritual component to the Jesus side of the blessed spiral.

As painful as some of these times were in the thick of it, looking back now, I am so grateful. Had it not been for these dark, hard times, I never would have known the goodness of the Lord the way I do today.

I want that hope and goodness for you, no matter what dark, hard times you have had to walk through.

A PRAYER FOR YOU

God gives us what we need when we need it—if we have ears to hear what the Spirit is saying. I'm no angel, but I know that God wanted me to share this message with you. If we were sitting on my porch swing, where Jennie and I sat with Lisa, I would pray this for you.

Lord, I thank You for the incredible gift of this moment. That out of all the people on this earth, the two of us get to share in this exchange. I pray that Your child would feel seen and special right now. I ask that they would sense Your protection over them, that You indeed have given Your angels command to watch over them. I pray that they would know Your love in a unique way, how high it is, how wide it is, how deep it is, and how past finding out it is. A literal ocean of love.

Right now I think of how Jesus kept His wounds when He rose from the dead. There is awe, wonder, and mystery in the fact that He chose to keep them in heaven. His body was risen and glorified, able to pass through walls, immortal and capable of flight—and yet still scarred.

I thank You that You don't intend to take away the pain we have faced, the trauma we have endured, or the indignities and failures we have experienced—it's much better than that. You intend to redeem and heal them.

Somehow, some way, You will receive glory. And we will take more joy from the healing and the scars than if You had waved a magic wand and removed the experiences altogether. We will carry our scars not as a reminder of human failure, evil, or pain but of Your divine love that prevails, overcomes, and never gives up.

Thank You for grace that is sufficient in weakness, powerful kindness that overcomes our smallness, and beauty that rises from ashes. We worship You now in this moment thinking of how the nail scars in Your wrists and feet and the spear wound in Your side don't make You less glorious but more. We humbly ask for the faith to see that wondrous potential in our own wounds. Heal them and help us to believe that the day could come when, given the choice, we, too, would choose to keep them. May they be a pathway to greater empathy, humility, and tenderness.

I close this prayer like Thomas, reaching out for Your wounds, not in stubborn unbelief, but because You invite us to. We ask for Your wounds to heal us. May Your holiness touch us from the top of our heads to the soles of our feet, sanctifying us spirit, soul, and body.

I ask in Jesus' name for Your power, might, and glory to course through Your child's past, present, and future. Purify, prepare, and redeem all the old and hard and stale.

I ask for flowers instead of weeds. Grass where there is only dry ground. And roses in place of desert sand.

I come against every evil spirit that would seek to divide, devour, and destroy, in the authority of the name of Jesus; I instead speak blessing and safety. I speak the name of Jesus over shame, abuse, regret, and self-centeredness. I speak Jesus over anger, loneliness, depression, anxiety, and fear. In His name I come against any other emotional baggage that may be holding them hostage. And I ask for Your glorious light to heal broken feet so they might dance.

In the beautiful name of Jesus,
Amen.

CHAPTER 17

SPRING, SUMMER, FALL, AND SMOKE

I AM FOUND on the mountain.

I am prepared to leave this world.

My midlife spiral at being over the hill proved surprisingly blessed, pointing me to the distant shores of heaven. I can see that there is more for me there than this life can hold. There is more before me than behind me.

Be not far from me, God.

I went astray. Jesus sought me and found me. He put me on His shoulders. He sang as He walked with me back to the flock. We are family.

Here's my heart, Lord, take and seal it.

This world is not my home. One day it will be—when the New Jerusalem comes down, when the horse's bells will be as holy as the high priest's breastplate. Meaning, the most common thing on earth, then will have as much glory as the holiest object in the history of the world. The entire earth a holy of holies, where God will dwell with His people. We will drink from God's river of delights without a filter of faith. The entire world will be covered with a weighty blanket of glory like the oceans currently cover the earth.

Holiness to the Lord.

Until that day I won't grab at bigger barns, trying to stifle emptiness with success. I will hold earth's blessings with a light touch, knowing true significance in Jesus along the way, and be prepared to let everything go.

Peter, James, and John got a peek at the coming glory on a high mount when Jesus transfigured before them. As if that wasn't astonishing enough, Moses and Elijah stepped away from heaven for a bit to appear also. It was like a scene from *Bill and Ted's Excellent Adventure*, a significant movie from my childhood (along with *Encino Man* and *Ferris Bueller's Day Off*). Like Bill and Ted hanging out with Genghis Khan, Napoleon, and Mozart, Peter, James, and John stood blinking at the two long-dead icons of the Jewish faith in their midst.

Now, Moses never got to step into the promised land; he only saw it from afar. I have to wonder if, at the transfiguration of Jesus, there wasn't a glimmer in Moses' eyes as he looked down at his feet and noticed his sandals were in the promised land. Of course, his focus was on Jesus and the conversation was about the cross, but how redemptive that he got to touch what he'd only been able to see all those years before.

And that is just the beginning.

Moses will live in the promised land forever. And it will not just figuratively flow with milk and honey; the ground will run with wine—the best aged wines. The trees of the field will clap their hands, and the mountains will somehow join in singing songs of praises to King Jesus. The new heavens and new earth will be stunning.

Will animals talk?

Maybe. Did you ever notice that, before the fall, Adam and Eve didn't bat an eye at the talking snake? They argued with him about what he said, but there was no shock that he spoke. When Balaam's donkey spoke to him, he replied without skipping a beat—then his rational brain convinced him it was outside the norm.

Universally, children assume the speech of animals and give them voices while playing with them. Might we discover in heaven that the adult perspective of "knowing better" is actually losing wisdom, not gaining it?

Some speculate that fairy tales with speaking trees and animals with noble character are not fiction but prophetic, illustrating a coming day when things will be lifted from the spell of evil and returned to the state they were in before the long winter of sin. We will have to wait for the Prince's kiss to find out for sure.

What we can know is that what is next is greater than what is now.

The latter glory shall be greater than the former.

So you don't have to cry. To fear being a nobody. To cling to any peak status. To despair at thinning hair, an expanding waistline, or the thought of irrelevance.

This is why it is such a grievous error to store your eggs of joy in this world's basket. There is an enormous hole in the bottom!

Whatever doesn't fall through immediately is fleeting at best. Heaven's joys, on the other hand, have no end. If this life is a dusty raisin, heaven is the juiciest grape.

C. S. Lewis said that heaven will work backward, turning even the worst of earth's sorrows into radiant reward. We will make up for lost time—nay, we will experience delight that is enhanced by lost time.

HEAVEN IS BEING WITH JESUS, AND YOU CAN DO THAT NOW.

When my family and I have been apart due to travel, the moment of reunion brings immense joy. The happiness I feel driving home from the airport, knowing I will see my children and hear their voices, blasts through the sadness of a temporary separation. FaceTime is a gift, but nothing compares to a family pile on the couch—to Lennox's laughs or Alivia's smiles, to the smell of Daisy or a story from Clover, to a kiss from my bride.

How often I have thought of Lenya in those moments. In our first hug in heaven, will we not feel the delightful impact of our reunion? Will it not overpower our season of separation and bring us the most serious happiness? I can only speculate, but I imagine the shock of her death, the agony of her funeral, and the coldness of decades apart will be overpaid in the tears of joy we will shed as we laugh until we hurt in the sunshine of that distant land.

There we will see each other as we actually are: glorious, holy, and made in God's image. We will glance up at the nail-scarred wrists of our Sovereign, who died to bring us to an unending life in His kingdom. What vacation, purchase, or social media following could—even multiplied a million times over—compare to one speck of the gratitude we will feel as we kneel before God's throne?

IMAGINE THERE IS A HEAVEN

Hear me: Heaven can't wait. Let it spread into your imagination now, even if you can only get limited glances from the top of this mountain. Make it a painting with sixty-seven million colors you frame, surround with lights, and place at the center of your attention. Otherwise, you will live as though this life were the pearl of great price instead of that which you must leverage to have a greater ownership of the Treasure that is Christ.

Heaven is being with Jesus, and you can do that now.

If you do not, you will look to lesser things, and you always will feel like an earthly peg trying to fit in a heavenly hole. Ever since we were banished from Eden and separated from God due to sin, we have not been home. With a sword drawn, an angel guarded the way back in and sent us out east; ever since, we have longed to get back to God's garden.

Abraham's nephew Lot was drawn to the well-watered plain near Sodom and Gomorrah. When he saw it, he called it "the garden of the Lord" (Genesis 13:10). Linguistically the narrative shifts and it is not the voice of the narrator but Lot's heart crying out this phrase. It's as though he was saying, *If I can have this, I will have peace.*

How did it turn out for Lot in Sodom and Gomorrah?

About as well as San Francisco did years ago, ironically not long after Teddy Roosevelt used Lot's same phrase, "the garden of the Lord," to describe it. As the ninth-biggest city in the United States in 1906, it seemed to be an oasis. Then an earthquake that, according to some estimates, was the equivalent of an 8.3 on the Richter scale (which hadn't been invented yet) ripped through the mostly wooden city in the early morning hours of April 18, resulting in an event more powerful than the nuclear bomb that decimated Hiroshima.

The equivalent of six million tons of TNT caused the earth's crust to slip by as much as twenty-one feet. A fire followed. The city's sprinkler systems and fire department were of no use, since the earthquake had snapped almost all water mains going into the city. The death toll rang in with a loss similar to September 11, 2001, as San Francisco burned to the ground. Thousands perished. In all, it was one of the most destructive natural disasters to take place in any North American city in history.

The "garden of the Lord" it was not.

When we proclaim that something other than heaven will do what only heaven can do, we set ourselves up for disaster.

DON'T KICK BEFORE THE HOME STRETCH

Many people conflate their view of retirement with heaven. If they look at retirement with lustful fancy (or with terror), they are forgetting about the true heaven.

Terror may stem from the loss or their status as a worker and producer; for these people, they will no longer have the opportunity to idolatrously draw their identity from their workplace achievements. Without a career to worship, they will wither and die.

The lustful fancy is part of seeing retirement as a carrot; they will do whatever they need to do to get it as early as possible. They may scheme to jump to retirement, sometimes following the acronym FIRE (financial independence, retire early). Achieve a million by thirty and have no responsibility as long as possible.

It can be a god of our age. And it can be a trap.

Yes, by all means, we ought to be good stewards and procure wisely so we might have a return on investment to pour into service of the King. But to view work as an enemy is to forget that, before the fall, before there was sin, there was work. Without it, things inside of us will be deficient. Just as retiring from a career that gave us identity will kill us, so will finding our identity in not having to work.

In his book *Twelve Rules for Life* Jordan Peterson wrote,

> A naively formulated goal transmutes, with time, into the sinister form of the life-lie. One forty-something client told me his vision, formulated by his younger self: "I see myself retired, sitting on a tropical beach, drinking margaritas in the sunshine." That's not a plan. That's a travel poster. After eight margaritas, you're fit only to await the hangover. After three weeks of margarita-filled days, if you have any sense, you're bored stiff and self-disgusted. In a year, or less, you're pathetic.

I once read a news article about a thirty-three-year-old mom who made $760,000 a year in passive income from her blog. "We've saved enough to retire whenever we want," she said. "This has allowed me to live my ideal lifestyle: I work just ten hours a week and travel full-time on our sailboat. I am regularly out snorkeling, exploring, and hiking."

Living a travel poster will be terrific for a weekend, but for the back nine of our lives, it might just kill us.

Whether we believe retirement guarantees happiness or we refuse to quit until we drop dead, we are on a path of wasting our lives.

Instead, we need to find our purpose, identity, and worth in

Christ. Realize that He gave everything, *everything*, to buy this world—not because He wanted to buy the world, but because it would allow Him to get to you. Sell all you have to be found in Him. See nothing as "yours"; see it all as His. He is the Treasure, because He treasured you.

Whether you stay in a job is not the issue. In heaven God's servants will serve Him, so why wouldn't we get a jump start on that now, however that looks?

We can aim to be like Graham, whom I read about on CNBC. He retired early on passive cash flow and now is freed up to serve the King. He is using his money to live out his destiny of funding nonprofits and his church. He is currently giving 30 percent to kingdom work but is shooting to get to 50 percent.

Goals. If you no longer have to work a career, you will be freed to focus more on your calling.

Bottom line, whatever your situation, invest yourself in the life of heaven as much as you can.

ONE MOMENT AFTER YOU DIE

Remember when Paul got to go to heaven on a day pass? Afterward he said it was so insanely great that to dumb it down enough to put it into human language would be against the law.

Far better. That is perhaps the best description of heaven in Scripture.

Take the most epic sunrise. I saw a banger today. Heaven will outdo it.

Take the best meal. I can't wait for heavenly enchiladas because the earth's are pretty good—and the earth's are just the raisin.

Isn't it interesting that Paul didn't come back from heaven and say, "I just want to go to Rome and have the pasta. To ride a hot-air balloon in Napa. To go climb Mount Everest"?

Of course, Paul probably knew how to enjoy a good meal and take delight in the beauty of nature. He did write Romans 8, after all, so he knew that all creation proclaims God's praises. He also was aware that God gave us all things richly to enjoy—he wrote that verse to Timothy. And yet he also prized heaven over the earth, knowing the resurrection changed everything. Eternity is ours. We have all the time in the world to swim with sharks, hike the jungles, and explore the mountains of a renewed universe. All of it will be *far better* versions of anything we could include on an earthly bucket list.

We also will move around in bodies that don't get wounded, sick, or worn down. There will be no broken bones, diseases, or even exhaustion. I tripped getting out of my truck last night and have a cut on my shin that almost made me cuss. My dad has been sick with a stomach bug that has made him queasy for half a month. That will never happen when we get to the place we can only see from the mountain now.

While early retirement may not be a goal, it can be a motivation . . . only it's not the fire of a false finish line. Retire with financial independence so we can get to the good stuff. It's not FIRE for the sake of putting our feet up and living on a sailboat; it's the fire of knowing our works will be judged as gold, hay, silver, wood, straw, and precious stones.

When Christ's eyes look on my works in this life, I want Him to find them full of the worthy, not the worthless. On that day the worthy will be rewarded and the worthless will go up in smoke as it is judged by fire. I don't want the total of my life to be spring, summer, fall, and smoke. I want to have more than travel stickers and shoes. I want to have spent my life enjoying God's goodness, yes, but also to have poured it out for a worthy cause and receive an eternal reward. I want my life to be spring, summer, fall, and glory!

Nothing matters more.

So, we can kick the earthly bucket list.

Get our bearings and face our shadows.

Hear His voice calling us further up and further in as we look to Him for our significance.

Just as we rely on Jesus for salvation, we also rely on Him for our daily security, sense of direction, and deep, abiding peace. When we find ourselves feeling lost, slipping and falling down a mountain, we can cry out and He'll come to us. We don't have to wander on the mountain afraid.

THE BEAUTY IN THE NOSEDIVE

I started this book talking about spiraling in a scary, dangerous, out-of-control way. If your spiraling feels like that today, take heart. There is a key tucked inside your pain that can unlock whole new levels in your story through praise.

One of God's most glorious Easter eggs He hid in nature is a spiral. When I was in graphic design school, I learned about something called the Fibonacci sequence. It is a progression of numbers that is infinitely expandable and builds in a predictable way. If you add two consecutive numbers, the result always will be the number that follows in the series. For example,

1, 1, 2, 3, 5, 8, 13, 21, and so on.

This is because

1 + 1 = 2 and 1 + 2 = 3 and 2 + 3 = 5.

What's crazy about this series of numbers is that it provides the mathematic dimensions needed to make a perfect spiral. All you have to do is draw squares with sides that are Fibonacci numbers, and then connect the corners of these squares (see illustration below). It is mathematically and artistically perfect. These Fibonacci spirals are found in seashells, rams' horns, the arrangement of seeds of sunflowers, the scales of pinecones, the shells of snails, the winds of hurricanes, and the rings of galaxies.

The Fibonacci sequence also gives us the "golden ratio," which is 1.618, a number that shows up when you divide a Fibonacci number by the number before it. This golden ratio, or mean, is a division of space that the eye finds pleasing and satisfying without really knowing why. It can be found in the design of the Parthenon in Greece, the *Mona Lisa*, the pyramids of Giza, and Notre Dame.

Okay, interesting, you might say. *But what does all of this have to do with my real-life spiral?*

You'll see soon. Hold onto that Fibonacci spiral insight while we consider another spiral in nature that shows the devastating sign of sin's curse: the tornado.

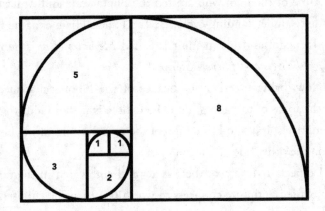

The twisting winds of a cyclone are one of the most powerful phenomena on earth. The terror of the twister is that it can upend your life and everything in it without any notice. You can feel blindsided by a spiral that seems to come out of nowhere and deprives you of what you thought life was supposed to be like.

Interestingly, a tornado is not a singular event. In a massive tornado, like an F5 that can spread out for miles, there are tornadoes within tornadoes. This explains why one house can be left standing next to another one that is demolished.

Even when a tornado passes by, not everyone faces the same level of hardship, even when it seems they are facing the same circumstance. You can endure virtually the same event but have a vastly different experience. If you sense you are spiraling on a different scale than the people to your left or right, don't take any meaning from it. It's always a mistake to compare pain.

Also, tornadoes don't get ranked until after they pass. It's not like you can look at the sky and declare, "That's an F3 if I ever saw one!" Experts determine a storm's size based on the devastation it wreaked after the fact.

The *F* in these tornado categories, by the way, stands for the last name of the man who created the Fujita scale and dedicated his life to understanding cyclones: Ted Fujita. His nickname was Mr. Tornado, and his memoir is called *Memoirs of an Effort to Unlock the Mystery of Severe Storms*.

Now, bring together the beauty of the Fibonacci sequence and the force of tornadoes. How incredible is it that God wove a redemptive spiral into His design of the universe, promising blessing on the other side of a storm?

I especially love that there is a spiral embedded in the ram's horn, which Scripture connects to worship. When the children of

Israel marched and shouted as the walls of Jericho fell, they also blasted a ram's horn. Spiral!

As Gideon's three hundred men rushed to destroy the Midianites with the power of the Lord and the sword of Gideon, the soundtrack was a blowing of the ram's horn. Spiral!

As the Lord descended on Mount Sinai to give the Ten Commandments, a sound of a trumpet signaled God's presence. Spiral!

According to the New Testament, when Christ returns, we will hear a trumpet ring out—of course we don't know which sort of trumpet it will be, but my money's on the ram's horn. Spiral!

And, finally, God's people used the ram's horn to declare the new year, the Day of Atonement, and the Year of Jubilee. Spiral!

Every end is a new beginning.

And for every wall you run into in life, there is a ram's horn of worship waiting to be blown. There is goodness to discover in it, just like the hidden numbers in the Fibonacci sequence. Around and around, closer and closer to the center. In time you'll see that God has a secret plan to turn each and every emotional tornado that comes your way into an instrument of praise.

After all, condemnation is not your master. *Christ is.*

Trauma is not your template. *God's truth is.*

Shame is not your story. *Salvation is.*

Panic is not your preoccupation. *Prayer is.*

And worry is not your warfare. *Worship is.*

You don't just have to spiral down into chaos; you can spiral your way up to breakthrough.

YOU DON'T JUST HAVE TO SPIRAL DOWN INTO CHAOS; YOU CAN SPIRAL YOUR WAY UP TO BREAKTHROUGH.

UNTIL NEXT TIME

New beginnings, new blessings, new mercies. This is what God offers you.

Your sin has been atoned for, paid in full. It is finished. Spiritual debts have been canceled, slaves have been set free, and the land the Enemy took has been restored.

You are a child of God.

From life's first cry to life's last breath, there is hope. You can look for a glimpse of coming glory, let it shape you, and then walk with Him, fighting to bless others in Jesus' name until you walk with Him in His country.

The *agape* love of God takes the desperation out of how we handle the other loves. Our *storge*, *eros*, and *phileo* loves mean more, not less, when we do not expect them to fulfill us.

Just as there are tornadoes within tornadoes, there is grace inside grace. So when you feel like you are in a free fall of chaos, remember there is art, beauty, and order within it. There's not just a blessing in your spiraling, there's a spiral in your blessing! Choose to see the spiral not simply in terms of how it feels but what you believe God is doing through it. He is Mr. Tornado. The spiral galaxies were His idea. He painted the spiral onto every shell on the seashore. And He. Loves. You.

I began this book on Valentine's Day—a day all about human love—and I am finishing it on Good Friday—the day of God's love. His divine love is the key to understanding what is earthly and the key to our earthly loves lasting forever.

If we are in Christ, dear reader, no matter how long our separation, we never have to say goodbye. Not even death can cause us to say farewell. If the story Jesus is writing is true, then I don't have to say farewell to you as I end this book. I can say to you what I have said to my wife and children many times: "Should we get separated, let's meet up in heaven, and the way to get there is simple. Jesus."

So no, it's not goodbye.

It's "Until next time."

AFTERWORD
Wow, Wow, Wow

I WROTE THE first fifty-thousand-word draft of *Blessed Are the Spiraling*, originally titled *The Surprising Delight of a Midlife Crisis*, in February and March of 2023. I began on Valentine's Day and finished on Good Friday, working throughout the season of Lent. During Holy Week, as I was in the final push to complete the manuscript, I spoke with my dad daily like we always did. He complained of a stomachache that grew worse as time went on. This made it into one of the chapters as an illustration of the aches and pains of life.

When the abdominal cramps became unbearable on Good

Friday, he was admitted to the hospital for testing and pain management.

It became clear that it wasn't a stomach bug.

The following Tuesday, he learned that it was an incurable cancer. Pancreatic.

So he drove to a scenic spot, parked his car, and, as he watched the sun set over the city skyline, he called each of his five children in birth order to tell them the devastating news.

Smack.

The next year was full of adrenaline, prayer, tears, and flights across the country to sit with him for chemo treatments and support him through a dangerous surgery meant to prolong his life.

I can see now that, for me, it was another massive growth season, much like puberty. Another chaotic stage of development that felt like hitting a wall (though it was truly a stairstep), this one a baptism by fire. I was working on a book about the shifting seasons of life, and now they were shifting on me big time.

Spiraling? Yes.

Blessed? Not on the surface. But it was in there.

Everything I had written about mountains was now there for me to live out as I slipped and slid and tried to find my way on this one.

You are never ready to not have a father. My dad, the picture of strength and best man at my wedding, dissolved before my very eyes. Yet he modeled true masculinity, faith, and selflessness the entire way.

"I am closer to God than ever, Levi. I'm not scared to die," he assured me. His biggest complaint throughout the initial stage of diagnosis was canceling a mission trip to Uganda.

But there were many low moments.

The chemo sickness was awful. It was disorienting to see him crawling around in such pain that, through his moans, he kept repeating, "I don't know what to do." Then, as I cradled him in my arms, he profusely apologized for inconveniencing me with his suffering.

Another time, he texted me at one a.m.: "I am going to miss you so much."

Gutted.

But there were sweet moments too. At Christmas all of his kids and grandkids gathered, and he led us in Communion. He put his hands on each grandkid's head and blessed them in Jesus' name.

We took a special fishing trip.

Had long hard talks.

Cried bitter tears.

And some tears of laughter.

There were apologies made.

There was gratitude expressed.

Ups and downs followed on the roller coaster that is cancer.

As the new year approached, I invited him to come with us to Passion 2024, a gathering of college students in Atlanta, Georgia, in Mercedes-Benz Stadium. He came, even while fighting through the chemo sickness, even if he did have to curl up in his seat for much of it. When a spontaneous rendition of "Agnus Dei" broke out in the arena, he summoned his strength to stand, raise his hands, and join the song of heaven with glorious abandon. The image of him in that moment stamped into my mind and would return to me as my brothers and I later carried his casket to the grave.

He was in that room when it happened.

He is now in *the* room where it's happening.

All through that next year, I continued to research and refine this book project, which had taken on new meaning as I went through the ordeal with my father.

As the Lent season of 2024 approached, we were lulled into a false hope that we had more time with him remaining than we did.

The surgery appeared to be successful, and it seemed that on the right protocol of chemo, he could live two or three more years. The doctors gave us a promising outlook.

A week before Easter I was traveling for a speaking engagement, so I stopped in to visit him. I was there for only a few days, but the next Tuesday we had plans to be together at a family reunion in Scottsdale, Arizona. Beyond that, we were charting out how we'd do a Father's Day interview together for our church and a trip to fish for bull trout in the Bob Marshall Wilderness. We'd go to my oldest daughter's state tennis tournament and high school graduation. Defiant hope. Lots of life to live!

I took him to buy birdseed for his feeders in his backyard. He'd been craving clam chowder, so we swung by Whole Foods to pick some up. Later we sat in his backyard together; he grabbed his Bible, and we spent time together before I flew out. The last night I was there, I tucked him into his bed in the living room, then came back to find him with his finger resting above the pause button on his phone; he was listening to a Bible study by Pastor Chuck Smith to comfort himself.

Those hands had held mine.

Had handed me a Bible.

Had folded to pray for me.

Those strong hands.

He took a turn a few hours after I flew out.

The stomach pain had returned with a vengeance, and he was checked back into the hospital on Wednesday.

I spoke to him on Maundy Thursday.

"Do you want me to come down?" I asked.

"No need now," he replied.

We talked about his excitement for church on Easter. "I'll be out of the hospital by then," he promised. "Wild horses couldn't keep me from the sunrise service."

On Good Friday we all received a catastrophic curveball.

It happened while I was on speakerphone with Dad, my siblings either in the room with him or on the phone as well. I was leaning on our foosball table after printing out my preaching notes when I heard a doctor from Dad's end of the line say, "Sir, can you hear me? The oncology team has agreed there is nothing more we can do. We are nearing the end of your life, sir. Your body is shutting down. All we can do is focus on comfort."

His undoing resulted from pausing chemo, a requirement while he recovered from surgery that repaired a hip replacement. It'd been malfunctioning due to all the weight he'd lost. (Three or four times he had experienced the agony of his hip coming out of joint and having to have it violently shoved back in.) The chemo break proved to be all the cancer needed to viciously regain control of what remained of his pancreas, as well as his stomach, liver, and lungs—all without our knowing, all within a matter of weeks.

I handed Jennie the notes. "You have to preach tonight," I managed, then got on the next plane.

I wept the whole way there. My dad was dying.

I vowed I wouldn't leave his side until he was in heaven or better and no longer in bed.

The next few days were a traumatic, frantic, Holy Spirit–drenched disaster.

By Easter Sunday, Jennie and the kids joined me and my family at my dad's side in the hospital. We watched his church's service online with him; the wild horses had prevailed and he didn't get to attend. But in a touching tribute, they dedicated the service to him. He passed in and out of consciousness as it streamed in the room.

Then his caregivers loaded him into an ambulance, and we formed a caravan bound for his home. Alivia drove his Mustang convertible behind the ambulance, and the rest of us followed in an honor guard, listening to his favorite music and wiping away tears on the long road home.

With every hour that went by, it seemed another year passed onto his body, like more vitality kept falling away from him. We pushed the pump to control his morphine when he couldn't reach for it, and we wet his cracked lips with a sponge on a stick. We cried while he groaned and begged God for a miracle.

We thanked him and held him.

Sobbed onto his shoulder and worshiped around him.

Slept at the floor of his hospital bed like sentries.

Death rattled in his lungs, but so did life. Jesus was calling him home.

Raising his hands, curling and uncurling his fingers, trying to sit up, forming words that wouldn't come. Twice he ripped the tubes out of his arm and nose and tried to run. I don't blame him; I wanted to run away with him. Far from that bed and those tubes and that gurgling, awful sentence of death.

"Why don't you give him water?" we asked the hospice worker.

"We find it just prolongs things" was the answer.

Smack. Jesus help me.

My dad died at twelve thirty a.m. on Tuesday, April 2, 2024, the day we were supposed to meet up at the family reunion in Scottsdale.

Strong hands now held his.

Hands that created the cosmos.

Hands that carried the cross.

Those strong hands.

I was sleeping beside him when it happened, just six inches away when his soul left his body, bound for the distant shores of heaven. I slept through it.

My brother woke the rest of the siblings up, convinced Dad had died.

"No, he didn't. He's right here," I insisted.

"I heard him stop breathing. He just died," he repeated.

Once while I was hiking up a snowy mountain in the dark, my headlamp died, and panic clawed at my mind as I fought to stay calm. Then I remembered there was a little flashlight built into my watch. I flipped it on and used it to see the terrain and get to safety. The night my dad died, we were in a pitch-black room, and I used that same watch flashlight to discover that my brother was right. Only this time the small light's glow caused my heart to sink. I knew instantly he was not there.

All of a sudden, I was in the dark on a cold mountain.

I began slipping, sliding, and spiraling in the dark of this new, unfamiliar terrain. And yet there was a holiness to the moment, as I knew he was with Jesus and with our little girl, far from pain. He had gone home.

It was one year to the day from when he had called us to tell us the news of his diagnosis. Between the two mountains of those

Easter weekends, a book now called *Blessed Are the Spiraling* and the end of my dad's life collided.

We held his service as an eclipse not to be seen again for twenty-plus years in North America took place. A totality. Though the following weeks and months were dark, painful, and full of grief, there was blessing, strength, and the presence of God in it.

I was not ready to not have a dad. Again, one never is.

But God was with me.

My counselor helped me put my grief into bins:

What I had lost: Daily phone calls; his presence at major family events. (Grieve it.)

What I hadn't lost: The lessons and memories. (Cherish it.)

What I couldn't lose: His presence in heaven in my future. (Look forward to it.)

Through hard work and the loving support of my family and community, the glory of God eclipsed the sorrow. It didn't go away, but it was covered with His goodness. Totality.

I found new resolve to continue to refine this message that I was living without the protective shade of my father as a branch above me in my family tree. I long to be the man who my dad prayed for me to be. And I know that, in his going to heaven, he has helped me move up the spiral staircase in that direction, just as he did in life.

I can see now that just as he had taught me to live a glorious life—how to catch a fish, love black coffee, and pray before going on a date—he was, in this final season, teaching me how to die a glorious death.

I leave you with his last lucid, intentional words, which he repeated multiple times over the final few days he still had power of speech.

"Wow. Wow. Wow."

A tornado of wildflowers indeed.

ACKNOWLEDGMENTS

I AM INDEBTED to many people for the book you presently hold in your hands. Over the course of the two years it took to bring it to life, there was a relay race of encouragement and contribution I would like to express my appreciation for.

Alivia, Daisy, Clover and Lennox: Thank you for the daily kindness and extraordinary generosity in cheering me on every time I clocked in to write and emerged having slain the dragon of that day's word count, edits, or revisions. I don't deserve such lavish support. I love you so much. Thank you for humoring me when I gushed about a connection I made, or new insight that came to me. I will never forget our shared excitement when watching *Cars 3* and discovering Lightning McQueen's arc.

Jennie, thank you for bearing with me through all of life's crises (thus far). You have my heart and I adore you. Let's keep spiraling together.

Thank you, Mom, for generously allowing me to share my perspective on the events that shaped my younger self with respect to the difficult seasons of life in our home during the 1990s. I found our conversations about the connections I made in therapy to be healing, and I am so thankful to continue to see our relationship grow as we both do hard work to be the best versions of ourselves. I love you and I'll never give up on you!

I am grateful for my long time agent and friend, Austin Wilson. It took a hot minute to land the plane, but you were steady all throughout, and I am eternally grateful.

Damon Reiss, thank you for the partnership that I am so proud to see continue. I trust and respect you and am so glad this book is with W.

Carrie Marrs, I love working with you on words. You are an editor par excellence, a worthy sparring partner, and there is zero percent chance this book would be what it is without you. For starters, it would have a much worse title. You are brilliant, kind, and a joy to work alongside.

Debbie Wickwire—I am so glad I get to type that! I loved getting the band back together on this one. Your comments, notes, suggestions, and vulnerability on the first pass brought such nostalgic import and brilliant editorial insight to the journey. Additionally, you were so generous with your vulnerability. Thank you for letting me know how the content hit you where you are in your season of life.

To Rachel and Eva, thank you for your contribution to this project on the sprint to the editorial finish! Even the dark saga with "her who shall not be named" ended up for good, as it prompted a few edits I wouldn't have come to on my own without the spiraling I did on the way to the end zone.

I am indebted to Katelyn Deitz for deciding to work on *Blessed Are the Spiraling* after all. Thank you for your dedication and hard work on this, and all the things! Elisha Gregory, thank you for always coming bearing gifts, for your steady leadership, and for hitting the cover *out. of. the. park*—without even realizing what you had done. It took my breath away the moment I saw the tornado of wildflowers. Your art helped the book become what it is. A picture might be worth a thousand words, but in this case, that's an understatement. Thank you, Kevin Guido, for bringing Elisha's masterpiece to life.

Ollie and Claire, thank you for letting me see this book through your eyes, and for your valuable insight on how this book landed with you.

Thank you to Micki Martin, who ran point in our office when I began writing this book. Another thank-you to Jeremy Jackson, who took the baton and ran with it—here's to spinning in chaos! You make it look good. You and your family are a gift to the Luskos. Thank you, Em, for your work in our home throughout this process.

Thank you to the rest of the Creative and Lead teams, the entire Fresh Life Staff and church, and online Fresh Life family, and to the Lusketeers . . . thank you for your prayers, partnership, support, and encouragement.

Thank you to all my friends who were, and are, in the weeds of my life in the midst of my spiraling in such tender and beautiful ways—you know who you are. Muchas Gracias.

On the heavenly side, Dad, I am so grateful I got to tell you all about the book and that you knew it was going to be dedicated to you. I can't wait for the first cup of coffee together in heaven. Lenya, I miss you always.

Thank you most of all to Jesus for bringing beauty out of every nosedive. You are the true Treasure.

And to you, the reader, for trusting me with your time and allowing me to share my words with you. Thank you.

NOTES

Introduction

xiv **That is the essence:** Matthew 5:1–12.

xiv **And as Warren Buffett:** Warren Buffett, chairman's letter to shareholders, February 28, 2002, in *Berkshire Hathaway Inc. 2001 Annual Report* (Berkshire Hathaway, 2002), 10, https://www.berkshirehathaway .com/2001ar/2001ar.pdf.

xvi **It was C.S. Lewis:** C. S. Lewis, *The Four Loves* (Harcourt Brace, 1960).

Chapter 1: Going Up

4 **I wasn't just scared:** 2 Corinthians 4:16.

5 **Poet William Butler Yeats:** W. B. Yeats, cited in Christopher de Vinck *Only the Heart Knows How to Find Them: Precious Memories for a Faithless Time* (Viking, 1991), 21. The spiral or "gyre" concept, as Yeats called it, first appeared in W. B. Yeats, *A Vision: The Revised 1937 Edition*, ed. Margaret Mills Harper and Catherine E. Paul (Scribner, 1937).

6 **But what that means:** Harv Powers, *Reemptive Leadership: Unleashing Your Greatest Influence* (Illumify Media Global, 2018).

7 **Studies show:** Arthur Brooks, *From Strength to Strength* (Bloomsbury Publishing, 2022), 192.

7 **Author Bruce Feiler:** Bruce Feiler, "Lifequakes," chap. 3 in *Life Is in the Transitions: Mastering Change at Any Age* (Penguin, 2020).

9 **Zacharias had:** Luke 1:5–23, paraphrased.

11 **Living a glorious life:** Matthew 16:24.

13 **Strive to win:** 1 Corinthians 9:25.

13 **According to Jesus:** Matthew 11:11.

Chapter 2: From Death to Resurrection

18 **Not just for José:** "From Farmworker to NASA Astronaut with José Hernandez," *Hey! It's the Luskos,* YouTube, March 20, 2024, https://www.youtube.com/watch?v=jt72UjxotCg; José M. Hernández, *Reaching for the Stars: The Inspiring Story of a Migrant Farmworker Turned Astronaut* (Center Street, 2012).

18 **I want you to:** Timothy Keller, "American Christianity Is Due for a Revival," *Atlantic,* February 5, 2023, https://www.theatlantic.com/ideas/archive/2023/02/christianity-secularization-america-renewal-modernity/672948/#.

19 **As novelist:** G. Michael Hopf, *Those Who Remain: A Postapocalyptic Novel* (CreateSpace Independent Publishing, 2016), Kindle. See also "Hard Times . . . ," on G. Michael Hopf's official website, accessed September 12, 2024, https://www.gmichaelhopf.com/hard-times.

23 **It spreads over:** "Pando—(I Spread)," Fishlake National Forest, Forest Service, accessed November 25, 2024, https://www.fs.usda.gov/detail/fishlake/home/?cid=STELPRDB5393641#:~:text=Pando%20is%20an%20aspen%20clone,of%20over%2040%2C000%20individual%20trees.

Chapter 3: Don't Blow It

31 **You should:** 1 Corinthians 9:24–26.

32 **If you start:** Dean Keith Simonton, "Creative Productivity Cap Through the Adult Years," *Generations: Journal of the American Society on Aging* 15, no. 2 (1991): 13–16, http://www.jstor.org/stable/44877717.

32 **Thereafter the likelihood:** Benjamin Jones, "Age and Great Invention," Review of Economics and Statistics 92, no. 1 (2010): 1–14, https://www.doi.org/10.2139/ssrn.608701.

32 **Simonton found:** Dean Keith Simonton, "Age and Outstanding Achievement: What Do We Know after a Century of Research?,"

Psychological Bulletin 104, no. 2 (October 1988): 251–267, https://doi.org /10.1037/0033–2909.104.2.251.

33 **Many tech entrepreneurs:** Arthur C. Brooks, "Your Professional Decline Is Coming (Much) Sooner Than You Think," *Atlantic*, July 2019, https://www.theatlantic.com/magazine/archive/2019/07/work-peak -professional-decline/590650/.

33 **Harvard Business Review reported:** Walter Frick, "How Old Are Silicon Valley's Top Founders? Here's the Data," *Harvard Business Review*, April 3, 2014, https://hbr.org/2014/04/how-old-are-silicon-valleys-top -founders-heres-the-data.

33 **Sylvester Stallone once said:** Sylvester Stallone, *Sly*, directed by Thom Zimny (Netflix, 2023).

33 **According to researchers:** "New LinkedIn Research Shows 75 Percent of 25–33 Year Olds Have Experienced Quarter-Life Crisis," Censuswide online survey conducted for LinkedIn, October 31–November 3, 2017, LinkedIn Pressroom, November 15, 2017, https://news.linkedin.com/2017 /11/new-linkedin-research-shows-75-percent-of-25–33-year-olds-have-e.

33 **One in four Americans:** Elaine Wethington, "Expecting Stress: Americans and the 'Midlife Crisis,'" *Motivation and Emotion* 24 (2000): 85–103, https://doi.org/10.1023/A:1005611230993.

33 **One in three people:** Oliver Robinson and Alexander J. Stell, "Later-Life Crisis: Towards a Holistic Model," *Journal of Adult Development* 22, no. 1 (2015): 38–49, https://doi.org/10.1007/s10804–014–9199–5.

33 **One study even reported:** Wethington, "Expecting Stress."

37 **According to:** Psalm 139:16.

37 **There was a man:** Matthew 13, paraphrased.

39 **To put it bluntly:** C. S. Lewis, "The Inner Ring," in *The Weight of Glory* (HarperCollins, 2001), 141–57.

40 **In an interview:** Hans Zimmer, interview by Leslie Stahl, *60 Minutes*, January 8, 2023. For transcript, see Leslie Stahl, "Hans Zimmer: 40 Years of Music for Movies," CBS News, January 8, 2023, https://www.cbsnews .com/news/hans-zimmer-60-minutes-2023–01–08/.

41 **Herod received:** Acts 12:21–23.

Chapter 4: Put Your Hands on What Is Yours

46 **Ask the man who:** Luke 18:18–23.

48 **A 2024 survey:** Rachel Lustbader, "2024 Wills and Estate Planning Study," survey conducted December 3–4, 2023, Caring.com, updated July 30, 2024, https://www.caring.com/caregivers/estate-planning /wills-survey/.

50 **Philip James Bailey said:** Philip James Bailey, *Festus*, 4th ed.
    (Benjamin B. Mussey, 1847), 80.

51 **Regarding time:** Stephen R. Covey, *The 7 Habits of Highly Effective
    Families: Building a Beautiful Family Culture in a Turbulent World*
    (Golden Books, 1997).

52 **At age four:** White House Historical Association, "William J.
    Clinton," The White House, accessed September 17, 2024, https://
    www.whitehouse.gov/about-the-white-house/presidents/william-j-clinton/;
    Britannica, "Bill Clinton," updated December 15, 2024, https://
    www.britannica.com/biography/Bill-Clinton.

52 **He then turned:** Jason Vest, "Bill Clinton's Handshake with History,"
    Washington Post, July 25, 1993, https://www.washingtonpost.com/archive
    /lifestyle/1993/07/26/bill-clintons-handshake-with-history/895dcfeb-8aa9
    –49bc-ab56-dcccb5a832a9/.

53 **And when he had:** Matthew 8:23–25.

54 **When the storm came:** Matthew 7:24–27.

55 **Many children:** Jordan B. Peterson, *12 Rules for Life: An Antidote to
    Chaos* (Random House of Canada, 2018), 296–97, Kindle.

56 **Mark Twain called:** Mark Twain, *The Innocents Abroad* (1869; repr.,
    Bod Third Party Titles, 2020), 555.

58 **Studies show:** Anne Fishel, "FAQ," FamilyDinnerProject.org,
    accessed September 13, 2024, https://thefamilydinnerproject.org
    /resources/faq/; Sharon M. Fruh et al., "The Surprising Benefits of the
    Family Meal," *Journal for Nurse Practitioners* 7, no. 1 (2011): 18–22, https://
    doi.org/10.1016/j.nurpra.2010.04.017.

58 **Many homes:** Tim Chester, *A Meal with Jesus* (Crossway, 2011), 46,
    Kindle.

Chapter 5: I Replaced My Mom with Pornography

65 **C.S. Lewis once postulated:** C. S. Lewis, *The Four Loves* (Harcourt
    Brace, 1960), 121.

69 **Sometimes he will:** 1 John 2:16.

70 **Also if all:** Matthew 22:37.

71 **This kind of healing:** John C. Maxwell, "The Law of Process," chap. 3
    in *The 21 Irrefutable Laws of Leadership: Follow Them and People Will
    Follow You*, 10th anniversary ed. (HarperCollins Leadership, 2007).

Chapter 6: On Taming Your Shadow

75 **After striving:** Thomas Cahill, *Desire of the Everlasting Hills: The
    World Before and After Jesus* (Anchor Books, 1999), 18–27, 60–61.

75 **Alexander is reported:** Alexander the Great, quoted in Plutarch, *Plutarch's Moralia: Twenty Essays*, trans. Philemon Holland (E. P. Dutton, 1911), 158–59.

76 **You say rightly:** John 18:36–37, paraphrased.

77 **Alexander shot back:** Cahill, *Desire of the Everlasting Hills*, 17.

78 **His shadow:** Philip Freeman, *Alexander the Great* (Simon & Schuster, 2011), 22–24, paraphrased by author.

80 **Ronald Rolheiser has said:** Ronald Rolheiser, *Sacred Fire: A Vision for a Deeper Human and Christian Maturity*, 15th anniversary ed. (Image, 2014), 4.

80 **In his book:** Ronald Rolheiser, *The Holy Longing: The Search for a Christian Spirituality*, 15th anniversary ed. (Image, 2014).

81 **The older brother:** Luke 15:11–32.

81 **Success still:** Rolheiser, *Sacred Fire*, 8.

83 **This scene:** Luke 10:38–42.

84 **When Lazarus:** John 11.

86 **To paraphrase:** C. S. Lewis, "Letter 8" in *The Screwtape Letters* (HarperOne, 2001), 40. Paraphrase by author of "Do not be deceived, Wormwood. Our cause is never more in danger than when a human, no longer desiring, but still intending, to do our Enemy's will, looks round upon a universe from which every trace of Him seems to have vanished, and asks why he has been forsaken, and still obeys."

88 **He was addicted:** Judges 13–15.

89 **That's what Paul meant:** Romans 13:14, paraphrased.

90 **But without God's power:** Romans 7:15–20, paraphrased.

90 **You will:** Isaiah 40:31, paraphrased.

Chapter 7: Monuments Versus Moments

94 **He appeared:** 1 Samuel 10:22.

94 **When the prophet:** 1 Samuel 15:17, paraphrased.

94 **As the late:** Adrian Rogers, *The Incredible Power of Kingdom Authority: Getting an Upper Hand on the Underworld* (B&H, 2002), 66.

95 **We see:** Isaiah 14:12.

95 **So he dug:** 1 Samuel 13–15, paraphrased.

96 **Rather the question:** Henri J. M. Nouwen, *Life of the Beloved: Spiritual Living in a Secular World*, 10th anniversary ed. (Crossroad, 1992), 92–93, paraphrased in Ronald Rolheiser, *Sacred Fire: A Vision for a Deeper Human and Christian Maturity* (Image, 2014), 19.

96 **He was saying:** Inigo Montoya, *The Princess Bride*, directed by Rob Reiner (Act III Communications, 1987).

96 **God told him:** 1 Samuel 13–15, paraphrased.

97 **His technical cause:** 1 Samuel 31; 2 Samuel 1.

98 **Ronald Reagan kept:** *Welcome to the White House*, Ronald Reagan Presidential Library Digital Library Collections, 12, accessed September 14, 2024, https://www.reaganlibrary.gov/public/2021–12 /40–108–7564766–061–031–2021.pdf?VersionId=RklslsiTpf _KU0hcf3DiFmULrtpDX0Zu.

98 **If people don't believe:** Chris Williamson, host, *Modern Wisdom*, podcast, episode 691, "Jimmy Carr: The Secret Hacks for Living a Fulfilled Life," Chris Williamson, October 9, 2023, https://podscripts.co/podcasts /modern-wisdom/691-jimmy-carr-the-secret-hacks-for-living-a-fulfilled-life.

99 **Jesus said that whoever:** Mark 8:35.

99 **Early in:** 1 Samuel 31:11–13; 1 Samuel 11.

100 **Jesus said if:** Matthew 6:23, paraphrased.

101 **It's like trying:** Matthew 17:4.

102 **Remember:** Luke 9:23.

103 **And Samuel tried:** 1 Samuel 6:7, paraphrased.

Chapter 8: Become Yoda

111 **It's a universal:** Joseph Campbell, *The Hero with a Thousand Faces*, 3rd ed. (Pantheon, 1949; New World Library, 2008).

112 **Star Wars is:** Ken Miyamoto, "The Hero's Journey to Breakdown: 'Star Wars,'" The Script Lab, October 11, 2019, https://thescriptlab .com/features/screenwriting-101/12309-the-heros-journey-breakdown -star-wars/.

113 **Truly Wonderful:** *Star Wars: Episode II—Attack of the Clones*, written by George Lucas and Jonathan Hale, directed by George Lucas (LucasFilm, 2002).

113 **The pneuma wind:** The Greek word for "spirit," "breath," and "wind" is *pneuma*. Similarly, the Hebrew word *rûaḥ* can also be translated "breath," "wind," and "spirit," as in Ezekiel 37, where it is used in all three senses. In his commentary on Ezekiel, John Taylor stated, "Part of the artistry of this chapter is the skilful use of the Hebrew word *rûaḥ*. This appears in three different translations: as *Spirit* in verses 1 and 14, as *breath* in verses 5, 6, 8, 9 and 10, and as *wind* or *winds* in verse 9. But in reality it is the same word every time, and no English translation can do justice to its variety of meaning. The Greek word, *pneuma*, shares the flexibility of the Hebrew, and LXX was able to use it consistently in this passage. It is the same word that lies behind the double meaning of wind and Spirit in John 3:8. At its root *rûaḥ* denotes the sense of 'air in motion', i.e. wind or breath. This can extend from a gentle breeze to a stormy wind, or from a breath that

is breathed to a raging passion. It comes to mean both man's spirit, or disposition, and also emotional qualities like vigour, courage, impatience and ecstasy. It covers not only man's vital breath, given to him at birth and leaving his body in his dying gasp, but also the Spirit of God who imparts that breath. Such is the rich variety of the word used here by Ezekiel" (John B. Taylor, *Ezekiel: An Introduction and Commentary*, Tyndale Old Testament Commentaries, ed. Donald J. Wiseman, vol. 22 (InterVarsity, 1969), 230–31.

114 **As Eugene Peterson:** Eugene H. Peterson, *First and Second Samuel*, Westminster Bible Companion (Westminster John Knox Press, 1999), 99.

115 **G. K. Chesterton wrote:** G. K. Chesterton, *Orthodoxy* (Ignatius Press, 2011), 66.

116 **Now that:** C. S. Lewis, *Of Other Worlds: Essays and Stories*, ed. Walter Hooper (Harvest, 1966), 25.

117 **As I have:** Matthew 6:19–21.

120 **George Santayana said:** George Santayana, *The Life of Reason, or, The Phases of Human Progress*, ed. Marianne S. Wokeck and Martin A. Coleman, vol. 1, *Introduction and Reason in Common Sense* (MIT Press, 2011), 172.

121 **George Bernard Shaw encapsulated:** George Bernard Shaw, quoted in Bob Buford, *Halftime: Changing Your Game Plan from Success to Significance* (Zondervan, 1994), 59.

121 **This is what:** John C. Maxwell, *The 21 Irrefutable Laws of Leadership: The Law of Explosive Growth* (Thomas Nelson, 2007).

123 **She sorts out:** Liz Wiseman, "The Multiplier Effect," chap. 1 in *Multipliers: How the Best Leaders Make Everyone Smarter* (New York: HarperCollins, 2010), Kindle.

124 **Eighty people can:** CEO, quoted in Wiseman, *Multipliers*, Kindle, loc. 369.

124 **All these years:** Joe Rogan, host, *Joe Rogan Experience*, episode 1620, "Nate Bargatze," produced by Jamie Vernon, March 16, 2021, https://youtu.be/3LcLIVDVyso?si=o365gQlr_wvWzyx-.

Chapter 9: What a Friend I've Found

125 **The thief comes:** John 10:10, paraphrased.

128 **This is why:** 2 Kings 3:15.

129 **So when:** Tim Kight, "Chronos vs. Kairos," A Call to Excellence, February 27, 2023, https://www.acalltoexcellence.com/chronos-vs-kairos/.

134 **The pilot expected:** Marcel Schwantes, "Warren Buffett's Brilliant 25/5 Rule Was Fake. Here's What he Really Said About Achieving Success,"

Inc., March 13, 2020, https://www.inc.com/marcel-schwantes/warren
-buffetts-brilliant-25/5-rule-was-fake-heres-what-he-really-said-about
-achieving-success.html.

134 **Augustine was right:** St. Augustine, *The Confessions*, trans. Henry
Chadwick (OUP Oxford, 2008).

Chapter 10: Leave No Claw Marks

140 **Ultimately he decided:** Philippians 1:23.

141 **Some say it:** Acts 14.

141 **Then he got up:** Acts 14:19.

142 **Paul chided:** 2 Thessalonians 3:6–12.

145 **The American told:** Erin Loechner, *Chasing Slow: Courage to Journey off
the Beaten Path* (Zondervan, 2016), 195–96. Based on a modernized
translation of a story often attributed to Heinrich Böll.

145 **What does it:** Matthew 16:26, paraphrased.

148 **It was rumored:** "How Did Elizabeth I Die?," Royal Museums
Greenwich, accessed September 16, 2024, https://www.rmg.co.uk/stories
/topics/little-known-or-unknown-facts-regarding-queen-elizabeth-death.

149 **Did you know:** Luke 16:9.

150 **The more he gave:** Paul Lee Tan, *Encyclopedia of 7,700 Illustrations: Signs
of the Times* (Bible Communications, 1996), 475.

150 **Consider this:** Derek Carr, quoted in Tim Ellsworth, "Raiders' Carr
Says Tithing Tops Priority List," Baptist Press, June 26, 2017, https://
www.baptistpress.com/resource-library/news/raiders-carr-says-tithing
-tops-priority-list/.

150 **John Rockefeller who:** John D. Rockefeller, quoted in Mark DeMoss,
The Little Red Book of Wisdom, rev. ed. (Thomas Nelson, 2011), 112.

151 **I've heard it:** Based on ideas in Richard Rohr, "The Two Halves of Life,"
chap. 1 in *Falling Upward: A Spirituality for the Two Halves of Life*
(Jossey-Bass, 2011).

152 **Augustine said that:** Saint Augustine, cited in Bob Buford, *Halftime:
Changing Your Game Plan from Success to Significance* (Zondervan, 1994), 18.

Chapter 11: Create Open Space

155 **It's been said that:** Gary Brecka (@garybrecka), "Aging is the aggressive
pursuit of comfort" a quote everybody should live by," TikTok,
accessed September 17, 2024, https://www.tiktok.com/@garybrecka/video
/7264731632660253994?lang=en.

155 **The largest soda:** Damon Zheng, "How Many Ounces in McDonald's
Large Cup: Compare Size 30 Oz.," Get Bio Pak, September 12, 2024,

https://getbiopak.com/how-many-ounces-in-mcdonalds-large-cup-compare
-size-30-oz/?srsltid=AfmBOorpugptXQ90JMbKcdNMIBQE6btwpqZFlr
NVOqwm8qC5I_zV7loT.

156 **When he bragged:** Matthew McConaughey, *Greenlights* (Crown Publishing, 2020), 133.

156 **In one of his:** Matthew 13.

158 **The average person:** Jena E. Pincott, "Wicked Thoughts," *Psychology Today*, September 1, 2015, https://www.psychologytoday.com/us/articles/201509/wicked-thoughts.

158 **Theologian and philosopher Søren:** Søren Kierkegaard, *For Self-Examination: Judge for Yourself!* trans. and ed. Howard V. Hong and Edna H. Hong (Princeton University Press, 1990), 47.

158 **In a lifetime:** Marshall Goldsmith, *Triggers* (Crown, 2015), 21.

158 **We form:** Based on concepts presented in James K. A. Smith, *Desiring the Kingdom: Worship, Worldview, and Cultural Formation*, Cultural Liturgies 1 (Baker Academic, 2009), 52–55, 80.

159 **That's why Solomon:** Ecclesiastes 1:14.

160 **After his dreams:** "Tim Ferris, host, *The Tim Ferris Show*, podcast, episode 647, "Mark Manson—The Path to 'The Subtle Art of Not Giving a F*ck,' the Ups (and Downs) of Success, the Craft of Writing, Personal Reinvention, How to Build a Lean Team, Protecting Boundaries, Decompressing with Fiction, and More," Spotify, 8:30, December 30, 2022, https://open.spotify.com/episode/06TzbZL1klcYGIObWfQxU5?si=d7VWFCGYQcOidID7pAHw5Q.

160 **Celebrated author Seth Godin:** Carey Nieuwhof, host, *The Carey Nieuwhof Leadership Podcast*, podcast, episode 576, "Seth Godin on His First Job at Age 14, The Best Question to Ask, Artificial Intelligence and the Future of Work, and How to Get Your Team Motivated, Enrolled, and Engaged," The Art of Leadership Network, June 12, 2023, https://careynieuwhof.com/episode576/.

161 **The problem with:** Katy Waldman, "The Rise of Therapy-Speak," *New Yorker*, March 26, 2021, https://www.newyorker.com/culture/cultural-comment/the-rise-of-therapy-speak.

161 **But as Charles Spurgeon:** Charles. H. Spurgeon, "Anywhere for Jesus," in Charles H. Spurgeon, ed., *The Sword and the Trowel* 10, no. 233 (May 1884): 206.

162 **In fact almost all:** Richard G. Tedeschi, "Growth After Trauma," *Harvard Business Review*, July/August 2020, https://hbr.org/2020/07/growth-after-trauma.

162 **Cancer survivors tend:** Mayara Goulart de Camargos et al., "An Explorative Analysis of the Differences in Levels of Happiness Between

Cancer Patients, Informal Caregivers and the General Population," *BMC Palliative Care* 19, no. 106 (2020), https://doi.org/10.1186/s12904-020-00594-1.

162 **Contrast all:** Mark Abadi et al., "20 Lottery Winners Who Lost It All—as a $925 Million Powerball Jackpot Is Still Up for Grabs," Business Insider, March 30, 2024, https://www.businessinsider.com/lottery-winners-lost-everything-2017-8.

162 **Professional athletes are:** Tim Parker, "Why Athletes Go Broke—and What the Rest of Us Can Learn from Them," Investopedia, updated February 27, 2023, https://www.investopedia.com/financial-edge/0312/why-athletes-go-broke.aspx.

163 **When Eve was thriving:** Genesis 3:5, paraphrased.

163 **It's called:** 1 John 2:16.

163 **Again naked:** Job 1:21, paraphrased.

164 **Meanwhile according:** C. S. Lewis, *The Screwtape Letters* (Macmillan, 1943), 143.

165 **It is within:** Mark 3:17.

167 **To paraphrase:** Teresa of Avila, *The Collected Works of Saint Teresa of Avila*, trans. Kieran Kavanaugh and Otilio Rodriguez, vol. 2, feat. *The Way of Perfection*, *Meditations on the Song of Songs*, and *The Interior Castle* (ICS Publications, 2012), 195.

167 **His presence is:** Psalm 16:11, paraphrased.

167 **Regularly fan it:** Psalm 119:11, paraphrased.

168 **The Pharisees once:** Mark 2:18–20, paraphrased.

170 **Thomas Merton wrote:** Thomas Merton, *In the Dark before Dawn: New Selected Poems of Thomas Merton*, ed. Lynn R. Szabo (New Directions, 2005), 65.

Chapter 12: See the Northern Lights

176 **There was a sharp:** Tunku Varadarajan, "Jonathan Haidt on the 'National Crisis' of Gen Z," Opinion, *Wall Street Journal*, December 30, 2022, https://www.wsj.com/articles/the-national-crisis-of-generation-z-jonathan-haidt-social-media-performance-anxiety-fragility-gap-childhood-11672401345.

176 **In his book:** John Eldredge, *Get Your Life Back: Everyday Practices for a World Gone Mad* (Nelson Books, 2020), 36.

176 **Studies prove that:** Dacher Keltner, *Awe: The New Science of Everyday Wonder and How It Can Transform Your Life* (Penguin Books, 2023); Eben Harrell, "The Power of Everyday Awe," *Harvard Business Review*, January/February 2023, https://hbr.org/2023/01/the-power-of-everyday-awe.

178 **He pointed out:** Cal Newport, *Deep Work: Rules for Focused Success in a Distracted World* (Grand Central, 2016).

179 **People have tried:** Matthew Walker, *Why We Sleep: Unlocking the Power of Sleep and Dreams* (Scribner, 2017), 134–35.

179 **Another person would:** Daniel H. Pink, *When: The Scientific Secrets of Perfect Timing* (Riverhead Books, 2018), 69–76.

179 **Seth Godin in:** Seth Godin, *Linchpin* (Portfolio, 10), 1.

180 **Perhaps this:** Matthew 18:3.

Chapter 13: You Don't Have to Be a Rancher

187 **By design:** Stephen Guise, *Mini Habits: Smaller Habits, Bigger Results* (Selective Entertainment, 2013), 34.

187 **But like Bob:** Bob Wiley, played by Bill Murray, in *What about Bob?*, directed by Frank Oz (Touchstone Pictures, 1991).

188 **As Harvard professor:** Arthur C. Brooks, *From Strength to Strength: Finding Success, Happiness, and Deep Purpose in the Second Half of Life* (Portfolio, 2022), 27–28.

189 **So while fluid:** Richard E. Brown, "Hebb and Cattell: The Genesis of the Theory of Fluid and Crystallized Intelligence," *Frontiers in Human Neuroscience* 10 (December 2016), https://doi.org/10.3389/fnhum.2016.00606.

189 **It's been called:** The concept of jumping the curve is often attributed to Joel A. Barker, popularized in his book *Paradigms: The Business of Discovering the Future* (HarperCollins, 1993).

190 **With God's strength:** Psalm 18:29, paraphrased.

190 **And with the wisdom:** Guy Raz, host, *How I Built This*, podcast, episode 506, 1:05, "Orangetheory Fitness: Ellen Latham," Wondery, April 10, 2023, https://wondery.com/shows/how-i-built-this/episode/10386-orangetheory-fitness-ellen-latham/.

191 **One survey asked:** *Funding Longer Lives: Preparing Americans for Greater Financial Security and Well-Being in Retirement*, Corebridge Financial Longevity Survey, conducted May 2–11, 2023 (Corebridge Financial, 2023), 5, https://crbgdoc.jaggedpeak.com/getDocument/?email=defalt@crbg.com&Source=default&catalogID=M6525WP1.

192 **Over time:** Gary Keller, *The One Thing: The Surprisingly Simple Truth About Extraordinary Results* (Bard Press, 2013).

195 **Peter was raised:** Genesis 25:26.

195 **Chariots of Fire:** Eric Liddell, in *Chariots of Fire*, directed by Hugh Hudson (Enigma Productions, 1982).

199 **Interestingly enough:** Rob Hardy, "Cincinnatus," George Washington Presidential Library at Mount Vernon, Center for Digital History, accessed September 19, 2024, https://www.mountvernon.org/library/digitalhistory/digital-encyclopedia/article/cincinnatus/;; Julie Miller, "George Washington,

'The Greatest Man in the World'?," blog, Library of Congress Blog, December 15, 2022, https://blogs.loc.gov/manuscripts/2022/12 /george-washington-the-greatest-man-in-the-world/#:~:text=West%20said %20He%20believed%20He,private%20life%20at%20Mount%20Vernon.

Chapter 14: Albert Einstein's Dirty Little Secret

201 **The word Einstein:** Walter Isaacson, *Einstein: His Life and Universe* (Simon & Schuster Paperbacks, 2007), 7–9, 16, 21.

202 **Albert considered:** Isaacson, *Einstein*, 7, 13.

203 **To paraphrase Gates**: Marcel Schwantes, "Bill Gates Predicted People with This Critical Skill Will Thrive in the Future of Work," Inc., July 7, 2020, https://www.inc.com/marcel-schwantes/bill-gates-future-of -work-skills.html.

203 **Leonardo da Vinci too:** Walter Isaacson, *Leonardo Da Vinci* (Simon & Schuster Paperbacks, 2017), 5, 178–79, 398, 525–26.

203 **Centuries later:** Rebecca Heisman, "The Amazing Secrets of Woodpecker Tongues," American Bird Conservancy, June 10, 2021, https:// abcbirds.org/blog21/woodpecker-tongues/.

204 **You were created:** Tim Tebow (@timtebow), "On purpose for a purpose," Instagram, July 2, 2023, https://www.instagram.com/timtebow /reel/CuMrVfjP5Qx/.

206 **For every person:** John 3:16, paraphrased.

206 **The group at Babel:** Genesis 1:28.

207 **He sought:** Genesis 28:17, paraphrased.

207 **As the famous:** Augustus Toplady, "Rock of Ages," public domain.

207 **Because Jesus:** John 10:9–10.

209 **Jesus says done:** John 19:30, paraphrased.

209 **Jesus says lose:** Mark 10:21.

209 **It's His way:** Romans 1:20.

214 **Jacob had wrestled:** Genesis 32.

Chapter 15: Fame or Flame?

218 **Anheuser-Busch secured:** Dave Roos, "Beer Ads and Wild West Shows Hyped the Myth of Custer's Heroic 'Last Stand,'" HowStuffWorks.com, August 10, 2020, https://history.howstuffworks.com/american-history /custers-last-stand.htm.

219 **George Custer was raised:** Biographical information in this section is taken from Ted Behncke and Gary L. Bloomfield, *Custer: From the Civil War's Boy General to the Battle of the Little Bighorn* (Casemate, 2020); and "Last Stand at Little Big Horn," *American Experience*, produced by Paul Steckler,

narrated by David McCullough, season 5, episode 6, November 25, 1992, 58:04 min., https://archive.org/details/american-experience_20220511.

219 **He got into:** Edgar Irving Stewart, *Custer's Luck* (Univ. of Oklahoma Press, 1955).

219 **He graduated:** Stephen E. Ambrose, *Crazy Horse and Custer: The Parallel Lives of Two American Warriors* (Open Road Media, 2014), 132, Kindle.

220 **As one of:** Elizabeth Bacon Custer, *The Boy General: Story of the Life of Major-General George A. Custer* (C. Scribner's Sons, 1907).

220 **He rebranded:** Stephen E. Ambrose, *Crazy Horse and Custer: The Parallel Lives of Two American Warriors* (Open Road Media, 2014), 501, Kindle.

220 **In the words:** "Last Stand at Little Big Horn."

222 **Perhaps it is:** Haggai 1:6, paraphrased.

223 **But he has found:** John 4:35.

224 **He won't leave:** Luke 16:22; 2 Corinthians 5:8.

226 **Jesus had seen:** Luke 10:17, paraphrased.

229 **It's like the widow:** 2 Kings 4.

229 **That is a demonic trap:** John 10:10.

229 **That is why:** Isaiah 40:6.

230 **The ruling caesars:** John F. Walvoord, "Revelation," in *The Bible Knowledge Commentary: An Exposition of the Scriptures*, ed. J. F. Walvoord and R. B. Zuck, vol. 2 (Victor Books, 1985), 976.

230 **Every time the crowd:** Warren W. Wiersbe, The Bible Exposition Commentary, vol. 1 (Victor Books, 1996), 636.

231 **As Tim Keller:** Tim Keller, host, *Gospel in Life*, podcast, "The Final Temple," Gospel in Life and Redeemer City to City, August 27, 2021, https://podcast.gospelinlife.com/e/the-final-temple/.

Chapter 16: There's an Angel on My Porch Swing

234 **A resting heart rate:** "Tachycardia: Fast Heart Rate," American Heart Association, September 24, 2024, https://www.heart.org/en/health-topics/arrhythmia/about-arrhythmia/tachycardia—fast-heart-rate#:~:text=The%20normal%20rate%20for%20a,Ventricular%20Tachycardia.

247 **I come against every:** Psalm 51:8.

Chapter 17: Spring, Summer, Fall, and Smoke

250 **Here's my heart:** J. H. Thomas, "Come, Thou Fount of Every Blessing" (pub. by author, 1872).

250 **This world:** Zechariah 14:20.

251 **When Balaam's donkey:** Numbers 22:21–39.

251 **The latter glory:** Haggai 2:9.

252 **C.S. Lewis said:** C. S. Lewis, *The Great Divorce* (Macmillan, 1946), 67.

253 **Linguistically the narrative:** Tim Keller, "Real Riches and the Ambitious Man," in "The Gospel According to Abraham" sermon series, GospelinLife .com, April 29, 2001, MP3 audio, 42:19, https://gospelinlife .com/sermon/real-riches-and-the-ambitious-man/.

253 **About as well:** Teddy Roosevelt, quoted in *The American Experience*, season 1, episode 1, "The Great San Francisco Earthquake," written and produced by Tom Weidlinger, narrated by F. Murray Abraham, October 4, 1988, MP4 video, 54:38, https://archive.org/details/american -experience_20220511/American+Experience+-+S01E01+-+The+Great +San+Francisco+Earthquake+(October+4%2C+1988).mp4.

253 **Then an earthquake:** "What Was the Magnitude?," USGS, accessed November 29, 2024, https://earthquake.usgs.gov/earthquakes/events /1906calif/18april/magnitude.php.

254 **Was the equivalent:** *The American Experience*, "The Great San Francisco Earthquake," transcript, Subslikescript.com, accessed September 20, 2024, https://subslikescript.com/series/American_Experience -94416/season-1/episode-1-The_Great_San_Francisco_Earthquake.

254 **The death toll:** "The Great San Francisco Earthquake."

255 **In his book:** Jordan B. Peterson, *Twelve Rules for Life: An Antidote to Chaos* (Random House of Canada, 2018), 207–8.

255 **I once read:** Michelle Schroeder-Gardner, "This 33-Year-Old Mom Makes $760,000 a Year in Passive Income—and Lives on a Sailboat: 'I Work Just 10 Hours a Week,'" CNBC Make It, July 12, 2022, https://www.cnbc.com/2022/07/12/mom-makes-760000-a-year-in -passive-income-and-lives-on-a-sailboat-i-work-just-10-hours-a -week.html.

256 **We can aim:** Graham Cochrane, "'I Work Just 5 Hours a Week': This 39-Year-Old Makes $160,000 a Month in Passive Income—a Look at His Typical Day," CNBC Make It, August 6, 2022, https://www.cnbc.com /2022/08/06/this-39-year-old-makes-160000-month-in-passive-income-a -look-at-his-typical-day-i-work-5-hours-a-week.html. He writes more about this in his book *Rebel*.

257 **On that day:** 1 Corinthians 3:13–15.

258 **When I was:** *Britannica*, "Fibonacci Sequence," updated September 9, 2024, https://www.britannica.com/science/Fibonacci-number.

259 **It is mathematically:** Lily Trestan et al., "A Mathematical Analysis of Animal Horns," *Bioengineering Hyperbook*, (McGill University, 2024), https://bioengineering.hyperbook.mcgill.ca/a-mathematical-analysis-of -animal-horns/.

259 **The Fibonacci sequence:** *Britannica*, "golden ratio," September 10, 2024, https://www.britannica.com/science/golden-ratio.

259 **This golden ratio:** *Britannica*, "Pyramids of Giza," updated December 19, 2024, https://www.britannica.com/topic/Pyramids-of-Giza.

260 **The F in these:** *The American Experience*, season 32, episode 6, "Mr. Tornado," written and produced by Michael Rossi, May 19, 2020, MP4 video, 52:50, https://archive.org/details/american-experience _20220511/ American+Experience+-+S32E06+-+Mr.+Tornado+(May+19 %2C+2020).mp4.

ABOUT THE AUTHOR

LEVI LUSKO is the founder and lead pastor of Fresh Life Church. He is a bestselling author, podcast host, husband, and father of five, and travels the world speaking about Jesus.

Levi is the author of several books, children's books, and devotionals including *Through the Eyes of a Lion, I Declare War, The Marriage Devotional, The Last Supper on the Moon*, and his latest, *Marvel at the Moon*. He and his wife, Jennie, cohost their podcast, *Hey! It's the Luskos*.

Levi and Jennie have one son, Lennox, and four daughters: Alivia, Daisy, Clover, and Lenya, who is in heaven.

ALSO AVAILABLE FROM LEVI LUSKO

Through the Eyes of a Lion
This is not a manual for grieving but a manifesto for high-octane living. Learn to find incredible power when facing impossible pain.

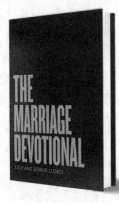

The Marriage Devotional
God wants you to have a strong, thriving, and fun marriage. In these 52 devotions, Levi and Jennie will point you to God's word and help you experience a depth and beauty you may have never thought possible.

I Declare War
Discover four keys to winning the battle with yourself. It's time to stop being your own worst enemy and become the person, the spouse, the parent, and the leader God intended you to be.

levilusko.com
Available wherever books are sold.

MAKE UP YOUR MIND
FREE EBOOK

**4 Decisions That Will Transform
Your Relationship With God**

Every day, we make 30,000 choices, shaping our lives decision by decision. In this devotional, we're exploring the pivotal choices that shape our spiritual lives: walking in the Spirit over the flesh, embracing obedience in uncertainty, seeking God's presence over worldly pressures, and choosing victory over victimhood. We are learning that our thoughts and decisions make up the people we become.

Download at
levilusko.com/make-up-your-mind

FREE RESOURCES FROM LEVI LUSKO

If You're Raising Kids...

There is power in gathering around the table. It's more than the food. It's the conversation. These conversation cards can be used for any age and are a fun way to help you get the dinner table conversations flowing!

If You're Married...

Prioritize your relationship by spending time with your spouse! Download twenty five date night ideas and meaningful conversation starters to freshen up your date night.

If You're Leaning Into Growth...

Discover the most important thing you can say today. Unlock a life you love by learning about the importance and weight of your words.

Download at
levilusko.com/resources